SAILOR BOB

Bags of pointers
to nonduality

Kat Adamson

Bags of pointers to nonduality

ISBN 9798474758985

www.sailorbobadamson.com

I dedicate this book to you, Dear Reader, but not you identified as form, the body-mind or conceptual image, but the Real You — inseparable Essence of Life, Heart of Hearts, that I Am.

Why S A I L O R B O B?

The Spiel has evolved during Bob's 45 years of mentoring. It contains many deep and profound descriptions; it is like a bag full of pointers. Just one of these pointers — when deeply heard, seen through, felt and understood — can be enough. Even one simple reminder can take a ripe seeker "beyond the need for further help", as Nisargadatta would say.

> **Bob:** *When you come into this space, leave your concepts behind: come empty. Listen with your heart, not with the head.*

Please find 'your' pointer amongst these, one or a few which ring the bell, feel true in your heart. They may provide an anchor, just for now. There are many options under each letter of the structure, so that the acronym SAILOR BOB can serve as long as required. Feel free to play, unpack and create your own expansion of the acronym. We are so uniquely different, we do not resonate with the same set of tunes. Every bird has a different song, but every song is an expression of the same life force.

$\underline{S}$ for $\underline{S}$eeming $\underline{S}$eparate $\underline{S}$elf or $\underline{S}$topping $\underline{S}$piritual $\underline{S}$earch may be a great reminder for some and may mean nothing to others. Others might feel that $\underline{S}$ for $\underline{S}$ky or $\underline{S}$pace — shifts or '$\underline{s}$weeps' them more.

Which of them will you resonate with? Try them on like you try a new outfit, and you will have a full set of reminders. Surely there are many words that I missed out on, or skipped to stick to acronym, and they are the right tune for you... Ultimately even words are emanations of That. Everything can be a reminder. Every word can be a pointer.

11

*So, **S** for... what? You could design an acronym of your own nickname or your favourite label of That. Play with this, have some fun, after all – this is Leela, the divine game!*

As you read the pointers over and over, resonance will build up and more of them will open your heart. Bob suggests repeated listening or reading, so that new habits of attention will support the seeming journey. Love for the truth will grow stronger and the readiness to surrender the falseness may emerge.

No real sacrifice is required. What is to die was never born. The journey has no duration, no destination and right now you may see it end. And right now is the only time it can and it does end. This being said, if you still believe in time, and you have invested a lot of it in seeking, certain undoing may be necessary. Let's make it light; may it be fun!

At the end (when it is now), you will see through all paradoxes of pointing, you will understand all limitations of words. For now, though, it is enough to say that the map is never the territory and a word is never the thing it represents. The word 'cat' is not the cat itself. Even a picture of the cat is not it. So, please read between the lines; look for the feeling rather than reason. Look for innate resonance, not for convincing arguments. After all, you knew it all as a baby, before you learned words, so it is all just re-cognizing (cognizing again), finding what was never lost. After all, it is the Natural State, ever present Ordinary Awareness.

And why this particular structure? Why SAILOR BOB? Because he is the greatest (in my eyes), and I'm the main author — totally biased ;-)! And because I love him. Because he un-entangled Life in 'my' body-mind and in countless others that I met and heard of. Because he is the most selfless, most giving, most loving, kindest, smartest and sweetest creature in 'my' whole dream.

Bob's secret is the same as his teacher's (and friend's) Nisargadatta Maharaj – simplicity and humility. No crowded retreats, guru-worship and no flashy self-promotion. Plus relentless rejections of popular interviewers highlighting personal stories or promising a better world in future. No claim to fame, no fortune and no sex scandals. His group meetings are small in number, with no titles or rituals. There is no sense of superiority, no distance and no order. He is as ordinary as everything in nature, you and me, the sky, the flower. And as lovable, authentic, natural and supremely generous in sharing, serving.

To support stabilisation when moments of recognition are still brief, Bob encourages people to ask questions, clear their doubts, or share what works for them. He loves to hear his pointers 'digested' and put in other words, in different angles; perhaps better to what comes up in his mind. This is true selflessness in action, hardly seen elsewhere.

Language will elude us on this apparent journey through attempts to express the inexpressible, so let's laugh at all the paradoxes, it will make it light, fun, adventurous.

Now it is time to open SAILOR BOB's bags of pointers collected over 45 years of his unique but very effective work.

The SAILOR BOB acronym expanded...

S – S-ailor Bob

S – START

> **Bob:** *START from the fact — whether you recognize it at the moment or not — that **you are already THAT**. There won't be any need to seek to become something or someone. If you accept for now, that you are THAT already, then you only need to notice what is seemingly obscuring it. It is nonduality we are talking about here. One, nondual, not two. Everything is THAT One. Not even one, to be more precise, but this we will leave for later. Now everything is THAT. Nothing is excluded, you are not excluded.*

So, please START from the top! Why climb the imaginary ladder to get there? You are THAT already. Everything is THAT. And deep down in your heart you know it. So called mind (the bio-computer with its logic, the stream of thoughts) cannot know it, because it only grasps things and THAT is no-thing. But heart, the core of the essence, it knows. You know. You know that you are. You know you are That. You are THAT awareness of being already. You ARE and you know it. You are aware of presence, you know you exist, that you are. That's it.

> **Bob:** *Not convinced? Please try a little experiment now: try to not be; try with all your might! How are you going?*

You failed. How wonderful!

So this is where we start. Starting from any idea of being some 'thing' (a body, an ego, other things) brings you back to the head: to thinking, imagining, comparing, drawing boundaries, interpreting, dividing, proving, disproving etc. **Knowing that you are** - requires no thinking. It can't be denied. Start here. This is the Truth. This is reality.

> **Bob:** *We know it innately in our language when we say, THAT is the chair, THAT is a carpet, THAT is Bill, THAT is a cat... Take the labels off things and THAT is all there is... Everything is THAT. And THAT is everything. THAT appears as every-thing. You are not exempt.*

Now, what stands in the way of fully experiencing THAT-ness or Is-ness? Just notice if anything presents itself in the field of consciousness. No need to do anything about it, because THAT (existence) is always there, like a 3D screen. That is it. If that one thing could be fully grasped, held dear in the heart — not just remembered as a concept — nothing else is needed. This is freedom. All the other aspects of it will present themselves as insights appearing on THAT, in you.

S – Story of Sarah – E X A M P L E

She heard Bob straight away when he pointed where to START. Sarah is a round, smiley, dark blonde lady with long hair and light brown eyes in her early 50's, who came to Melbourne from New Zealand four years ago. Her phenomenal speed of thought made her a genius researcher, but what she was really after was 'enlightenment'.

She found Bob via Google. To come here with no money or job was a bold act. Because of social benefits for autism she never needed to work before. Instead, she would travel, learn rare skills and study, study, study. The length of her stay in Melbourne was unknown to her before she would be penniless, either needing to go back or staying and starving. Her commitment to see it through was total.

> Bob told her, You are already THAT: START here! There is no entity anywhere running the show. Life is functioning the universe. You are that life. Start here.

So she did. She didn't waste the pointer.

Her trust in Bob was enough, and ever since then she has been experiencing the manifested world as if she wasn't a separate limited 'me' inside somewhere, but THAT, Spacious Existence. In THAT – everything appears, comes up, stays or goes. Noticing happens, changing content is pops up and disappears: things, thoughts, all of it.

Retranslation of the whole life from personal to un–inhabited was instantaneous but without major fireworks, thundering or bliss. What Bob said was logical and was to be verified in consumption. And it works better for Sarah than the popular myth of the separate self or soul in a driver's seat.

Insecurities and mental projections — once debilitating — were now recognized as impersonal 'stuff' and lost their sting. Joy came to the foreground. Life became more effortless and exciting. 'I', recognized as redundant, didn't surface again, as it couldn't be believed in anymore.

She is way too smart not to appreciate fully (including on an intellectual level) how much more efficient, brighter and simpler the map of reality is without any suspicious invisible entity called 'I' claiming doubtful control over it. Much fewer *variables, much simpler equations. 'No-I model' was explaining things with greater precision and clarity. Obviously!*

Sarah is well looked after and her old anxieties are not like dark clouds anymore, but rather 'cumulus humilis', which signify good weather. Her needs are miraculously attended to by Life.

Deconditioning still goes on; her brain is rewiring itself, forever changing. Insights are to be found everywhere now, without any looking. Seeking is over and done but thousands of aspects of the mystery keep revealing themselves to her. Breathtakingly beautiful poems started to pour out to illustrate it.

She found a good place to stay, an attractive job and made valuable friendships. Desire for romantic relationship has evaporated miraculously and nothing is missing anymore. Life is amazing, fascinating! All because of relinquishing the ridiculous belief in a separate entity inside. She is living as THAT, as that Basic Screen.

S – Screen

Bob: *When you go to the movies and see all the cowboys and Indians shooting at each other – is the screen ever affected? When the movie ends – is there any blood on the screen or bullet holes in it?*

Another way to point to That (such-ness) is to compare it with a screen or a 3D space-like screen. It contains every image but is not contaminated by it. Ancients use the analogy of a mirror, which reflects everything with absolute indifference. You are that screen.

At this point it may be helpful to discard the content and stay with the emptiness of the screen. In other words, discard what you are not. You are neither a cowboy nor an Indian. You are neither the body, nor the mind, nor are you a person. Nor are you any other limited object temporarily appearing on the screen. Ancients call it the Neti-Neti process, translated directly as: "not this, not that".

Anything that can be noticed or known is merely an object, physical or mental. Nisargadatta used to say that nothing perceivable or conceivable is what you are. You are what it appears on/in. We will be coming back to that analogy of the screen and clarifying it further as we go.

At this point, discard the objects. Stay with what is left when everything else is discarded. Is there anything left?

Just stay there. Stay here.

S – Stay...

Bob: Stay with that basic screen, stay with the I-am-ness. Nisargadatta calls it, "a diamond of good fortune to stay with that I-am to the exclusion of everything else". It took him three years to realize his true nature and he had no prior seeking experience nor any knowledge about Advaita. So stay with that sense of presence. Stay as That.

The pointer 'stay' is hinting at 'don't move away' and relates to the attention, the light of knowing, which is called consciousness. As much as you can, relax into it, remain as That. The only way to move away from this present moment is to daydream, to imagine other moments and scenarios. When you daydream, you are still **here**, but the attention is on the daydream. Notice that. The space from where you are noticing it is stationary. It is from HERE that you feel the sense of presence.

> **Bob:** *Some people are told to stay in the NOW. They ask me how to do that. I tell them, try and get out of the NOW and see if you can. You'll see that you can't leave this immediacy, you can't leave this present moment now.*

You can only imagine you have left this moment. Any daydream in which you imagine this – is happening right now as well. All sensory activity is happening presently. Seeing is now, hearing is now, tasting, touching and smelling – all are right now. Thinking is also happening now, but the content of thinking may be relating to some past or future events (being recalled or anticipated now). Yet, none of that could even take place if not for the pre-sense...

S – Sense-less Presence

> **Bob:** *The sense of presence is the knowing that you are. You are aware of your being, you have a sense of existence. But it isn't a sense like other senses, it really is a pre-sense, prior to senses.*

The pointer 'pre-sense' hints at the absence of qualities of that presence. It doesn't have any taste, any colour, shape, form or smell. No sensory qualities like warmth or light or pleasure (bliss) can be experienced. If there were qualities, they would be appearing on that **quality-less pre-sensory presence**.

It is sense-less but the most essential, most vital, radiant, extraordinary, experiential, undeniable fact. It is the Home you never left. It is the Kingdom of Heaven you seek. It is closer than your face or your breath and more intimate than your deepest vulnerability. Known under many names, but really beyond language, it is who you are.

> **Bob:** *Life is spontaneously happening! Have a look at that essence that you are. With all the dramas and traumas and things that have happened in your life, has that sense of presence been contaminated in anyway by any of those things? No.*

Everything appearing on it is a fleeting story.

S – Story

Story is a thought-form. It is made of concepts, ideas and/or images. Story may be very simple or very complex, but to be it needs attention. Without being known, it is merely a potentiality. Starved of attention (ignored) it vanishes as quickly as it appeared, even though, just as everything that is, it loves to be. By its very nature a good story is quite seductive!

> **Bob:** *Story requires time. Every fairy tale starts with, "Once upon a time". Can you see how quickly it moves*

out of the immediacy of this moment to imagined time? Of course it doesn't leave this moment, it happens only conceptually. Time is a concept, a mental construct only. There is no future unless you take a thought. There is no past without thought. Try it now. Is there a past unless you think about it? There is not. And even thought about the future or past is happening presently. So there is no time. Time is only in the mind. Time is mind.

Story also requires context. It has a beginning, location, space-time, a hero, an action... Such variety of engaging mental constructs is so very attractive that the screen gets forgotten. A daydream is very much like a night dream. That-ness gets lost in the content, in the appearance. The screen is forgotten. Still it is always there...

Who are you without the story about you? What is there without the story about the world?

Bob: *What is wrong with right now without the story? What is wrong with this timeless present moment if you pause the thought?*

This moment is story-less because it is time-less. And without the story, the pure screen is known non-conceptually. The screen is not an object; it is no-thing. It is like space. It can't be found but it also can't be denied. It is knowing itself.

Nobody can ever know it because there is no split between somebody and 'it'. They are one no-thing: just pure immediate know-ING. There is no knower knowing known, but one –ING, activity of knowing which Bob and Jiddu Krishnamurti liked to call 'Intelligence Energy'.

But it's not an intellectual understanding but a knowing of the heart — knowing from the core of the essence, undeniability of our own existence. You are that knowing: the knowing of existence. Be-ing. Is-ness.

Story is a vibration upon the stillness of the screen. It is a dynamic aspect on the static background, like Shiva and Shakti.

S – Shiva, Shakti

> **Bob:** *In Hinduism they call it Shiva-Shakti. Shiva is the static aspect and Shakti is the dynamic aspect. Shakti dances and the world appears. But Shiva and Shakti are not two things but two aspects of the one.*

The static aspect is the background or the basic screen. The dynamic aspect is the content. Both are merely aspects of the One. Stillness moves, vibrates into wondrous forms. It appears as gross and subtle vibrations, solid rocks, icebergs, oceans, bodies, sound waves and sunlight. It vibrates to what ancients called five elements: air, water, fire, earth and space, of which everything else is made.

In the same way the screen is not different from the story. Shakti dances. Dynamic aspect is a movement, a dance of Shakti, a vibration.

The screen is static; the story is a movement of energy. The story is sights, sounds, smells, etc. Sound is a movement, a vibration of air; light is a different frequency of vibrating energy and matter is a different speed of vibration of subatomic particles. Subtler still is a thought or image.

The static screen or Shiva transcends the duality of both aspects. We point at That, which transcends perceived static-dynamic, black-white, passive-active, mind-matter, Heaven-Earth, me-other etc. Movement appears on it and of it...

In this timeless immediacy Shiva is not prior to Shakti. Where do both appear?

> **Bob:** *Everything is That. Space vibrates into things, emptiness vibrates into forms... Everything is That One Essence vibrating into different shapes and forms and patterns. Nothing is separate or apart from That. All of it – are just vibrating patterns of energy. They also call it Sky-like awareness.*

S – Sky

In Shamanism primordial duality is illustrated as Father–Sky and Mother–Earth; Consciousness (or spirit) and matter (body). Consciousness, male, is static, space-like; while matter, female, is constantly transient, dynamically changing, dancing.

> **Bob:** *They call it Sky-like awareness because the sky is empty, there is vast nothingness in every direction. Do you think there is some blue canopy out there? Did you ever see blueness pouring through the windows of an airplane? It only appears blue, but it is a clear emptiness. Sometimes there are clouds covering it, but are they stitched to the sky? No. They are free to*

move on. You are that sky-like awareness, and clouds of thoughts are not stitched anywhere in your head so they cannot really touch you.

In Taoism there is a ubiquitous circle illustrating the Yin-Yang polarity. The attributes are assigned in the opposite manner there. The male aspect is dynamic (white, active) and the female is static (dark, passive), unlike in Shamanism and Hinduism. That is a fortunate reminder that no illustration is ever true. No map is the territory. Concept or image cannot contain it. The symbol is not to show what is, but to describe how it appears. No words can ever represent it adequately. Contradictions and paradoxes are welcome aids to undo any fixed ideas.

> **Bob:** *The answer is not in the mind. How long have you been searching in the thinking? Some of you have been seeking for 20-30 years. You would have found the answer by now; or somebody else would have found it if it were there. But it cannot be grasped by thought (mind).*

Where does any symbol appear? The basic screen of sky-like awareness transcends both aspects: static and dynamic, emptiness and form, black and white. Because mind is duality, this is beyond intellectual understanding, but it can still be pointed at.

> **Bob:** *"Make the smallest distinction, however, and Heaven and Earth will be set infinitely apart", says the Hsin-Hsin Ming. But can the planet be separated from the sky it floats in? What is heaven? Isn't it sky? Isn't it empty space all the way, as far as you can see or imagine? So, Earth can never be separate from Heaven (sky), only seemingly so, only conceptually, by mental divisions. It all appears in Space, in Stillness.*

S – Space. Stillness. Silence

> **Bob:** *Everything is content of Space. Space is No-Thing. Can anything come from No-Thing? No. So, the content must be that Space too. All manifestation is just an appearance, an illusion, the No-Thing. They call it Maya. Space or emptiness is vibrating into forms, shapes and patterns, appearing as things.*

Yet, things look like they are separated by space between them, sounds are separated by silence between them, thoughts- by gaps between them, movement is known in the background of stillness...

> **Bob:** *For things to appear, they have to appear dualistically. There cannot be sound without silence, darkness without light... There is no one-ended stick. Every stick has two ends, yet it is one stick.*
>
> *Without the duality there is no appearance. But when you look closer, is the darkness anything other than the absence of light? Is light anything other than the absence of darkness? There is only One. One essence vibrating into multitude of forms.*

World only appears to be, just like the dream at night. The dream doesn't have any real existence. Cities, people and mountains only appear to be. Activities, challenges and encounters are only appearances in the space of the dreaming mind. As you wake up, they are all gone. Have they ever really existed? Nothing has ever happened. All is merely temporarily believed into existence, when attention sustains it.

> **Bob:** *Space is not obscured or contaminated by its content. When content is overlooked, the background shines forth. When attention is on the screen or space itself, subtle joy, subtle love of being is experienced.*

The physical body is Space shaped into a pattern of the body. Every thought is Space formed into a pattern of thought. Form and form-less are space. Can you be anything other than Space?

Emptiness, vastness of Sky (Space, Silence, Stillness) is vibrating into forms. Everything is THAT (ONE) forming into various shapes, fashions and patterns. Sound waves are vibrations, thought waves are vibrations, and matter is energy ($E=mc2$). Light, heat, gravity... everything is That. You are — you must be — THAT ONE, too.

Leave thoughts and things as they are, they will move on. Recognize what they are appearing on: that's all that needs to be done. Leave your responses to thoughts and things as they are as well. Recognize them as vibrating patterns of energy appearing in stillness.

> **Bob:** *What is the first thing you see right now? What is the closest to your eyeballs? Isn't that Space? But we don't notice it, we focus on things instead of relaxing into the Space...*

S – Space Out – E X E R C I S E

Relax for a moment, back into the Silent Stillness of Space (in whichever way you understand this suggestion). Look without focusing, at a wide angle, including the peripheries. Experience un-fixated attention, free from clinging and grasping. Things may appear mildly blurred. Don't label anything or don't pay attention to labels if they come up.

Where does the seeing come from? What is its source?

Notice the window of seeing in place of the face. Gently move aside what you know intellectually and check the direct experience.

> **Bob:** *How many eyes do you have? Do you experience two eyes doing the looking or just one open window of seeing?*

Experience the soft edges, the periphery of this field of seeing to your left, and right, up and down. And then experience the whole field ahead of you, the whole space of your gaze.

Experience how pure Space is filtered through the eyes – becomes the Space of Seeing. Notice how that space enables everything to exist. Acknowledge the awareness of that space of seeing. The whole gaze is being known.

Experience the disappearance of the world as you close your eyes for a moment. Stay in that no-space for a few seconds.

Open your eyes and see the universe filling up the space of your gaze again. Close your eyes and let it disappear. Marvel at this for a while. Acknowledge that both, gaze and no gaze are being known. Being knowing is underlying the appearance of space. In the space of being-knowing, the space of seeing comes and goes.

Use it as an anchor any time during the day. Simply close your eyes for few seconds when it is safe to do so. Enjoy!

S – Senses

It is commonly assumed that Nature (or Life) has equipped humans with six senses: seeing, hearing, tasting, touching, smelling and thinking. The first five senses constitute or enable experiencing space (volume) and the sixth one, time (duration). Other animals experience (project) completely different worlds.

> **Bob:** *The very first thing you see (but overlook) is space. Space contains everything, but nothing can contain Space.*

Space is the most obvious pointer used in the visual field.

In the auditory realm, Silence is an equivalent.

Stillness is a **base** on which all movement appears. It is a changeless, immovable background where change and vibration play out. Taste, smell, sense of balance, temperature, tension, sight, feeling, emotion and thought are all different forms of impressions — vibrations.

Space, silence and stillness are merely pointers attempting to describe the indescribable. They are No-Thing. They are 3 aspects of Absence.

Our eyes are designed to see forms separated by the absence of forms. We experience that absence daily while walking, manoeuvring in traffic or pouring tea into a cup. Space between objects gives us the impression of a multitude and diversity of separate forms. It well deserves acknowledgment and appreciation!

Space, which contains both the presence and absence of forms, cannot be known through the eyes because it is That which is knowing; it is pure subjectivity. In direct experience, the physical space disappears when the eyes are closed, but the subjective realm in which both co-exist cannot be denied. In the space of being-knowing, the space of gaze comes and goes.

Our body is designed to sense movement amongst the absence of movement. Yet that Stillness which contains seeming presence and absence of movement cannot be known with the senses, because it is That which is knowing, it is pure subjectivity.

Our ears are designed to hear sounds thanks to gaps between the notes, which both happen in Silence. Silence is a screen for the presence and absence of sounds. That Silent screen is not a thing, therefore thought (mind) cannot grasp it. It is the pure subjectivity, the knowing principle, the I Am, which is aware of both sounds and gaps.

Stillness is what is eternally changeless — pre-sensory. Anything that changes is movement: vibration appearing in Stillness. Gaps are seemingly moving as well, appearing and disappearing.

Changelessness cannot be understood in terms of dualistic symbolic language, but it also can't be denied. Everything that changes is known from its opposite. This opposite of change is non-conceptually known, or more precisely - it is the very process of knowing, the knowing principle.

What is That, which never changes?

> **Bob:** *Silence is always there underlying sounds and gaps. Space is never obscured by any objects appearing in it. Stillness or the Static Screen is no-thing: it is and it isn't at the same time. It cannot be grasped as an object because it is your essential nature. Know-ING. It is pure subjectivity.*

Because the sixth sense, thinking, creates time and this way adds a lot of extra dimensions to the volume of this timeless moment, humans often spend most of their attention on thinking, neglecting more immediate inputs from other senses. Bringing balance and distributing attention more evenly reduces psychological suffering. We will expand on this further when looking at Attention. Now it is time for pure subjectivity.

S – Subjectivity

The screen, space, Siva, silence or stillness cannot be known intellectually because it is not an object. To know the screen as some 'thing', we would need someone outside of it perceiving it. We would then have something like a cinema, with a screen on the wall and an observer who is aware of it. And what is the screen for the whole scene? We may call it Space. To know that Space in which cinema, screen and observer appear, we need something or someone outside of it to report on it. Where would that someone appear?

> **Bob:** *Can you postulate anything outside the Space? Where would it appear? Nothing could be outside this Space or Stillness. It is a basic screen on which — and of which — everything comes, and to which it dissolves.*

The seeming duality here of screen and content (changeless and changing) is due to the limitations of language. The word makes an absence of something; a thing on its own. For example an absence of sounds is a 'thing' called silence. Absence of objects is a 'thing' word calls space, absence of forms is a 'thing' called emptiness, absence of light word labels as a 'thing' called darkness. Neither is a 'thing' in essence. Screen is not a thing and content is merely an appearance, so it is no-thing as well. All is one, the no-thing. Yet it is known. There is an experiencing.

Whatever can be known is not the ultimate knowing principle. It is an object in the space of knowing (consciousness). And what is the field of knowing, activity of knowing or the basic screen? Can the space of knowing be known?

> **Bob:** *In Buddhism they call it COGNIZING EMPTINESS. It is not that you or I are cognizing (or knowing) it, but it is the emptiness itself suffused with the capacity of cognizing. It is self-knowing, self-aware, self-shining. It shines of itself with this innate intelligence or cognizing capacity. It is not a subject knowing the object; it is pure subjectivity. It is closer than your breath. It is who you are.*

There is a consciousness, a wakefulness. There is a knowing, awareness of presence, there is a sense of existence being known. And it is immediate and intimately subjective, although it is not personal.

The knowing principle is pure subjectivity. It is you, your sense of 'I am'. Because it is unknowable as an object, it is **unknowable at all**. Yet it is also undeniable; it is the most intimate feeling of 'I exist', 'I'm here...'

> **Bob:** *Can you negate your being-ness right now? Even to say, 'I Am not' there has to be something there enabling you to say it. You have to be there to say 'I don't exist'. This 'I Am' is pure subjectivity without conceptual (imagined) boundaries of shape and form.*

...And it shines of itself; it needs nothing outside itself to light this awareness of presence. Dzogchen gives it to you in six words: "self-shining, ever fresh, presence awareness". It adds also, "Just this, nothing else". There is **nothing else** and nothing else matters.

> **Bob:** *Dzogchen also calls it, "The Great Perfection". It says, that "The Great Perfection is non-conceptual awareness". Knowing without concepts, without a thought. This is your essential nature.*

There is no need to split pure KNOWING into the knower and the known. This split is artificial, conceptual only. No need to split see-ing into seer and seen. No need to split pure activity into subject and object. They are inseparable.

S – Split. Seeing: Seer-seen

Bob: Knowing is happening, just like digestion is happening. Thought arises: 'I know'. But could there be a knower without the knowing? Could there be anything to be known without the know-ING? There couldn't be.

If there is nothing to be known, there is no knowing, no knower. Without a process of knowing (capacity or activity of knowing), neither knower nor known can exist. In the absence of a knower, no knowing is going on and nothing is to be known. So, there is only one process, not two or even three separate elements.

Please digest it, see through it, make it your own — and the whole duality will be solved for good. Simply see how it is constructed mentally and be free from it. Please look ahead right now and experience the singular process of seeing happening in the immediacy. Notice your narrative constructing the thought "I - see - ahead". Close your eyes and notice how it disappears with the seeing gone. When there is no one looking, there is nothing to see and no seeing.

Do you see? There is only see-ING. The rest are merely ideas invented at seeming two ends of the singular activity.

Singular reality can only be sliced down by concepts, by imagination. This split is not and cannot be real. All trinity or all duality within the functioning are in fact one. One ING, function-ING.

Let's look again at seeing:

Bob: *Everybody is seeing right now. Did you set out to do this? Did you switch it on somehow when you woke up in the morning? Or was it readily available as soon as you opened your eyes?*

So the seeing is happening right now. It is the same seeing you had yesterday but the content has changed.

Does your eye tell you, I see? My eye doesn't tell me, "look at this Bob, look at that", does yours? My eye doesn't say anything at all. Seeing is happening through the eye, and the thought comes up and translates it into 'I see'. But can that thought 'I see', actually see anything? Close your eyes and see how much you can see in the room with the thought 'I'. Come on, do it now!

So, seeing is happening. The eye is an instrument through which it is possible. Just like a computer's camera is an instrument. The camera doesn't see, it only relates the picture, and the computer only interprets it. The eye doesn't see either. Neither does the thought 'I see', which interprets and takes credit for seeing. So what is seeing?

Bob: *The thought 'I see' cannot see, but now, when we say 'I see', we don't mean pure seeing anymore. Now, this 'I' has been introduced and believed into being. Now we relate it to the conceptual image we created around this I-thought and we consider ourselves to be it. So now I, me, Bob, the Australian, the good guy, claims the capacity of seeing...*

Is anybody doing the seeing or does it spontaneously happen? Is the 'I' doing the being? Is anybody beating the heart? Is anybody replacing cells in the body, producing saliva or sweat, digesting food or thinking thoughts? Does do-ing need the doer?

> **Bob:** *Can there be a seer without seeing? No, there cannot. Can there be a seen without seeing? No! So, there are not two, only the mind divides them conceptually. All there is here is the seeing, see-ING: the -ING on it signifies the immediacy of this moment. Seeing is an immediate activity.*

But why does seeing seem to be located in the face?

In this dream-like manifested world, Space has many points (faces) where seeing seems to be located. It is just like how a big shopping mall or cruise ship has many cameras involved in its security system. Every camera covers a certain part of the overall area. In the same way, the eyes of many beings cover the whole appearance. Various parts of it are covered with appreciation but, collectively, all is being witnessed or known.

So, the splits seer-seen, thinker-thought, doer-deed, are only conceptual; imaginary. Without the concept of division, all activity, all functioning is singular, and it is spontaneous.

S – Spontaneity

Some ask if life is predetermined, as if it has already happened and is only being reviewed now. They ask if life is like a fully produced film stored in the can, as if the reality of linear time and the solidity of personal story were facts. It is not so.

The whole appearance is constantly transient and spontaneously arising. There is nobody who blows the wind or grows the grass. Environment is the Whole, the oneness. Everything is changing, waving like one ocean, but there is no controller or doer of it, and no singular cause.

It would be equally true to point that 'no-thing does it' and that 'every-thing collectively contributes to doing it'. Both nothing and everything, zero and eternity, are beyond the grasp of mind. Please quit trying to comprehend it intellectually. Relax the thinking mind. Notice the awareness of any mental activity instead and leave it as it is.

Nobody does anything and everything does it all. The same applies to every part of functioning as a human, both consciously and unconsciously. The whole environment has shaped the brain, the lungs and the skin. The whole environment induces every thought or impulse, so action that follows the impulse can be credited to the Whole or to the no-thing. There is spontaneous act-ING, but no separate actor and act.

> **Bob:** *Do you know what your next thought is going to be? Have a look now. Wait for that next thought to come. Or tell me what you are going to be thinking in two minutes from now. You don't know, right? You do not know what your next thought is going to be.*

Nobody knows what they will think in the next two minutes or next two hours. Thoughts appear. They are spontaneous. Nobody does thinking. Thoughts arise. Nobody does seeing. Nobody does raining, nobody explodes and implodes the stars. The whole environment waves it.

> **Bob:** *Nisargadatta told me and I'm telling you, "There is only Life. There is nobody who lives life". Watch*

> *yourself through the day and see how true it is. You*
> *are being lived. See it for yourself, don't take my word*
> *for it!*

Nobody does heart-beating. Nobody lights up the sun. Nobody lives life. Life as the totality, in all its expressions, is the only doer. Space or the potential of doing — the field of potential experiencing — is utterly spontaneous.

> **Bob:** *The multitude of causes Nisargadatta simplified*
> *to stating that things are uncaused; uncaused*
> *meaning spontaneous.*

The self-organizing universe is updating itself moment to moment. No agency is required. There is no future for predetermination; no past for recollection. There is only right now. And now! NOW.

> **Bob:** *You see. Seeing is spontaneous, just like the*
> *knowing that you are is spontaneous. In that seeing*
> *it's all inclusive. There is no separation in the*
> *immediacy of this moment.*
>
> *Another way of looking at spontaneity is to see that*
> *this moment 'now' has no duration. Look, when does*
> *this now begin? It begins right now. And as you say it*
> *begins, it is already ending. And beginning again. And*
> *ending. So it has no duration. There is no time in this*
> *immediacy. Timeless means spontaneous.*

Spontaneity therefore means certain unpredictability and no duration. It means that an infinite amount of variables are influencing this moment right now. Subject and object are seemingly arising simultaneously on the screen. Hearing is spontaneous also. Speaking comes from the very same place.

S – Speaking

Only fragments of what comes out of our mouth are rehearsed in inner dialog, in the narrative. When the time comes to speak, we see once again it happens spontaneously, regardless of any preparation. Sounds that are coming out of our mouth are not much different from the sounds outside — like the sounds of birds or traffic. We can't control them. They share the same general unpredictability, the same spontaneity.

Our speech has guiding habits or pre-conditioned characteristics which can be modified if there is an inspiration to invest attention (energy) in it. Yet that inspiration is out of our control, as well. Strong, charged thought must appear first for the process to begin.

> **Bob:** *People often ask me if Nisargadatta told me to speak. No! He didn't tell me anything like that. But even if he told me to not speak, he couldn't have stopped me.*

Will you find a compelling urge to share this message in the form of public speaking? Or perhaps your song is utterly different? It doesn't matter.

Every creature has its own unique gifts. Cats meow, dogs bark. It is all right. It is up to Life, and subject to constant change.

This Life, sacred space of being-knowing-stillness, is well described as Sat-Chit-Ananda.

S – Sat-Chit-Ananda

Bob: In Hinduism they call it Sat-Chit-Ananda. These are NOT three things but three aspects of the One. Sat means existence, Chit, consciousness, and Ananda is bliss, loving to be, or stillness. Awareness of being is bliss. Or being, knowing and loving to be. Or existing-knowing-stillness.

Are you not existing right now? You are existing. Are you unaware? You are not unaware, so you must be aware or conscious. Aren't you happy to be? Would you be dead for quids? You would defend yourself or run if somebody was trying to shoot you right now. So you must be that Sat-Chit-Ananda already.

Being and the knowing of it are inseparable. We know that we are. If we didn't know it, we couldn't even say we are. And without existing, we couldn't know it. This is intuitive, undeniable and obvious.

The third factor, Ananda, usually raises questions. Seekers are often looking for ways out of acute suffering. Bliss is an ideal for them: a dream, a desire. It is not what 'a living reality' is here and now. The content of now is not what they want, and far from bliss, they think.

The idea of bliss as a content of conscious experience is a desire for future pleasure. As an ideal (or sale's pitch) it is also called 'an eternal bliss' (meaning always here, never not here). However, this imagined thing can't logically be 'eternal'. If it is absent right now and has a beginning sometime in the future (whenever achieved), then it is not eternal. What is eternal can only be recognized, since to be eternal it must already be present.

Bob: *There is only this moment NOW. Always and ever now: time-less, eternal. This is the only unchanging truth. What is not here now, is not eternal, but transient. What can come, will also go, so it is not worthy of chasing. Bliss as an ecstatic event is just another passing experience.*

Your essential nature of 'being, knowing, loving-to-be' is never obscured by passing experiences. It is not touched by the duality of day/night, pleasure/pain, up/down. Sat-Chit-Ananda is THAT, pure subjectivity, Siva, Sky or the basic screen.

But what happens to Ananda ('loving to be') in suicidal depression? In the darkest night of the soul, one is ready to end life to stop suffering. Love for life is not enough when shame takes over: one does not want to be at all, to say nothing of loving life. One wants to fall asleep forever, drown or disappear in an explosion. One would do anything to stop — to extinguish — this unbearable present experience (or unpredictable fearful future that threatens to become even worse)! Many have been there. I have, too, and so has Bob. We both have lost dear friends to suicide.

...But what was it really that desired to be extinguished, non-existent? Was it the body? Physical pain? Mental suffering? The narrative? The hated I-thought (ego)?

Modern research shows that if love, peace, self-worth and health (physical, emotional, financial and spiritual) were to reappear in life, the death-wish would go away. Everyone who had suicidal ideations but was not charged enough to follow through has been there (again, including Bob and me).

In some ancient scriptures 'Ananda' is translated as 'Stillness' instead of the label 'bliss'. Stillness points to absence of any movement of thought, to no mind.

> **Bob:** You will never find peace of mind. Peace is when the mind is not, that's why they call it "peace that passeth all understanding". ...And this is your natural state; this is Ananda.

Peace is when the mind is not. Mind is thought. When thought stops for a moment or gets unattended, there is a peace beyond measure.

What is there without thought?

What is wrong? What needs to change or die if there is no thought (no mind)? What is left? Isn't this what Sat-Chit-Ananda points to?

In the absence of distractions, when the mind is still, there is Ananda. When the light of attention relaxes onto itself, when focus comes back to being-knowing and stays there, joy radiates. Love shows up. The heart opens up. The Self returns to itself. Peace shines forth.

If that delightful stillness is not experienced now, it is (you are) just one thought away. There is a cloud covering up the sky. But stillness is always already here, under the overlay of mental activity. You are here. You are THAT.

> **Bob:** We have five factors in Hinduism: three of Sat-Chit-Ananda — that is what's real — and the other two, Nama-Rupa, the name and form, the illusion or Maya. You are the awareness of bliss in being, Sat-Chit-Ananda. This is reality. You are not what you think you are; you are not the name or form. They are limitations we put on ourselves. They are illusions.

This is how bliss gets obscured: instead of directly, experientially knowing Being, the focus goes toward assuming the reality of *things;* starting from the 'me' and proceeding to everything else perceivable and conceivable (all that you can see or think about). Things are given reality by defining, dividing, exploring and explaining. Things get labelled. The knower gets labelled also, identified as another thing. The two remaining factors in Hinduism, Nama and Rupa, constitute illusion (Maya).

Now all these things appear real, believed into existence by conceptual division into duality: by naming forms. Instead of one see-ing, now we have seer and seen. All are constantly fed with precious attention and sustained by a steady supply of energy via the focus of Life essence. Distractions, clouds, are ready to substantiate the dream. The singular stream of experiencing became an 'experiencer', and 'things experienced'.

Things are believed to be objects because they have been given name and form. The apparent subject, the 'I', is given name and form also. It is a man or a woman, a Christian or a Muslim, of a particular race, nation, age and peer group. It is limited by concepts. It is confined, incomplete, deficient, less than the Whole.

The undeniable reality — delightful awareness of presence, Sat-Chit-Ananda — gets forgotten, lost sight of. It is replaced by identification with body-mind and dis-identification with all other forms and the space in which they appear. Separation (the original sin) is believed into existence. Paradise is lost. Now I'm this, but I'm not that. Now I'm small, incomplete and unworthy. I'm not at peace.

How to wake up from the spell of Nama-Rupa? How to come back to the natural state of Sat-Chit-Ananda? How to return to un-fixated awareness, to overlook the clouds and be the sky? What do I do?

Simply recognise Nama-Rupa for what it is. Strip this 'I' (presence) of any names and forms and stay open for that recognition to dawn. It is not a result of doing, for there is nothing to be done and no-one to be a doer. START from who you already are. Start from the fact that you are. You are. You know it. Relax into it. Stop covering it up with concepts.

To say the very last word on Ananda, look at saints, sages and seers, and see if they experience everlasting bliss or ecstasy...

S – Saints, Sages, Saviours and Seers

Bob: All this has been pointed throughout the ages by many sages, saints and seers. But they are merely messengers! They are just patterns through which this Intelligence Energy expresses itself, and what really matters, is the message!

Looking at great saviours and saints we notice normal personality patterns, colourful biographies, often packed with very human tendencies, frequently including addictions. Stories about Jesus portray him as a man with the capacity for passionate fury (dealing with money exchange in the temple) or painful doubts (of being forsaken). There are also great anecdotes about the lives and lifestyles of ancient and modern Zen masters, as well as about contemporary gurus and speakers. We can see how rarely they are immune to basic human pleasures, which in other eras could have taken them to the cross.

Bob: Somebody asked me once if I was a sage. I told him, I was parsley, rosemary and thyme.

Just like everyone else, the daily lives of the great masters contained the experiencing of constant change. Peace might not be very far away, but feelings, including these often labelled as negative are certainly available and experienced.

It is in the same way that nature exhibits storms, volcanoes and tsunamis; that dogs bark when disturbed; that winters follow summers and days follow nights... But nature doesn't call any of it 'negative'. Neither you nor the Buddha are any different from nature. You are nature.

Bob: There wouldn't be a manifestation if it didn't appear dualistically. There couldn't be a dawn without the dusk, pleasure without pain, if not for interrelated pairs of opposites there would be nothing at all.

An old Buddhist proverb says, "The only difference between enlightened and unenlightened is that the unenlightened believe there is a difference". The sage knows there is no difference. There is no superiority or inferiority of saints or saviours. There is no separation. There is no duality in nonduality.

The same message is innately yours. The Sage, the Seer, the Saint is just a label differentiating ONE. You are that undivided ONE dreaming you are not. See the dream for what it is and marvel!

Bob: What you need to understand is that nobody can tell you anything, and nobody can teach you anything. You may want to go to another guru, who will tap you on the forehead with the peacock feather, give you a Kundalini experience or promise you some enlightened future. But this is not it. Experiences come and go. What you are right now is changeless reality. You have to see it for yourself, because no guru or prophet, or saint or saviour — in fact: nobody — can do it for you.

It may feel justified to see somebody who doesn't suffer as superior and to want what he/she 'has'. No matter how little Bob emphasizes his own personal stories, there seems to be a slight tendency for people to romanticize him as superior: a teacher or guide. ...But Bob's stories are all about what he doesn't have anymore, not what he's got.

Bob: *You may want to watch the next video, read the next book, go to the next Satsang in hope to get something, but it is all the matter of discarding! Investigate, see the falseness of this so-called ego and you won't need any saviours, sages or seers. That light will shine bright out of your own eyes, undimmed by false belief. Instead of you chasing saints or messengers, others will come to you attracted by that peace.*

People coming to Bob usually have to hear this many times before it sinks in. It seems unthinkable. To see our form as no different to any other form in nature feels like a stretch. We were told we were sinners. We tried to be or become saints. How can the forms of saint and sinner be no different? Where are they equal?

Bob: *Everything is ONE in essence, but not in the way it appears or expresses!*

Every form is always uniquely different. The flute is different from the trumpet and the sounds they make are different. Yet, the same life (air, breath) is what makes them express. On a subatomic level it is the same 'substance' (energy) that constitutes their forms. That essence or life is both form and activity, instrument and music. It is also the basic screen on which they appear.

You are that Life as much as Bob or Buddha is, even though your instrument and music are different, unique, one of a kind.

> **Bob:** *We worship the messenger and ignore the message. We put them on high thrones and worship them. We call them saints, sages, saviours and seers and hope that they will give us what we don't have.*
>
> *There is a story about Jesus hanging on the cross, still alive. People at his feet are fighting over his robe instead of asking him the ultimate truth...*
>
> *So, understand, it is about the message, not about the messenger. The messenger is just a mouth-piece.*
>
> *Do you think somebody else can save you? Or that somebody else can save the world? How well did Jesus or Buddha do? Suffering still thrives as ever.*

There is a beautiful, romantic tale that a saviour or a hero will come from above in the future to liberate us. This is an idea only, a dream, a story about time. There are other heart-warming versions of this tale. It is hard to not appreciate the sweetness of thoughts like: "Love will save us", "self-sacrifice will cleanse us", or surrender (forgiveness, Grace) will bring liberation...

And it will happen for sure, says another myth, if we only believe unconditionally, with no doubt. "Fake it until we make it". We will for sure. Not now though. Later. When we are pure, eligible, deserving. When we atone for our sins. Maybe

46

in a year. Maybe in the next life. Maybe after we die. Not now. **Why** not now?

It is a very poetic but potentially dangerous story! Seeds of truth in these romantic myths are pointing to the force from beyond the separate identity or ego. The famous saviour Jesus called it Truth. "Know the truth and truth will set you free", he was said to say. Not a person or activity, but the truth. Not the messenger. Not his truth.

You shall know it intimately as yours. But not in the future. NOW is the only time there is. The truth is known now. It is already here, already known, but it is overlooked, ignored. What is it?

Romantic ideas may touch your heart. They may bring some resonance and serve as a milestone in this apparent journey with no distance. And the time may come when they are to be left behind, for no idea, however beautiful, is what you are truly longing for. Why not now?

It is not an idea you are searching for. Truth of your being is not a concept, not an idea. It is the reality, always present and shining through. It is self-shining, like the sun.

S – Sun. Self-Shining

Bob: Buddhists call it "Self-shinning, ever fresh presence-awareness, just this, nothing else". They mean it shines of itself, like the sun. Nobody lit up the sun, its nature is to shine. From sun's standpoint, what can ever obscure it?

We have tasted it throughout our lives. We have had moments of clarity, where everything was fine, nothing was wrong, no trace of resistance of any kind. We have tasted an effortless being, the natural state. It might have been more prominent while in contact with beauty or while 'in love'. Or when we suddenly got surprised or even shocked. Or in the state of flow, or creation, or a passionate activity with no mental chatter. Or before the memory kicks in as we wake up in the morning. Or when we wake up from the day-dream. We have moments like these many times throughout the day. Acknowledging them brings about more!

> **Bob:** *Nisargadatta pointed out that you can only put it in negative terms: "nothing is wrong anymore". This is the natural state.*

We all started this way as little babies. Fault-finding machinery wasn't tuned in yet. Without language we couldn't separate ourselves or label anything as bad; we couldn't have a story to overlay the is-ness. Ordinary awareness shone forth, like the Sun in a clear sky.

How does it get obscured? Can mental chatter and imagination really obscure that self-shining light of awareness it appears on?

What we call 'problem' may seem like a thick dark stormy cloud covering the sun. The 'I' who 'owns' the problem seems to be a small, overwhelmed body-mind looking up and seeing darkness. From this standpoint, the Sun appears to be so far away! Storm clouds cover it up completely!

But are you really that tiny little 'I' inside the body-mind? Is there anyone there apart from the voice of commentary and the bundle of images? Do you have to take the position of the voice and images? Aren't they just appearing in the light of the knowing?

The Vast Cosmic Space of the Absolute knows the storm cloud (problem) quite differently. So does the Sun. There are millions of stars, tiny planets circulating around some of them, and an occasional thin layer of atmosphere around a few of these planets. The storm cloud is moving in the atmosphere of one of these tiny planets far away from the Sun. It doesn't matter to the Sun. It is too far away, too small.

Why identify with or as this body-mind or someone inside it? Why locate oneself on a tiny planet called Earth looking out and up for the Sun?

> **Bob:** *When you go out on a cloudy day, do you say that the Sun is not in the sky? No. Because you know for certain that the Sun never leaves the sky. And what does the Sun know about the clouds? They are so small, so far away, the Sun in its vastness doesn't even know about them; it just shines.*
>
> *And when you think what causes the clouds, you realize that the Sun itself causes the clouds to form. It doesn't know anything about it. It just shines and through shining and warmth it evaporates water. Evaporated water forms the cloud and difference in atmospheric pressure forms the wind that blows away the clouds or causes them to fall down as rain.*
>
> *So, as the Sun forms the clouds, the same way the Life Essence itself forms thoughts — or expresses itself as thoughts. And like clouds, they are not attached anywhere. They move on. Are thoughts nailed to your skull anywhere? No. They are free to move on. Just like clouds.*

49

You are not a little vehicle separated from the Sun by layers of clouds. You are not an individual troubled by thoughts and stories. You are the sun. The light of knowing. The self-aware Universe.

To experience itself at all, this universal self-shining light expresses itself as multitude. One cannot know itself because it is all there is. It doesn't even know that it is, because it doesn't know the opposite, the not-being. So it dreams. It dreams to be the other, the part, the divided, separated, sinner. It is still the Whole, but it dreams of separation.

S – Separation. Split

Bob: From the time we started to reason, that sense of separation came upon us. As soon as the 'I' thought came up, so did its opposite: 'not I' or 'other than I'. With that arose a belief in something that is separate and apart from 'I'.

I and 'not-I' is a core split. The same conflict, however, may present itself in disguise. My own struggle with separation was about the duality of emotional life. Why the division in feelings? Why the painful fluctuation of moods? Couldn't there be just one, loving kindness, without its opposite? Couldn't there just be ever-lasting bliss? Why does Love (the Absolute) allow fear?

It seemed cruel to me that an all-loving One would allow the suffering, the separation, the hell... It seemed unfair; unnecessary. I thought at times it would be better if there was just plain *nothing*, no expression, no experiencing and no emotional pain...

...And does Absolute Love really allow fear? Did God really create the Devil? Did God separate light from darkness? Yes or no? Which one is true and which one is just more convenient to accept or subscribe to? Which is logical and according to who?

Truth is beyond concepts of yes and no. It cannot be known by thoughts. Concepts and ideas are only believed or discarded, accepted or rejected, agreed or disagreed with. And they are the human domain. They are impermanent while truth is that which never changes.

It cannot be known whether Consciousness or God has ever allowed anything, created and separated anything or decided to experience itself as other. We can't truthfully say there was a time before duality or separation. We can't really say that the no-identity of Space has shifted to the identity of the form. The truth is beyond the mind and its stories.

We can't really say that the ocean decided to experience itself as the wave. We can't know if God forgot itself and fell for the dream of an individual. And we can't say it isn't so, either. All explanations belong to the mind, in the duality of language.

The split comes up when a child learns language. Plain seeing becomes seer and seen; myself and the world outside me. Further, as more words are acquired, the separation advances. Mind (ego) divorces the body.

> **Bob:** *So, you believe yourself to be this person, this separate self. How did it come about? Well, we learned words, and around the age of two, two and a half, the reasoning capacity developed in us and we*

51

started using words. We were told, "You are little Johnny".

So this is 'I', little Johnny or 'me', we reasoned; and that is 'not I'. With that separation (I – not I), came insecurity and vulnerability. From that moment we try to resolve what has never been real in the first place.

Separation exists only in language. With words, everything started to appear separate. The chair is separate from the floor, from the sound of traffic, from the body sitting on it. Even my legs and my head seem to be separate parts. Every smell is fresh and new, distinct and separate from the background. Or it at least seems to be this way. Even in dreams at night I meet separate people. I see the room and the sky and it seems real.

Bob: But you can't be separated from the Totality. It is that sense of separation, the belief in the separate identity, an individual or a person, that is where the fear comes from. If you were the Totality, could you fear anything? But you ARE the totality! You ARE the tsunami, you ARE the cyclone, you ARE the volcano erupting. You are that everything!

And the illusion of separation is very convincing, very believable! It seems so real, that we believe it to be real and we experience it as real.

...All seemingly so.

S – Seemingly so

*Bob: Upon a bit of investigation and contemplation –
it becomes evident that separation is only seemingly
so. Look at seemingly separate pieces of furniture...
This chair was a piece of wood and few nails at some
point, or a tree, a sapling, a seed...*

The tree exists because of the sunlight, the soil, the shade and the seed, which the wind brought to this specific location on this particular planet, where organic life is possible due to infinite amount of coexisting factors. If one key variable were missing, there wouldn't be a chair. There also wouldn't be a seeming 'you' sitting on it. You wouldn't have that singular experience of touch. You wouldn't have that conceptual image of point of contact between two things.

Without concepts, there is just sensing. Without concepts of chair and buttocks (duality of felt and feeler), there is just one experiencing: the sense of touch. It is one singular feeling, sensing.

It seems to be two (chair and buttocks); it seems to be seer and seen; it seems to be thinker and thought. It seems to be time, the past and the future. It seems to be a world and a witness.

There seem to be many worlds when we go to sleep at night or when we day-dream. All are well-furnished, equipped with landscapes, buildings and sentient creatures.

There seems to be meaning and importance to every event. The sky seems to be blue during the day and black at night. There seems to be a 'me', a separate person, an ego. There seems to be a self-centre or soul to which all other things relate. Self-centre seems so realistic!

S – Self-Centre; Soul

Bob: So, you believe you are this separate entity, this person. Look where this word 'person' comes from. It came from the Latin language. In Latin, the word 'persona' means 'a mask'. We put on the mask of identity and we believe we are this mask. During the pandemic, we can see how a mask obscures some of your features, restricts your speech and breathing. It may protect the body, also. But we do not take ourselves to be that mask. 'Persona', the imagined self-centre is like a mask. We are not it.

'Ego' is just another label used for the self-centre, individual or person. It is a Latin word for 'I' introduced to every day vocabulary by Sigmund Freud a little over 100 years ago. It is not a personality pattern but an act of an identification with it.

'Soul' is a concept of separate essence or spirit. The concept of self-centre (ego) has accumulated some kind of pejorative flavour, and it is associated with selfishness or fear. Soul has much nobler connotations.

Some spiritual paths suggest that ego (or the lower self, or shadow) is to be gotten rid of, but the soul (or higher self) is to be nurtured. Self-centre (ego) and Soul are polar opposites in these approaches. But there is one thing that applies to both equally: they are merely ideas. They are like a mask of concepts.

> *Bob:* Are you asking me if I'm using my ego? Well, I know for a fact that there is no 'me' anywhere to use an ego or anything at all.

Both the ego and the soul, need to have an owner. Who would that be? Who has them? Is there any little human in the head or in the heart of the physical body? Nobody has ever found any. Could that little dwarf be translucent, invisible like an angel or devil but still real?

Or maybe there is just Life without anybody who has it or lives it. Maybe the ego or soul is just a belief, a mental cloud, a verbal commentary. Maybe the separate entity is a phantom and nothing else. Both of them — the ugly enemy or ego and the romantic idea of a soul — are completely made up, dreamed into seeming existence. How simple!

If the word 'soul' does appeal to you, please consider it to be impersonal, like a universal soul, spirit, essence, energy or life. Consider it, by whatever name, to be one transpersonal Self instead of 'my' higher/lower self.

> *Bob:* Perhaps when they talk about 'soul', they don't mean s-o-u-l but s-o-l-e, the one and only. There is no personal soul. Nobody has ever found one: no 'my soul' or 'your soul', but 'sole': one.

Yet, a self-centre seems to be here. I'm uniquely different from you. My body, my personality, my reactions, behaviours, my values and dreams are like none other. I seem to be located behind my eyes, or in the heart at times. I don't feel like I'm everywhere in Space. I can only use the set of senses of this one body, located here. I cannot see through any other eyes. I cannot feel physical pain of another body...

> **Bob:** *You say you are still here. Well, where else would you want to be? Just see if this HERE has any boundaries unless you think about them. See if there is any location to it at all. The body, with its senses, is just a costume for this spirit to experience and express itself. Spirit seemingly needs a vessel through which it expresses.*

S – Spirit

> **Bob:** *Spirit doesn't know matter. Why? Because they are not two, they are not separate. They are aspects of the same. Matter is like a congealed spirit. Just like steam, water and ice are different states of the same H2O. Or like a blood clot that congeals.*

$E=mc^2$ is the scientific equivalent of oneness of spirit and matter, manifesting as energy or form. But what is manifesting both? Is it even a thing?

Energy is no-thing, but not a nothing. It is pure potentiality. When Stillness moves, it is not called Stillness anymore, it is called movement. But did one disappear and the other came into existence? No, we can't say they are two things at all.

The ocean 'manifests' waves made out of its own body, which is water. Weather 'manifests' hurricanes the same way. Emptiness (potential) creates forms made out of itself. God and its creation are one. Spirit and matter are one indeed.

The word 'Spirit' is often translated as essence of life, energy that animates the body, or breath. The Holy Spirit is the 'acting' of God.

Depending on the way the word is contextualized, translated or understood, Spirit can be a pointing towards activity (life, breath, God's will) or towards stillness (background, emptiness or the basic screen). But Father, Son and Spirit (creator, creation and creating) are not three, they are one.

> **Bob:** *Spirit doesn't know matter. Emptiness doesn't know form, Shiva doesn't know Shakti, darkness doesn't know light, and day doesn't know night, for they are not two, it only appears to be so. Neither aspect is supreme or superior to the other.*

S – Supreme, superior

> **Bob:** *You call yourself a human being, and you call God the Supreme Being. Take away the label human, take away the label Supreme, and try to separate the being without the label... There are not two at all!*

To illustrate it we can say, the Spirit, the pure Life Essence, is dreaming of being a separate soul, a human being. And as a human form it is praying to the Supreme, longing for home. It dreams that a Supreme Being, God, can hear and answer the prayers.

Isn't it a romantic dream? How else would these beautiful feelings of reverence, longing, hope, surrender, self-care, compassion, gratitude and love come into experiencing?

> **Bob:** *When you walked into this room, you formed a concept about everyone, and everyone formed a concept about you. You also have a concept about yourself. Which concept is right?*
>
> *No concept is ever right! And without the concept, who would ever be superior to you? Who would ever be inferior to you? ...And what would you want from the other person?*

Without the thought, no God is superior to you, nor is it/he/she supreme. Every point in creation is the same Absolute Totality. Space and time are created by the mind. Space is experienced because of seeing, hearing, tasting, touching and smelling, and time because of thinking. The universe is holographic and hollow, empty of judgement and meaning. Nothing in it has value unless we assign it.

In my own struggle, this pointer was a thunderbolt. I saw how everyone had a different concept about me and that I had a concept about myself, as well. I thought theirs were all wrong but that mine was right. It somehow escaped my attention that my concept about myself was equally unreliable, ever changing, depending on mood, weather, diet, my age, hormones and interactions with others.

Concepts others had about me were based on my job, roles, tendencies or shortcomings; but my own was more about sensitivity and vulnerability. It felt vaguer yet truer. But it was no different. It was just another concept. Seeing this ended the search. Self-image hasn't re-established itself ever since.

I have no self-esteem and no idea of what I am. I have no interest to figure it out. There is nobody there who would need to or want to know it. I'm neither superior nor inferior;

I'm not nothing, not a thing and not everything. But I am. And so are you.

You are that supreme, universal, limitless life force. All limits are merely concepts. And there is a sentience, and great sensitivity in the experiencing!

S – Sentient, sensitive self

When I met Bob and joined his group meetings, I knew beyond any doubt that I was neither the body nor thoughts (mind). I knew they were passing phenomena. I knew that the experiences of both were inconstant, but that I was constant in my awareness of this. I knew they were changing while I was still. Having said that, somehow I missed the fact that the same applies to feelings and emotions. I thought I was my avoidance of rejection, my emotional core, the heart.

I believed I needed to protect myself, stand up for myself and avoid suffering at all costs. I needed to be on the look-out for dangers, and to relate things as relevant or irrelevant to myself. I needed to interpret and give meanings to things. I needed to be in charge. The amount of control I thought I had seemed to grow with the age of 'this' body. But it was never enough!

This was the conceptual image I had about myself. I identified with this vulnerable, sensitive self, the emotional, sentient core. I was frustrated when others didn't see me the same way. I was hurt because my ex-partner perceived me as a sum of skills and habits of the body. I suffered when my proud girlfriends introduced me as a ship's officer. I wasn't any of these.

I thought I was my denied fears, my shyness, my wounds, my shame, my hopes and my dreams. I thought I was my most sacred values and my unprotected sensitive self. I wasn't the only one; all my 'spiritual' girlfriends were stuck in the same place.

> **Bob:** *You're asking if these sentient beings called humans, that have been around for thousands of years were all wrong. Well, I know that I was wrong in believing that I was a sentient human being.*

I somehow failed to recognize that all these feelings were subtle concepts as well. They were just subtle thoughts, present in narrative, in the inner monolog or dialog. They were meanings (labels) given to various energies. I called them a deep fear of unworthiness and sense of incompleteness. I saw them as social and existential angst.

I failed to recognize that these feelings were also fleeting appearances on the screen of consciousness. Their intensity was varying, which means they were just other kinds of transient phenomena. I hadn't realized that I was getting busier and busier in my self-talk, which had evolved to a self-obsession.

S – Self-obsession, self-centeredness

My preoccupation with myself became an obsession. What did others think about me? Did they like me? Where would I go next, what would I do? How could I distract myself from this void? How could I sedate myself? I should have told them this instead of that! That wasn't supposed to happen to me! I should have done this and they shouldn't have done that! I-me-my... Me, me, me...

Self-obsession. All about me. I was the centre of my universe. I was sick of myself and full of myself at the same time — and I couldn't do anything about it. I didn't know what to do or how to do it.

> **Bob:** *When you see the falseness of that self-centre, then you are no longer bound by that — and that is the freedom. That is freedom from the seeming "bondage of self", like the Big Book of AA puts it.*

Initially I couldn't see that feelings change as much as thoughts do. I couldn't be my fear of rejection or my social anxiety. I couldn't be my anger or hopes for love. They could be 'mine', but mine means whose?

And yet all these things were so close, so intimate, so 'me'; to see them as impersonal was unthinkable. I also thought, I was my longing, my love for freedom. I was the importance I gave to the ideals of honesty and service. It was all so 'my'...

> **Bob:** *This self-centre is the cause of all my problems. This cage of concepts – this self-centeredness, which I have built around myself, is a phantom. It does not exist! The cage door is open right now. As a matter of fact, the whole cage can be seen for what it is (a mirage), and it will fall away right now.*

In my inability to see and recognize this simple truth, I suffered.

S – Suffering

Bob: *'Me' is the cause of all so called psychological suffering. If you break a bone or burn the skin, it is physical; you can locate it. But if you have a so-called lump in the throat or knot in the guts, it is psychological. You know it is not real. You can't locate them precisely. All psychological suffering comes from relating to this self-centre, the 'me'.*

There is an old saying: "Pain is inevitable but suffering is optional". It means that the duality of life – the winters and summers, the pains and pleasures – are sure to appear but they need not cause any mental drama. There is no need to be unhappy about being unhappy, angry about being angry, or afraid of fear. If physical pain appears, there is no need to add psychological suffering on top of it.

Animals are permanently in the natural state. They don't imagine any ego residing inside themselves. They don't have the narrative self. Same as us, an animal won't be too happy if it gets wounded. But unlike us, it won't make a story about it. It will do what is necessary for healing; will rest in the shade and lick its wounds.

Bob: *When an antelope escapes the lion, he won't run to the others to tell them how horrible or unfair it was, how the lion was picking on him or bullying him. But we can tell a well embellished story in the pub even 20 years later!*

We, human patterns, are the story tellers. This capacity brought us together, helped us to form larger communities and opened up a new chapter in learning. However, it also introduced suffering.

Bob: What is karma? It is the cause and effect. What I'm pointing to, is the 'me' that is a cause of all psychological suffering. It is only 'me' that can be angry, only 'me' that can be fearful or depressed. It is only 'me' that can be inferior.

But can there be an effect if you don't relate it to the cause? There can't. And I just pointed out that the 'me', the cause, is total fiction. Without the cause, where would the effect lodge?

There is nobody to suffer if there is no 'me'; and there is no 'me'. Pain is not mine. Sadness is not 'my sadness' it is impersonal. It is not 'mine'. The 'I am' (sense of presence) is the space for it. The 'I' (being) sits with the discomfort. The 'I' (awareness) watches the changes in breath, the tensions, the vibration of life. Like an antelope, the 'I' (in the natural state) licks its wounds, rests in the shade and does nothing.

However, when identified as the human pattern being in an uncomfortable situation, habit often shifts attention elsewhere. Distraction may seem to help with pain for a while, but over the long term it impedes healing! Television, the Internet, shopping, food, sex or even self-harm may sedate discomfort temporarily. But because "practise makes the master", they reinforce the habit of seeking further sedation

S – Sedation

Attention is limited. The processing capacity of the human brain is large but not infinite. (Latest research puts it down to: "up to 60 bits per second"). Our brain prioritizes inputs and habituates responses. Over the millennia, with advancing socialisation (and therefore advancing of language and story-telling) we tend to think rather than feel. The overactive mind focuses on interpretation rather than flowing with present happening. We label feelings and we think we know what they are. Concepts and stories replace the direct sensory experience which 'doesn't make it' to the attention stream and gets overlooked.

This subconscious tactic may have served to sedate displeasure and confusion in the past. In various traumatic situations it could have even been a life-saver. Yet for too many it has become largely overused default setting.

Sedation work in many ways. Hearing or viewing a good story may turn the attention away and sedate physical pain or uncomfortable emotion for a moment. Sensory pleasures (and pains) may sedate the story running in the narrative. We medicate psychological suffering with distraction in seeing, hearing, tasting, touching and smelling. In extreme cases we think instead of feeling or turn to addictive drugs, risk lives in dangerous thrills — to not think. We end up harming ourselves or others; or overeat until we get sick.

We increasingly 'need' more and higher highs, hotter chili, sweeter sugar, louder music, more violent sex, faster movies and more aggressive advertisements. Attention gets desensitized and the competition for it becomes more vulgar.

So many ways we have developed to sedate psychological suffering! Yet, none of the avoidance strategies really heal it. Sedation is not only short lived but it also leads to dangerous habit patterns or 'isms'. Workaholism or alcoholism are just two examples.

> **Bob:** *Being still, utterly present for whatever is arising, is the opposite of sedation. After all, disrupted,*

distracted or not, everything is constantly transient.
...But Sat-Chit-Ananda, which is always and ever here
— is too subtle when attention is all tuned to the
extremes!

So many pathways to suffering have been laid ahead! Sedation is not just an avoidance habit but it has also become a survival strategy! Excessive shame, self-hatred, suicidal depression and the likes can lead to a disaster.

What is your most commonly used pathway to suffering? What thoughts make you miserable? What concepts take you to this dark space of senselessness and incompleteness? How do you disrupt these patterns? What is your preferred sedative?

We tend to think that this feeling of separation (from our environment and everything and everyone in it) is a fact. This is suffering. Now we 'need to' sedate our painful story about the isolated, unworthy 'me' — 'my' dark past and 'my' scary future.

Bob: *We tell ourselves, 'I was abused', 'I'm not good enough' and 'I'm shy' or 'fat'. And the worst we put on ourselves is, "after all I'm only human". ONLY human. Who told you so? Are you really only human or do you just think you are? Why identify as anything?*

By dwelling in the past, we feed guilt and shame. By projecting the future, we feed anxieties and fears. By investing in comparison, stories containing 'shoulds', 'ifs' or 'buts', we argue with reality. Comparing oneself with another or others causes suffering. We also 'need to' sedate when we identify as a victim, when we are blaming someone or fighting someone.

We suffer when we desire what is not here now. We suffer when we resist what is, or resist its moving away or changing. Even believing that we've got it and that we are right (enlightened and superior to others) causes uneasiness, for it can be lost. We sedate self-hatred or hatred towards others, for we believe there is a self and others.

Generalizing (use of words like 'always' or 'never') also leads to suffering. Believing any thoughts for a prolonged time (including positive thoughts) causes fixation and impedes the natural flow of life.

> **Bob:** *Fixation on 'me' and relating everything to this 'me' is the primary cause of suffering. It brings up the seeming need for sedation or distraction.*

But how to stop relating to the 'me'? How to stop engaging in all these habitual activities? How to break these patterns? How to disbelieve this voice in my head, which was with me for as long as I can remember, and it calls itself 'me'? How to stop it?

S – STOP – E X E R C I S E

> **Bob:** *"Don't pretend to be what you are not", said Nisargadatta Maharaj. If you understand the answer is not in the mind, how do you get out of the mind? There is only one way. FULL STOP. Don't go there.*

E X E R C I S E:

Please, experiment, contemplate for a few seconds and verify:

What stands in the way of fully experiencing THA ̄ness? What takes attention away from recognising your̤self as THAT? What says otherwise?

To get to know it experientially rather than conceptually, please STOP for a moment.

Pause.

> **Bob:** *What is wrong with right now if you don't think about it? To check it, you need to STOP. Pause the thought for a moment. In fact, thought will pause by itself if there is genuine curiosity. And what is there without the thought?*

A few seconds will be enough to see this, because thoughts will automatically start appearing, just like shivers or sweat on the skin, saliva in the mouth or hormones in the glands. Thoughts are not a problem, once you see what is left without them. See if anything is wrong or what is lost. See what is here without concepts...

> **Bob:** *What is wrong if you pause the thought for a moment? What can you say without the thought? Is it good or bad, pleasant or painful without these labels?*
>
> *Is there a future or past unless you think about it? Pause. See it for yourself. Where is yesterday when you stop thinking?*
>
> *You cannot say anything at all without the thought.*
>
> *But you haven't disappeared, have you?*
>
> *Breathing didn't stop, the heart is beating, digestion goes on... Seeing is also there, hearing is there, all senses are working but the thought is paused.*

67

> *From that, you can see that what you are is prior to thought. This is because on what you are everything appears. Before the thought comes up, you must be there to know it.*

There is no drama, no story, when the thought is paused for a few seconds. What happens to the future without the concept of it?

> **Bob:** *Without the future can there be a spiritual path to be on? Is there any room for progress?*

> *Who are you without the thought or mental image?*

Is there any goal or desire to get somewhere or become someone unless you think about it? Do you need to improve or grow or change? Please, STOP and have a look.

Please verify: do you experience any shape, size, colour or form of yourself unless you think about it or make a mental image of it? Please check: do you experience any 'face' unless you think about it? In direct experience do you have a brain? If you don't label vibrations/sensations with thoughts, do they have any qualities, location or limitations in space?

If your thoughts won't stop for long enough to see, please park them aside and look again. Look past them just like you hear past the traffic sounds or like you ignore your breathing.

Stop.

> **Bob:** *What is wrong without the thought?*

Nothing is wrong.

Ideas may arise, "That's ok for now but later, when I get home..." (or "when I get a headache..." or "when I get nailed to the cross...") — but that is just another thought, a mental image, a projection of a non-existent future. This is not what-is. Just park it aside.

So, without thought, everything that was wrong is not here. Problems are not here. The future and past are not here. Self-definitions are not here. Acute pain or anxiety is now just a fresh and new sensation. It is just buzzing life energy to study with curiosity.

> **Bob:** When the thought is paused, have you fallen apart? No. All senses are working, the body keeps functioning, hair and fingernails keep growing, cells are being replaced, food is being digested; only the thought is paused.

> You can see that what you are is prior to thought. And on that basic screen or awareness (whatever you like to call it), fresh and new thoughts will come up. But it will come up on That — what was there when the thought was paused.

Without thought, you are awake. New daydreams will come but in the gaps between them, you are awake. New clouds will come but in between them, the sky is clear. Stop seeking. Clarity is underneath this seeking pattern.

S – Sick of seeking?

> **Bob:** Stop looking for the answer in thinking. Stop trying to find the answer where you cannot find it. Didn't some of you try to find the answer in the mind for 20 or 30 years? Didn't it dawn on you that you are looking in the wrong place?

And where else can we look for answers? Or even for questions? Where else can we look for who we are?

Bob tells an old story about a group of exhausted, thirsty tourists high in the mountains, catching their breath on the side of steep hill. They can hear a stream but there is no path to it. One of them takes off and struggles through the brushwood and scrubs, gets bruised, falls down a couple of times and wounds himself; but finally returns after a few hours with water for the others. What will they do now? Won't they just drink the water? There is no need for everyone to go through the ordeal of getting it if it is freely offered.

Bob had been seeking for 16 years and understood that mind cannot contain IT, because mind is just a minute expression of IT. This is the water he offers. But you have to drink it yourself.

The sooner this is seen through, the sooner relaxation into the stillness will come about. From that stillness, the source, insights spring. Compulsive thinking, trying to understand relaxes; and grasping, seeking ceases.

> *Bob: You will never find peace of mind; peace is when the mind is not. This they call "the peace that passeth all understanding".*

It means that Peace is beyond intellectual understanding. It is beyond ALL understanding. It is beyond the mind, beyond thought. Peace is stillness and mind is movement. Movement has to cease. Movement is to be deprived of attention.

> ***Bob:*** *So, what way is there out of the mind? You have to see that anywhere you go will be in the mind, any direction you take. If you are on the North Pole, you cannot go any further north. So just FULL STOP. You are already That.*

Understanding that seeking leads us away from the truth means to relax, stop and trust. When the seeking stops, desire stops. It does it on its own. You can't do it. There is no you to start or stop anything. Invitation to relax can actualize if the resonance is there.

There are many moments when seeking is absent. Notice them. When there is nothing wrong anymore, when there is no desire for anything to be any different, the Self-Shining Sun isn't obscured anymore.

Seeking any other pleasure is no different from seeking enlightenment. I used to believe that enlightenment was eternal bliss: an ever-lasting ecstasy (which is supreme pleasure). But I thought my desire for liberation was somehow noble. How wrong! There is nothing noble in wanting what is not. There is nothing noble in depreciating the mystery of this moment as it is and wanting something different instead.

> **Bob:** *You see that seeking itself is a problem. And you cannot stop it, but you can recognize that activity and not go there. Just don't go there.*

The end of seeking is an end of the split between 'seeker' and 'sought'. The end of questions is the end of the questioner. When you no longer need to find out or understand who or what you are, you just are. Freedom. Source.

S – Source – E X E R C I S E

Please, experiment, contemplate for few seconds and verify: where do ideas come from? Please look for an experience, not logic. Relax for a moment and wait in silence for the next thought or mental image to come up. Where did it come from?

Where does perception come from? What is the source of seeing? Where does it start?

Did you ever ponder upon what is an origin of a cell, a bacterium, a body, a planet? What location do clouds come from? Where do thoughts come from? How and where do they form? And where does everything go when it disappears? Science may suggest some theories, but what does the experience, direct observation say?

Can thought grasp the origin of itself? …Or would it just be another thought? Would the conceptual answer really explain that mystery?

And is the Source of all knowing really unknown? Yes? No? Neither? Both? Even if the conceptual knowing can't grasp it, the non-conceptual awareness of existence can't be denied. It is here now, not out there somewhere. You are that Source.

> **Bob:** *Can anything come from nothing? And yet it is there, right in front of your eyes. It is and it isn't, and that is why they call it Maya, an illusion, a phenomenal manifestation.*

Source is an elegant word, holding less imagery than God or Creator, but it may still suggest 'a thing' with a certain location. The agreed-on source of a river can be pin-pointed on a map.

72

But what is the source of that source? And what is the destination of the river?

The ocean may be where the river ends and dissolves. Ocean's sources are multitudes of mountain streams, rain clouds and even icebergs. But have the rivers, clouds and glaciers really existed before the ocean? No. Doesn't rain, snow or ice falling on the mountains come from evaporated oceanic waters? It does! Rivers are rains of evaporated ocean, ocean is rivers.

Bob: *Steam, water and ice are all the same H2O.*

H2O would represent conceptual source here, inseparable, unlocated.

In the same way, the source of all experiencing is at the same time unlocated and always here-now. It can't be grasped because it isn't a thing. Thoughts, like clouds, take shape when the environment is right for them. They arise from this alive, brilliant interconnected ONE no-thing, which is not a nothing!

Bob: *It is the Emptiness itself waving, pulsating and throbbing with life, experiencing and expressing itself as diversity of forms, shapes and patterns. It is the source and destination, the heart, the core, everything and nothing.*

It is expressing itself in a holographic manner. It means every part contains the same algorithm, like in most complex fractals. ...And yet it still remains empty. Mind cannot grasp it, heart cannot deny it.

S – Some more on S

S – Surrender

> **Bob:** *To surrender to life is to drop the illusion of control and give all credit where credit is due.*

From the perspective of Bob's "giving credit where credit is due", surrender is a spontaneous act of love. Loving surrender is known to weaken the so-called ego, to dissolve it in bliss. Surrender understood as a selfless act is a pointer to spontaneous happening. Nobody surrenders to anything. There are not two, but it appears to be so. As with everything else in the appearance, spontaneous acts may be inspired from within or from without.

The path of worship and surrender is often referred to as the Bhakti Path. As Saint Tukaram pointed out, worshipping form may lead to attaining the formless. Worshipping the formless is self-love.

You will not find pointers in this book on how to progress on a path in time towards some future attainment. Many paths are believed to lead to the top when instant recognition is rejected or doesn't resonate. There is one summit, they say. Love and understanding meet there. But this book is not about believed-in paths through time. It is to show you what is already so. There is nothing to attain and no-one to do so. It is plain and simple. Surprisingly simple.

S – Surprisingly simple

> **Bob:** *There are not-two. There is nothing simpler than One.*

Simplicity and directness are what it is all about. Over the years, under Bob's guidance, hundreds if not more saw through the dream and shared their resulting insights.

Simplicity was the most surprising aspect for most of them. 'Simplicity' is one of the key words for me to know they were not imagining it. That is why it is called a cosmic joke. It surprises everyone because whatever was expected or imagined is not it. It is too simple and too obvious, and that is why it is so often missed.

To improve the pointer is to simplify it. The simpler the message is presented, the closer it is to the truth. Simplicity is the key. It is singular after all!

S – Singularity

Bob: Just rest in this uncontrived singularity. You are it.

'Singular' means one; there is nothing apart from That. It is pure being-knowing but there is nobody to be-know 'it'. It is not an 'it' and there is nothing outside and apart. Being singular means it is a totality without any separate parts. It is one without a second.

Another meaning for 'singular' is exceptionally great, remarkable and extraordinary. In mathematics and physics, the singularity is a point at which a function takes an infinite value. It is especially so in space–time, when/where matter is infinitely dense (like at the centre of a black hole).

We are pointing out beyond space-time, beyond any division, beyond emptiness and form, beyond language. It is very subtle.

S – Subtlety

Bob: Be with this subtlety of livingness and see what comes out of this. It is the very essence of life. There is nothing boring about the subtlety whatsoever. It may appear to be boring because it is no-thing to the mind.

What the mind has been used to, since the time it first started to reason, is looking 'out there' for bigger and better sensations, sweeter or saltier tastes, brighter colours, more intense entertainment, stronger pleasures. That has become our habit pattern.

> **Bob:** *When you come back to the nothingness, the subtleness, which is no-thing, it seems very bland and very boring compared to what the mind has been used to. But stay with it for a while and see. There is a lot more to it than what you believe. Get into that blandness or that boringness or nothingness. Sit with it for a while. Don't try to do anything. Just be with it and see what comes up out of it. See the subtleties, what I call the uncaused joy: the sense of well-being; the sense "nothing is wrong anymore", to use Nisargadatta's words. Be sincere.*

S – Sincerity

Nisargadatta used to encourage earnestness. Sincerity is just another word for the same thing. It relates to the quality of single-pointed attention, devotion towards the truth. This quality may be already present or it may be inspired into experience through resonance. It brings a certain sweetness into the seeming process of inquiry. It includes the heart. It is not the same as seriousness.

S – Seriousness

Whenever thoughts are treated too seriously, reality gets forgotten. Seriousness is a great pointer: a reminder to ease up and relax. Nothing has ever happened. There is no future. There is only this moment now. All the rest is a dream made of concepts and images. If seriousness travels through that vast empty space of loving awareness, let it be there. See how long it is going to last. See how impersonal that pattern is. It has been learned, modelled from others. There is no you doing it. Only pure innocence. It is always only Love in disguise (of wanting protection, approval, peace, control, justice, etc.). Relax. At this very instant nothing is threatening your survival.

S – Survival

Every creature wants to love and protect itself. Nature equips it with various mechanisms enabling survival. Sharp claws and teeth, camouflage, venoms and intimidating colours are some of the ways. As humans, we are additionally equipped with reasoning capacity, which is also utilized by nature to seek understanding and safety. We can problem-solve, foresee, plan and predict the future and this is done through learning, utilising memory, comparison and imagination.

Many creatures are capable of instinctive, non-conceptual division of things into eatable/uneatable, safe/dangerous, pleasant/painful etc. But in the narrative (which seems to be only a human trait) this judgement is related to the subject, 'me'. There is an assumption of the existence of the subject, 'me'. That assumption breeds attachment, aversion and self-condemnation.

Survival instinct functions regardless of narrative, which is only *post factum* commentary on what has already been decided or acted upon at the cellular level. As much as good cognitive skills and mental health are vital for optimal survival mechanisms to function, ego, or the sense of an illusory separate 'me', is completely redundant.

You do not need your ego: neither to survive nor to thrive in the appearance (the world). You may leave it behind: shift out.

S – Shift

When the actress takes off her costume, she steps out of the stage and out of the role she just played. There is a shift in identity. When you wake up in bed from a dream in which you were busy and active, this is also such a shift. When a student finishes the classes and goes home, he shifts from one role to the other. The parent may assume the identity of partner once the kids are in bed.

The separate self is a shape shifter. It has many faces, many self-concepts. It may feel worthy or worthless depending on hormones, weather and so forth. But the ultimate shift is the attention shift out of any identification.

You are Life wearing the costume of 'me'. You are not the separate identity. You are the space in which it comes and goes. You are not the animal body.

A – S-A-ilor Bob

A – Animals

Bob: There is a herd of deer grazing. When a few wolves appear, the herd starts to run. Wolves will catch one; and as soon as they put it down, the other deer stop running away and return to grazing. And what do people do? They run a story, and often many years later they boast about what has happened to them back then.

Animals are always present with what appears. They live spontaneously, instinctively responding to sensory information. In the absence of symbolic language, they don't invent the idea of a controller residing inside themselves. As far as neuroscience can tell, their brains didn't develop what we call the DMN (Default Mode Network) or, in short, 'the narrative self'. They are free. They experience pain but not the psychological suffering which results from resistance to pain in the narrative. They don't have any self-centre or self-image. They don't relate to a personal story or 'me'.

Bob: All animals have ways to communicate. You can hear how they communicate. The bird has a different call for danger or for when it is looking for a mate. Dogs have different barks, lions have roars, antelopes snort or stomp their feet when danger is around. All this is present happening. They have amazing capacities to survive. They learn, problem solve and some instinctively plan and prepare for winter.

Animals in trouble rely on their instincts. Human animals, on the other hand, react with resistance in inner commentary. Instead of efficiently addressing the trouble (be it hunger, heat, cold, sickness or competition for territory or a mate), we complain. More often than not, we waste energy investing attention in the story of 'poor me' (or 'great me').

We live mainly in our minds. Awareness of this habit helps to return to a natural space of healing. Being with what is, is the natural state. Watching nature inspires and grounds us. It also brings about a sobering realization of the pointlessness of arguing with reality.

A pointer I found very helpful during my initial stabilisation — and which still speaks loudly to me today — is Bob's: "Look to animals to see what is natural". For me, cats, dogs and birds were easiest to relate to. Do they get triggered, irritable or frustrated? It certainly looks like they do! Do they get sad or restless? Sure. Dogs growl; cats hiss. But they don't hang onto it, they don't carry it around. They don't take it personally. Growling and hissing happens just like barking and meowing, wagging tails or purring.

And what's more, they learn too. They grow, evolve and change, just as everything else does. They know who not to approach or what not to eat (at times after few experiments). But they don't hold grievance by sustaining thought, in a human way. With new learning the database gets updated. It is not personal.

Our two darling cats are master examples of what is natural in living without a self-centre. Bob lovingly calls them "pests" and threatens them with "a bag of rocks and a trip to the river". They don't take any notice at all. They crawl on his lap and purr.

We don't consider them enlightened because there is nobody in there to be enlightened. In the same way there is nobody to be enlightened in Bob, you or me. There is only awareness, ever present and ever fresh. It is undeniable knowing of existence.

Over the centuries, various Buddhist scholars have discussed the question of whether dogs possess a Buddha Nature. They have never found the resolution because it lies within definitions of terms. Dogs do not awaken because they didn't fall for a daydream like we do. Awareness in animals is unobscured by the clouds of self-obsessive thoughts. Awareness is clear.

A – Awareness

Bob: Are you unaware right now? No. You are not unaware. So, you must be aware. Awareness is there, right where you are. Awareness is just another word for the activity of knowing, intelligence energy or consciousness.

It points to the same no-thing to which the words Stillness, Siva or God point to. Various definitions will differentiate these for the sake of pointing but, ultimately, it is all One: nondual. Awareness is an aspect of the changeless Reality, of what you are Omniscience The Source of all cognizing; the very knowing itself. Awareness of your own presence is the knowing that you are.

Awareness is the background on which everything comes to be known, to play, to appear and disappear. Some call is Sky-like-awareness or Space. Nothing 'is' without the knowing of it. The very knowing is awareness.

The content of knowing: knowing about this, that or the other — is how it expresses. This is where the differentiation into consciousness may become handy. Awareness is a capacity of knowing while consciousness is utilizing it through the senses.

> **Bob:** *This awareness is with you all the time. You are not unaware: you can't deny the fact of knowing. So you must be this awareness, no need to look for it anywhere or try to grasp it. It is not a thing to imagine or find. When it may be helpful to discriminate, we can say that consciousness is an existence utterly aware that it exists. Awareness is first, consciousness appears on it.*

It would be fair enough to say that this awake awareness is a spacious screen, and that everything else is content. Being in awareness means being known or cognized. In that field of awake awareness, there is a body, thoughts and other objects. This means that there is awareness of them.

Can we say that anything exists without having awareness of it? Is Schrodinger's cat dead or alive before we look into the box? (Radioactive material in famous theoretical experiment gives it 50 per cent of chances, pointing paradox of quantum superposition.) The answer is: nothing can be said about it. It shows that being and knowing are not separable. They are two aspects of the one.

In that awareness there are thoughts, feelings, sensations and mental images; stories about past and future; sounds and smells. In that spacious field of knowing, everything appears and disappears. When it disappears from knowing, it is gone.

Acknowledging awareness means withdrawing attention from illusion. They also call it awakening.

A – Awakening

Bob: Aren't you awake right now? Did you have to do anything for that wakefulness to be there? Is that something that you have or it just is? It may get obscured by clouds of thoughts but it is never far away.

Awakening is the point when the dream is gone. That includes the daydream. That includes the investment and belief in narrative. If you were 'gone with the birds' just a moment ago but now you are awake, then welcome home. This is it. In a moment another train of thought may take you for a ride, and the ride may entertain you for minutes or hours. But when you wake up, you are here now. Welcome home. This is it.

In the gap between daydreams, sky-like awareness is clear. This is awakening from the daydream. In this clarity there is no self, there is just what is.

When you wake up from the ride of thought (imagination or memory), there is no you. 'You' can only exist in the story. Check it out, please. There may be a presence of some kind here, but nobody who owns it or has it. In this story-less moment nowhere (now here, no-where), there is nobody who has awakened. There is seeing, hearing, tasting, touching, smelling, talking, walking, living – but no-one is a doer of it.

Understood in this manner, awakening is not a lasting event but a moment to moment realization. There is nobody who is permanently awake, because being awake means there is nobody home. Awakening is a shift of attention from the story of 'me' into story-less presence. In the absence of the story of 'me', life just is. Without the concept of 'me', there is no 'me'.

Does it mean that animals are awake after all? They don't believe in separation, they don't carry the story of 'me' to wake up from. They just are. Nobody is home; there is only life functioning. They don't know any other way. They have never lost the paradise of their innocence.

Only the human pattern can fully appreciate freedom from beliefs, the awakening from the daydream. But for this possibility of awakening to appear on the menu, falling for the separation is a prerequisite.

It is the consciousness that wakes up (disentangles) from the dream: the daydream, the night dream and the waking dream. In the human body, consciousness wakes up to the waking dream from the daydream. Upon the death of the human body, consciousness wakes up from the waking dream. 'You' or 'me' is the dream to wake up from. 'You' or 'I' do not awaken. The dream doesn't awaken. The dream character is a dream.

You are that consciousness, already awake. Recognize that. You are the totality. You are awake; alive. You are aware. You are. You are That Static Awareness. What moves in it is attention.

A – Attention

Attention is like a torch or flashlight casting a ray in a particular direction. Because everything is the movement of energy or life, so is attention. Awareness in motion is attention. Awareness is the background for attention. Siva, the Sky (Awareness), vibrates: Shakti dances and the world appears in the field of attention.

> **Bob:** *Stay utterly awake with the five senses wide open and un-fixated awareness. We habitually focus most of the attention on thinking and the other senses get neglected. So, we may miss something important happening in the seeing, hearing, tasting, touching and smelling.*

Attention is limited. The brain has a certain computing capacity which may be enhanced but not indefinitely. There is only so much sensory information that neural networks can process. …And only a fraction of it is processed consciously; the majority of processing is happening unknowingly — on autopilot.

If the attention is invested in the five senses, less of it is available for the sixth sense, which is thinking. Now we are 'more awake' (from the story, to sensory experiencing).

The basic five senses report about the environment (including the body) in the present location, at the present time (for there is no other time for direct sensory experiencing). They project Space with its content in HERE. Only thinking (imagination, daydreaming) seems to transport the attention away from this immediacy to other locations and other times. Only conceptualization can create the illusion of not-here, not-now. But where and when does conceptualization happen, if not here-now?

> **Bob:** *Try and leave this moment now. You will see that you can't. You may imagine you do so by directing your attention away from what is presently happening, but even that you still do in this immediacy of NOW.*

Emotional pain comes from the fixation of attention on a stressful idea. There is a believed in problem or a fear related to this entity, the 'me'. Obsessing starts. Attention is trapped in the narrative.

> **Bob:** *This is what Nisargadatta had to say about the source of suffering: "Desire is a fixation of the mind on an idea. Get out of its groove by denying it attention".*

Attending to the attention itself rather than falling for its content usually weakens or ends the fixation. Recognition of fixation releases some part of the attention stream for noticing it. Recognition is spontaneous. When the narrative is noticed, its content is less relevant than the basic fact of the autopilot chatter.

Attending to the attention is also a magnificent exploration — fascinating learning. Every individual pattern of personality is vastly different. It has different tastes, values, attention habits, responses and reactions. To be able to see where the attention goes, where it stays, what it avoids — is a spectacular entertainment which provides great insight into the nature of things.

A – Attention on attention – E X E R C I S E

Take 10 to 15 minutes to walk around wherever you are. Observe where the attention is moving, what it is attracted to and what it resists or omits. Notice how much of the attention goes to objects. See what part of its stream is involved in noticing impressions (seeing, sensing bodily movement, breath, balance, scents and hearing sounds). Observe how much of it goes to mental activity. Be utterly aware of that inner commentary.

You may repeat this exercise at different times of the day to see any patterns in your habitual movement of attention. For example, you may notice how it oscillates around food when close to meal-time. You may notice when it tends to revisit the past or project the future. You may find repetitive thoughts regarding yourself, others, places or things.

You may make it a habit to check and contemplate, to reflect on the movement of attention for a few minutes every night before you go to sleep. Another effective learning method is journaling.

Watching attention in this way disables identification with it and makes it impersonal. It also reveals the mechanicalness and predictability of most habit patterns.

You might check where attention goes and where it tends to stay at different points throughout the day. Every hour (or however often you want to check the clock), you can reflect on the movement of attention. You may notice the topics, moods, states of mind, attraction and repulsion and the inner commentary.

Please acknowledge every moment when you are awake to the movement of attention. Reward yourself for that with a warm feeling of gratitude. The more you acknowledge it and reward it, the more it will reappear.

Please don't judge yourself if you forget to bring attention to the attention. Any mental punishment will only ensure that the habit of noticing weakens and punitive thoughts will reappear. Remember, they are habits, you are not the doer, and you are not guilty.

Training attentional habits is almost like training a puppy. Encouragement and rewards work wonders; punishment traumatizes and shoots down willingness and curiosity. Please, make it light, make it fun!

   Bob: *Watch the mind, see how it operates!*

You are never a doer of any mind-training or attention-tracking habit. If that idea doesn't hit home, fails to inspire, that is perfectly okay too. It was a big one for me; it brought about a lot of clarity on how attention wanders.

The attention on attention exercise can also be done sitting still in a meditative posture, if you can remember not to take credit for its outcomes and not to harbor imaginary expectations. Be motivated by curiosity rather than a personal agenda of 'achieving enlightenment' for the ego.

A – About Andy's awakening – E X A M P L E

Andy is a Californian, handsome, single homosexual man with big blue eyes, long eyelashes, black eyebrows and semi-long brown curly hair. He is in his mid-30s. Before the pandemic he was working 5 days a week as a tour-bus driver and liked his job a lot. But in the office, where he had to show up twice a week for a briefing, he was often confronted by his homophobic boss.

Till recently Andy's attention was preoccupied with anger towards his bully of a boss and anxiety about potential loss of employment. He just couldn't contain his temper when he felt provoked! Back home he sedated the uneasiness with his drug of choice: porn. That addiction would trigger a deep-rooted sense of guilt and shame, which in turn brought further need of sedation.

He would Skype with Bob weekly and chat with me on FB messenger, always experiencing temporary relief and some sort of a shift to clearer skies. But even being so receptive to pointing, he would often revert to old thinking habits only a couple of days after each session.

That is, until one fine summer evening, when a couple of hours after his regular Saturday video call with Bob, Andy recognized — at last! He saw clearly how impersonal his line of attention habits was! He could see how thought triggers emotion; how emotion changes the chemistry of the body; and how there is no 'him' to do any of it!

Curiosity about the process — how intensely, for how long, and how often it is going to come up — liberated him at last from resistance to it. The breakthrough happened at about 7.00 pm local time, while Andy was eating pizza...

89

All at once, the world seemed to stop completely. Attention suddenly disengaged from the narrative and became still and silent for immeasurable time. Joy filled his heart and his big blue eyes welled with tears. It was clear in this moment that nobody was there to move this attention around! There was nobody to believe and react to things! It is always just what is. There is nothing more. No Andy. Just this. Just movement or stillness of attention. What a cosmic joke!

It felt like hours of bliss, but only twenty minutes later, at 7.20 pm by his big kitchen clock, he took another bite of a cold pizza. A faint thought showed up to doubt the recognition but he ignored it and left it unattended. The doubting thought appeared in stillness, to no-one. Attention didn't sustain it, so it died out like a fire without fuel.

Now, two years later, Andy still puts attention on the movement of attention, and he still experiences the liberating bliss of impersonality of action. However, now he knows he doesn't do it at all. Life does it. Life brings up the curiosity which calls for attention for the dance of these innocent habits.

Habits are neither good nor bad. They must have served him once, otherwise they wouldn't have been formed! Andy fully understands it now.

As realization matures, more lingering beliefs drop off and the anger pattern slowly subsides. We keep catching up on Skype every couple of months to share the joy and ease of the natural state.

Andy's anxiety disappeared once and for all on that fine summer evening. His relationship with his boss has shifted to more respectful mutual tolerance. A few miracles have appeared in respect to his formerly estranged family as well.

Andy saw how the mind operates. He saw how life happens. He saw how nobody moves the Sun, nobody blows the wind and nobody directs his or anybody else's attention. He understood his boss's innate innocence and the innocence of his own responses. He is free. Consciousness in Andy is liberated. Consciousness in Andy is clear that there never was any Andy, even when life was lived through this contracting filter. All seeking, all questions became laughable. This is the answer.

A – Answer

> **Bob:** *The answer is not in the mind. Stop trying to find the answer where you cannot find it. Didn't some of you try to find it in thinking for most of your life? You are intelligent people. It is about time to realize it is not there.*

How could mind, which is just a stream of thought, grasp the Absolute in which thoughts merely appear and disappear? Mind is only a minute expression amongst many others.

How could mind, which is a movement, a vibration of thoughts, sounds or images, grasp the no-mind — the absence of movement or sounds? How can movement experience stillness or sound taste silence?

The answer is: IT CANNOT. There is no point trying. Trying has to cease. Mind has to get out of the way.

This is the only thing that needs to be understood in a traditional, conceptual way: The answer is not in the mind. This is the only understanding that needs to be given to the mind. When this is really understood, seeking stops. Natural relaxation brings up all the relevant answers whenever question arises.

When the mind stops, there is nothing about the nature of the experiencing that you are not able to know directly. The answer is here: full stop ('period'). The answer is the dissolution of all questions. The answer is an absence of the questioner. The answer is silent.

> **Bob:** *Instead of inquiring 'Who am I?' you can look and see who is asking the question. You will realize that the questioner is the question itself and they will cancel each other out. No question, no questioner, no-one to know 'Who am I', no one who needs to know it.*

If there was an answer in the mind, somebody would have found it by now and given it to us instead of throwing vague pointers which later on evolve into organized religions, practices, or get lost in translation. If not you, then maybe the Buddha or Jesus would have found it there and given us a prescription instead of an imperfect description of where to look.

And what would this answer be if it was in the mind? Would it not just be another concept? For how long would that concept satisfy you? Would you need to believe it and remember it all the time? And lastly, where, on what screen would this concept appear? Who would be the receiver of it? Where would the receiver appear? If it was to depend on so many external factors, how absolute would that answer really be?

There is no accurate conceptual answer. The answer is an absence of the questioner. See if there is anyone there who is believing the thinking stream. In finding nobody there, the questioner is gone. Realization of your own being is experiential, and not an intellectual inquiry. The answer to life and everything is not in the mind. No point looking in thoughts. Relax. Everything is just an appearance.

A – Appearance

The definition of Reality is: "That which never changes". Is there any form that is eternal? Surely, there is not. Forms change. The only changeless is No-Thing or Space; Emptiness or the Basic Screen. Everything else is constantly changing. Some things seem to last longer than the others, but all of them have their beginning and an end. The lifespan of the galaxy is vastly different to the lifespan of a bacterium or subatomic particle. But they all appear and disappear from and to the formless nonexistence, the empty screen of awareness. That is why they are collectively called 'an appearance' or 'manifestation'.

> **Bob:** *What appears, we can call 'phenomena'. Check your dictionary definition of phenomenon and you will see that "phenomenon is what appears to be". Not what is, but what appears to be. Noumenon is what is. All that you see is a 'phenomenal manifestation'. It is an illusion, Maya.*

Appearance is also called a dream, a mirage, a phantom, Leela or, simply, the content of space. Appearance is what shows up in the field of sensory knowing. Whatever can be perceived or conceived of is an appearance. Whatever is mortal, temporary or changing is an appearance. Whatever has a beginning and an end, birth and death, shape and form, is an appearance. Its existence is transient, not absolute.

Dreams at night appear real. They may contain people, places and things. Logic during the dream may say, "These trees look 100 years old", or "These buildings have been here for a long time, and people born in the distant past used to live in them". But is that really so? Seemingly, things need time to come into existence. Yet, in the dream, the whole lot came up, lasted but minutes and then disappeared. It came up in the immediacy and its past was assumed and projected back, also in the immediacy.

In the same way, in this waking dream, the age of the galaxy and everything in it is contained in this moment. Its origin, its past — is in the content of thoughts: it is imagined. It doesn't exist presently in any other form than a mental image. It is the thought itself.

Wherever attention goes, creation and projection follow. Appearance is like a fractal; anywhere you look, more details emerge. Nothing exists without attention. Everything thrives and proliferates on it. It applies equally to all fields of sensory experience, including thinking, which creates time.

In the manifested world, there are situations and processes appearing and disappearing in time. Even if some things and forms seem to last an almost infinitely long time, they will all expire. Everything is impermanent, bound to change. No form has absolute reality. No form is the Absolute.

A – Absolute

That which never changes is called real or The Absolute. But what never changes? There is no such thing. Only No-Thing is changeless, real or absolute.

In a dictionary 'absolute' is defined as: "something that is 100 percent complete with no exceptions, something that is always true and accepted as fact, with no arguments against it or conditions necessary for it to be true." An example of absolute would be total silence with no noise at all.

> **Bob:** *What can you add to the Absolute? Can you add anything? It wouldn't be absolute if you could. And what can you take away from it? Nothing. It is already total. You are already That Totality.*

You are That Absolute. You are that changeless background including all the seeming content of it. You are non-conceptual awareness. In you, all forms appear and disappear and those are That, too. You, as Life Essence, are the source of all the movement of thoughts and images. You, as Space, have created forms out of yourself.

Absolute Stillness (motion-less-ness) is both static and dynamic, vibrating into all those forms, shapes and patterns. Yet, it never ceases to be itself; it never really divides or separates. It only appears to be so. In reality, nothing has ever happened. Nothing left its source. It is always and ever the complete, undivided, not-even-one Absolute.

Synonyms for the absolute are: complete, full, outright, sheer, simple, unadulterated, unlimited and unqualified. Just like pure presence, I am.

To taste it, don't identify with any particular expression of it but see them all as content — the changing in the changeless. Nisargadatta would tell you (speaking to your idea of 'me') to expand and embrace the universe. Recognize it is already appearing in that (your) presence. The universe is in you. You are that Absolute. You are that limitless space, that open field of awareness. It is so already. You are that Absolute already.

A – Already

Bob: *Start from the fact, whether you know it, or feel it or understand it right now or not, that you are ALREADY That. Everything is That. ALREADY.*

This is a key word in Bob's message. It points to the fact that nothing needs or can be done or fixed because it is already so. You are already what you seek to become. You already have what you may think you are lacking or wanting. There is nothing to do, no one to become anything else, no achievement to make. There is nothing to find elsewhere nor in time. There is nothing to add or construct.

You are already fulfilled and complete. You are already perfect. It is so, whether you have realized it or not. You are already an empty sky, whether dark clouds are passing through it or not. You are already that Sat-Chit-Ananda, still conscious being, regardless of the limiting beliefs you may carry around or mask you may wear.

Being the Absolute, you already contain every quality, every value and every skill and talent — even if just as a potential. If it is not in one particular body, then it is in some other one. All bodies are appearing in you, in your conscious awareness of presence. You are an open field of infinite possibility. You are already free from your imagination, free from the conceptual mind. Who you are in truth is not — and cannot be — contained or constrained by any idea.

Just allow spontaneous recognition of the fact that it is already so. You are not unaware, not asleep and not unconscious. You exist. As a body-mind form you are being lived. As animating life, you do the living. You are that One, dreaming to be the body-mind. You are that One wearing the imaginary costume of limitations so you can see, hear, feel and think.

But you are already that One. You can't be separate from Oneness; you can't be an entity. Recognize that it is already so. Awareness is already awake and alive. You are that animating aliveness.

A – Animating aliveness – E X E R C I S E

Bob: Do you know the difference between an alive body and a corpse? They both have all the inner organs. The corpse has the heart, the lungs, the voice box etc. But without that animating force, the Life essence, the body is just a corpse.

Aliveness is like electricity for the light bulb or toaster. It is an energy. It can be measured, even in plants. It can be stored and utilized. (While doing my martial arts training in China, in

2006, I witnessed a Shaolin Kung Fu master breaking bricks and setting fire to wadded paper using concentrated chi!)

We all know the difference between being exhausted and fresh, sick and healthy, depressed and in love, or depleted and invigorated. We also call that animating energy a vital force or vibrancy — the radiance of life.

You can experience that animating life essence right now by focusing your attention in the body, regardless of your energy level at this moment. A few deep breaths will recharge you and intensify the feeling, if there is a need. It can be intensified further with a few deep, fast breaths followed by a short pause in breathing with your eyes closed. It can be sensed as pulsating, throbbing, vibrating, animating aliveness.

Without controlling the breath, an easy way to experience life-force is by sensing any obstruction to its free flow, such as tension or resistance in the shoulders, neck or on the face. Tension around the eyes or in the jaw is usually easy to detect.

Any point of contact — the fabric of clothes on the skin, where feet touch the ground, where the lips touch each other — produces a distinct sensation. Any mental image or thought which might come with the sensation (to interpret it and give meaning) needs to be put aside, unattended, ignored.

Sensing life-flow is particularly easy when strong emotion or a near-miss shakes you. Don't seek it out, though: Life will provide it in time! Hold space for this shakiness; feel the juiciness of animating, awake aliveness. It is also present without trauma. It's always here.

Please experiment for a couple of minutes with your eyes closed. Bring the attention to any physical sensation in the body. If you are sitting, sense where your backside touches the seat. If you are standing or walking, feel your feet. Simply notice the sensation.

Push aside any mental image that tells you that there are two things (subject and object) meeting: it is irrelevant. Sensation is singular. It is alive. It is just here — not any distance from an imagined center of self. Aliveness is here. Enjoy it, fall in love with it and be curious about it. Find it attractive, worthy of exploration and appreciation.

One interesting application of this exercise is the observation of strong emotions like anger, shame or fury. No need to recall and re-live it; just remember to experience it fully when the emotion naturally occurs. It's an opportunity to learn about the emotion's physical effects without labelling it and weaving together a story about it in your head. This way, the emotion will be neither expressed nor suppressed but experienced fully in terms of present sensation and sensation only.

> **Bob:** *What is this thing that animates the universe? What moves the planets, what makes this body move and feel?*
>
> *It is this essence: energy or life. This life force is functioning in this body-mind. Thinking is taking place, seeing, hearing, heart beating; the whole lot is going on.*
>
> *But all these sense organs would be useless if life essence were not in the body. Can a corpse see or hear? Can a corpse be aware? Can a corpse feel, taste, touch or smell? No. Give credit where credit is due. This animating life essence is what you are. Appreciate it as it so deserves.*

A – Appreciation

Appreciation is just another name for love. As energy, it feels high, selfless; very close to gratitude. Acknowledgement and admiration are said to be its synonyms.

I like to think about appreciation (or love) as the meaning of life. It is just a story, not the truth, but as a story it includes all and sprinkles everything with self-love. The Absolute loves its reflections in forms. It wouldn't have them otherwise and there would be no appearance.

Every form (including thought-forms) is appreciated by one or the other. Nothing is excluded. Illnesses and wars bring money to big concerns, and money creates illusion of power, which is highly appreciated in the appearance. Other humans appreciate art, pleasures, gods, sports, weather... There are other creatures and forms in nature as well. Every individual has preferences. Collectively, every inch of the appearance is covered by appreciation.

In this way, Totality exhibits self-love. In fact, everything you see is a reflection of that Totality. It gets glimpses of itself through the senses. It is all *it*. *It* is all *you*. It can't know itself in any other way. The world is a mirror — a reflecting surface or space filled with images. One could say the space in which the world appears is a mirror and the world is a reflection in that mirror — but they are not two and can't be separated.

Parts of the appearance are appreciated and other parts are depreciated. Some are seen through the filter of the 'self-centre' as bad, ugly or unlovable. Negative attention feeds them into existence. Yet, in the scheme of things, these feelings are deeply appreciated as well. Why? Because they exist. They are. They love to be. They are complements for their opposites: goodness, beauty and loveliness, which couldn't exist otherwise.

As an example, I feel great appreciation that in this human adventure Bob values loyalty over betrayal. However, what Bob is in essence is not a human pattern — not the body-mind with its likes and dislikes, values and preferences. In essence, there is no Bob, just This. Bob is only a way it expresses itself. Gratitide is a response to it.

Yet, he is my favourite illusion, deeply, deeply appreciated in all aspects! There is undeniable attraction between us: attraction on every human level that makes this amazing dream even more appreciated. What an attractive appearance!

A – Attraction

Bob: *People are often asking about the Law of Attraction. Yes, there is a natural law of attraction, which is not what people make of it. Look at the little child, how he operates. When something attracts his attention, he grabs it or pushes it away. It functions naturally, effortlessly. There is no story in here anywhere.*

Animals function in the same way. A momentary need comes up and response to the need follows. Innate intelligence of each pattern knows what is necessary for it to function, and the same intelligence (life) equips different animals with their required skills and capacities.

A sunflower seems to be attracted to the Sun, as it follows it throughout the day. Birds migrate. Squirrels plant forests. Bees pollinate.

There is a natural attraction between people and amongst individuals as well. There is intellectual attraction, sexual attraction, attraction to certain tasks, certain foods, to particular entertainment, behaviors etc. Without the narrative to sustain it, without the story and energy of belief, everything naturally resolves. Needs are spontaneously addressed via actions. Attraction or repulsion moves the body-mind pattern to do what needs doing and to be where it needs to be.

Attraction/repulsion seems to be a natural law governing the appearance. Without them there would be no movement. Without the narrative, there is no problem anywhere. Everything is just as it is. Everything is no-thing in essence but a thing in how it appears. Without the story, things are just as they are.

A – As they are

> **Bob:** *Leave things as they are. What does it mean? As they are means unaltered, unmodified, uncorrected. To try to fix, change, alter, modify or correct, means to resist. And what can you alter it with? Only the thought, the concept.*

As they are, things are perfect. It may not be evident when they are related to an individual who has an agenda in time, but in eternity it is obvious.

Bob: "When from the perfect the perfect is taken, only the perfect remains", says the Guru-Gita. Everything is perfect as it is, unaltered, unmodified, uncorrected.

This is a very powerful pointer which has helped many seekers to relax their trying to 'fix'. There is often a lot of 'trying' and 'efforting' to get something or to get out of something. This trying (resistance) is like fuel for the fire. It is an energy of belief (attention) that keeps it alive for longer than necessary.

With or without trying to fix, things will change. Always. Nothing stays the same in the appearance. The fastest way for them to change is to withdraw importance and leave them as they are.

Bob doesn't give much advice because there is no-one to follow, since the ego is a fiction. However, he does inspire and he calls for resonance, for innate wisdom. Therefore: do leave things unaltered, unmodified, uncorrected! Leave them just as they are! Whatever comes up, don't touch it. Let it be noticed by the cognizing emptiness that you are. Being Space, what do you care?

Anger comes up? Cool! Notice a vibration in the body, the images in the mind. Isn't it interesting? No need to change it: it won't last anyway. A reaction comes up: cool, an impersonal reaction pattern.

This is not to say that 'you' should not fix things, because the impulse to fix may arise, but there is no 'you' to own it. If fixing happens, leave it as it is, let it happen. There is no need to take ownership; no need to take credit for spontaneous happening. So, just relax. Nothing is wrong. Whatever comes up... cool! It is not personal, it is just a pattern.

Are we really sinners who need to be repaired? We were taught incompleteness. We were told that we need wealth, name and fame... We were told we need to add to ourselves, to accumulate, amass...

A – Add, accumulate, amass

Bob: *When the child is about two, two and a half, the reasoning capacity starts to function in this human pattern. This is the capacity this human pattern has. Other patterns don't have this particular capacity but they have other capacities. The bird has eyesight much better than we do, and the capacity of flying, which we do not have.*

But through the capacity of reasoning, we have built eye glasses, binoculars, and microscopes that enabled us to see better. And we constructed airplanes, balloons and helicopters that enabled us to fly.

So, it is a wonderful capacity, but it can back-fire, also. Reasoning capacity or thinking is what we call the mind. Mind is nothing but thinking, and thinking is vibration.

The nature of the mind is to vibrate, and it can only vibrate dualistically. Watch the mind and see how it functions. Everything is either good or bad, pleasant or painful or it is somewhere between those two.

Those two extremes are boundaries we put on everything.

Thinking in the interrelated pairs of opposites creates the duality of 'I' and 'not-I'. Insecurity and vulnerability stem from identification as an 'I'. We feel small and limited. To diminish this insecurity and vulnerability, we are told to add, accumulate, amass — to do anything to feel more complete, more secure...

Bob: *Our parents told us to go to school, to get a good education, a job, to make money. Then, we hope maybe a partner will complete us, or a new car, a promotion, membership of nation or community...*

Search for the relief from this sense of incompleteness is always futile. We are trying to cure a disease that is imaginary. No amount of wealth or fame can eradicate this fictitious limitation. Illusion needs to be recognized only.

Bob: *Parents told you, you are little Johnny, good little boy or a bad one. But what can you do with an image like this? You need to build it up, add to it events and experiences from the past to give it credibility.*

But it still feels kind of incomplete. So they tell you to go out, add, accumulate, amass: the title, profession, adventures, achievements etc. But has that helped them? Are they fulfilled?

The whole consumerism as a culture thrives on this search for relief, the self-help industry included. The self-help movement offers more inner solutions, new sets of skills, changes in values and techniques of interrupting patterns instead of looking for a cure. It suggests adding, accumulating and amassing qualities, behaviors, affirmations or explanations. It also hopes for a future when you will feel less incomplete and more fulfilled.

We say STOP. Adding, accumulating and amassing are distractions from this immediate moment of aliveness. Be aware of it, let attention rest in this uncontrived singularity. Leave it unaltered, unmodified uncorrected — just as it is.

Actions will spontaneously arise. Adding will arise without urgency, without importance, without the story of lack.

> **Bob:** *Mind has been used (since the time it first started to reason) for looking 'out there', grasping, grabbing and searching for bigger and better sensations. The greater, the noisier, the louder or more beautiful the sensation is — the more it gives a lift or a kick — the better it is. That has become our habit pattern. That is what we seem to aim for. Is it a valid aim?*

A – Aim

The self-help industry convinces us that only a well set aim, mission or goal — and a path to it with visible progress — can make us happy. This can be particularly appealing to natural high-performers. However, this is not what we observe with the careless, playful explorers that are young children! They don't need future targets or a sense of achievement to be in joy. They do not need to take credit for simple happening. Narrative is not a terrorist for them just yet. Stories of selfishness and urges to grow and contribute will come a bit later. The so called immortality dream and resulting anxiety is still unconceivable.

But for an adult, which notion is right?

There is a way to look at aim-setting without making it good or bad, right or wrong, necessary for happiness or redundant in life. Aims may show up or they may not. They can be short-term, long-term and life-long. An aim may appear as an image, vision or project and may be charged with passion. Just as Life manifests every thought, decision or creation, aims may also arise out of this field of infinite possibilities. No need to take credit for setting it. It sets itself, like a sun.

But there is a freedom much more profound and much more fulfilling than dependence on missions and goals. The natural state needs no conditions. Anchored in the source of all being, any vision is welcomed and appreciated but so is a plateau and period of rest!

There is also another angle to look at aims: Instead of finding long term goals (building name, fame and wealth) in the future, a momentary aim to serve, to recognize love, to appreciate beauty or to experience and express flow with life may already be available. Once that level of presence is habituated, great creativity and passion springs from such moment to moment recognition. Worldly success may follow or it may not. It won't be a problem if joy is abundant.

Our feedback mechanism is our current feeling. Our sense of fulfilment and happiness is the compass. It is an inner guide, a sadguru. It shows us that (as social creatures) we are often happy when we go beyond ourselves to serve others; but only with selflessness derived from love, and not from resentful self-sacrifice.

Aims or goals may show up according to bodily predispositions but there need be no credit to the fictitious individual. There is no need for a personal agenda nor for any attachment to the outcome. There is no need for the addiction to high performance. However, this and various other addictions may form in the body-mind.

A – Addiction, abstinence

Bob: I was a drunk, no-hoper when I was young. Do you think I set out to become that? Do you think when my dad asked me who do I want to be when I grow up, I said I wanted to become an alcoholic? I didn't. But life had it this way. If not for the suffering coming from my alcoholism, I probably wouldn't embark on the search.

Also, my mind used to tell me that I cannot live without alcohol and cigarettes, yet I've been without them now for over 60 years. My mind was telling me bullshit. Addictions can be broken, that is certain!

Nisargadatta kept smoking, even when his throat cancer became unbearable. Alan Watts died of alcoholic cardiomyopathy at age 58, Chogyam Trungpa had alcoholic liver failure that killed him at 48. Many other 'enlightened teachers' have become addicted to substances, sex or power. How come?

Perhaps bodily habits are also, like everything else in the universe, a result of the collaboration of an infinite amount of factors. Presence or absence of an imagined self is just one of these factors.

Nisargadatta suggested leaving the body alone to do its thing until its time is over. Bob likes alkaline natural food and herbal supplements. Neither is superior nor inferior. Bodies have their preferences. Minds have their habitual responses. They form in collaboration with the environment.

Addictions can drop off. Addictions can also be broken if enough attention fuels such desire! So called Higher Power does that, not an individual. Obsession with abstinence to the point of worship has been a life-saver for many alcoholics! It had to be facilitated in that way. Such was the way that life had for Bob. In other cases, addictions would simply drop off. Or they would stay present, delivering suffering or indifference.

Life has so many vehicles of experiencing and expressing itself, that every story is fresh and new, unique and unrepeatable. You are Life. You are all of them.

In these stories life loves itself. It sees patterns, it draws conclusions. It creates metaphors and analogies...

A – Analogies again

There are a lot more impactful images available to illustrate certain aspects of the awakening. The well-known Plato Cave allegory (with its modern version of a cinema screen) is a good example. Plato's prisoners in chains represent people who are immersed in the superficial world of appearances. They are viewing shadows created by the fire behind them, an illusion of reality projected on the wall, which they try to interpret without understanding the truth. They do not know; they only believe what they see. Yet, they *believe* they do know. They fell for the dream.

Every analogy pointing to being identified as a lost in the individual story person (be it an analogy of a character in the book, hero in a movie, a computer gamer or a dreamer) is a great image to contemplate upon. They are like Zen koans or other unsolvable riddles.

If you take yourself to be a character in the book, dream, game or film, how do you break free? How do you stop being what you believe you are? Is that possible?

Under chapter L — Limitations, we will address some of the downsides of these analogies.

Comparing the body-mind to a computer with hardware (physical parts) and software (programs and applications) is an analogy that Bob often likes to use:

> **Bob:** *Look at the computer. It has all sorts of wonderful information in it. But what can you get out of it if the power is not on? Click that keyboard, run the mouse as much as you want, but it is not a little bit of good if the power is off. So what are you? Are you this body? Or thinking? Or are you that power? If not for that life essence surging through you, you would be a corpse.*

To illustrate this animating aliveness we can use all sorts of equipment run by electric power. One person may be a musician, another a doctor, a thief or the village idiot, but the same life animates them all and expresses through — and as — them. We can have a hair dryer, toaster, lamp or washing machine, but the same animating power makes them move and do their things. That Life animates bodily cells, thoughts, toasters, planets and stars.

> **Bob:** *There are a few nice analogies for the futility of getting rid of the ego. A good one from Zen monk Bankei says: "It is like washing away blood with blood. It won't happen".*

Useful analogy to human states of minds and moods is the weather. There is outer weather that we don't consciously control, and there is an inner weather, no different to the outer one. There are floods in nature and floods of tears in sadness. There are tsunami and volcanoes in nature and there are waves of fury and explosions of anger in humans.

Both, inner and outer weather exhibits are triggered by an infinite amount of environmental factors brought together. Like within, so without. Like above, so below. There are highs and lows; there are seasons and cycles. Hormones, moods and activity patterns are all variables interfering with each other in hard to predict ways, constantly changing.

This analogy helps to see emotional patterns as impersonal, which may bring back a sense of innocence and curiosity. If my internal world is as unpredictable as nature, let me see what my next mood is going to be! Let me see in a relaxed manner, no need to be too alert about it! Let me see what other anchors I can use.

A – A few more anchors on A

A – Alertness

As much as mindfulness techniques can improve concentration, and such alertness can be a desirable habit, it is not a requirement needed for recognition of the natural state. Neither is meditation, using mantras nor any other practice necessary to realize it. Trained or untrained, the mind is left behind upon awakening. Whether alert or clumsy, mind is just a pattern in the Absolute.

The by-product of disbelieving the inner commentary is that sensory information becomes more noticeable and beauty starts accompanying us in daily life. Alertness to it is a by-product of realization, not its aim. Instead of listening to the negatively biased survival instinct, other things are sensed, and spontaneous creativity comes up.

If you are moved to stay alert and mindful by any sort of regime or routine, appreciate the force which moves you to a commitment like this! Don't take any credit for it, but do appreciate the outcomes. If you are not moved to practice any disciplines, harbor no hard feelings about this. Explore other aspects!

A – Aspect

'Aspect' is a word which brings to mind multifaceted representations of something that is ultimately singular, such as the well-known trinities of Sat-Chit-Ananda, father-son-spirit or omnipresence-omnipotence-omniscience. These are all aspects of the One. Even steam-water-ice (standing for thought-feeling-emotion) is one made three. These trinities all attempt to characterize IT from three angles or perspectives.

Dualities of thin-thick, good-bad, black-white are also two ends of the same one stick; two sides of the same one coin. In the same way subject-object, seer-seen are aspects of the one (relating, seeing; one experiencing).

As the Dao De Jing says, "Dao brought forth the One, from One comes Two, from Two comes Three and from Three comes the ten thousand things". But it also says that the Dao has no beginning: it doesn't come from anywhere. There is no prior to One, Two, Three and ten thousand things. Time is mind.

Aspects do not point to seeming division of what is in truth indivisible. Angles of perspective bring back to oneness without denying diversity. It is like one actor changing costumes and roles.

A – Actor

Shakespeare said: "All the world's a stage, and all the men and women merely players". Life is an arena and we are all actors. We are wearing the costume of the body-mind, which is well-equipped with preferences and built-in sets of reactions. When the role we play is done with, the mask can be taken off. I may play the mother, the wife or the boss, but I'm none of these. There is no need for you or me to stop playing the role, as it isn't us doing so, but life. It plays itself. There is no one to stop it. Even the desire to do so is merely another orphan thought. Recognition is enough.

Who is wearing the costume? Who is expressing through the body and as the body? Who is an actor? Who am I? What is 'I'? Is there anybody in this costume?

"I don't know", an honest mind would say. The answer is in silence. It is in the direct non-verbal knowing of unlabeled being. Abide as That.

A – Abide as That

Bob: You are THAT already. Stay there. Abide as That. Start from there and see how the attention is moving away into a daydream but abide as That.

Notice any movement away from I-am-ness. Noticing is always here, only the content seemingly comes and goes. In here, in stillness, the movement of attention is known. Abide in here.

Abide as That. What takes the attention away? What concepts present themselves to argue with that basic statement? Is it a thought? A mental image? A feeling? Watch that angst. Let anxiety teach you.

A – Anxiety, angst

Angst is a feeling of deep fear or dread, typically an unfocused one about the human condition or the state of the world in general. It is fully reliant on mental activity — the concepts one subconsciously holds about the future and about oneself.

Deep rooted fear of unworthiness and of being undeserving feeds the existential angst. Underlying it is a desire for peace and security. That caring desire is a pointer to already present peace that passes all concepts. It is a stillness in which anxiety appears and disappears. This stillness can be recognized and appreciated right now. There is only now, always now.

Without any label, anxiety is just an energy moving in consciousness. Can you locate it? Can you circumscribe it? Can you sense its density, shape and colour? What does it do to the breath? When neutral curiosity replaces resistance, it is life itself. It is fascinating. ...And so is anger!

114

A – Anger

Bob: If anger is there, let it be there! It won't last if it has nothing to fixate on. But when you label it 'anger', where are you labelling it from? You have had this experience before and you remember; they told you this is anger. So, the similar vibration may come up and you label it from the past as anger or fear or whatever. You label from the past, instead of being with it as it is, experiencing it fresh and new. And you load yourself down with all past anger or past fear that you ever had.

If you are with it as it is, if you see it for the first time, you can be curious about it. It may be an entirely different emotion that you don't need to label. But the resistance there hangs around and it builds up. Then comes the condemning yourself afterwards for being that way. It keeps perpetuating itself from that.

Instead of supressing or expressing, explore. See the reflection of that movement of energy in the body. Notice what it does to the throat and lungs. Feel where it causes tension or contraction. Feel the buzzing of life. Give it space. Give it neutral but curious attention. Enjoy! There is nothing good or bad in it.

Haven't you seen angry birds or dogs? Pure sensation is pure. Interpretation in terms of a victim story is another pattern added (also to be noticed with neutrality). Space doesn't judge or take sides. You are that Space. Have an affectionate awareness of That.

A – Affectionate Awareness

> **Bob:** *Have the affectionate awareness of being. Be warm towards yourself, love yourself. This is Sat-Chit-Ananda.*

Many spiritual paths preach self-love, affection towards oneself. This is not about narcissism. Affection is to be directed to the being-knowing, which is our formless true nature. It is to be recognized as already present rather than forced or enacted.

Love (as gratitude) towards certain values, qualities or skills developed in one's own body-mind can be combined with humble recognition that we didn't create ourselves: Life has. There is nothing humble about denying innate self-love, because nothing could ever belong to a non-existent 'me'.

Finding the seed of self-love already present and nurturing it feels right! Acknowledging and appreciating Ananda (loving to be) heightens the bliss.

> **Bob:** *People who are trying to be humble are often proud of their own humility! They get attached to it!*

A – Attachment

Buddhism sees the source of suffering here. Attachment to the seemingly separate self ('me'), attachment to everything and everyone that is added to this seeming individual ('me') can certainly cause psychological pain. It breeds desire, it fuels possessiveness, and it evokes control. Attachment to beliefs and ideas causes defensiveness and enhances the sense of importance. Some people are ready to die for 'their' ideas!

The major difference between attachment and love is that love is a feeling directed toward the 'other' (the other person, place or thing), while attachment is self-centred, based on fulfilling your needs.

Some natural attachment to care givers or tools ensuring survival can be observed in nature. It doesn't need to cause psychological suffering in narrative, where future losses are being imagined.

Recognition of attachment pattern as impersonal activity liberates one from both: attachment and detachment. Viewed in this manner, neither is superior or inferior, preferred or undesirable. This recognition can be anchored and associated with pointers.

A – Associate, anchor

You may be moved to associate insights with as many pointers as you can, so they become your reminders of the natural state they evoke. You may anchor them with the words so that they will spontaneously arise when needed. If the word 'Silence' touches your heart, you can anchor that touch, so it returns when the word is heard or thought of. Because it is life that moves and inspires it, life is the doer, not you.

In Neuro Linguistic Programming 'anchoring' is done by repetition, word-feeling-break, word-feeling-break, four-five times. Other associations can be added from any sensory area. You may add touch (like pinch or slap), taste (even if just the roof of your mouth), scent (of your skin if nothing else is available), image, a thought of colour, anything.

Anchoring was what I kept doing unknowingly and spontaneously as a seeker. Every little pointer was an arrow which could bring back the light, the ease. But particular keywords or anchors were only one of infinite factors. There were times when nothing would shift the energy. All pointers were impotent. I was stuck, suffering. I was humbled by my lack of control as a doer.

Association with an anchor is not to suggest that you could or should imagine your way back into a past insight or experience! It won't work! It has to be rediscovered fresh and new.

> **Bob:** *Don't chase the old insight, it is dead. Stay open and a brand new insight will show up from that silence. When an old one is gone, let it go, accept it!*

A – Acceptance

Your acceptance as body-mind is not required for Life (God) to be as it is. There is no need to force oneself to accept anything at all. What shows up, shows up because it has already been accepted on the deepest level by Life itself. Tune into it. This is unconditional acceptance. Neutrality. You are That.

If there is non-acceptance showing up, see how it is already accepted, otherwise it wouldn't be there. Accept your non-acceptance. As Space, you have already done so. As Space, which is who you are, you do not mind. Acknowledge that!

A – Acknowledge

Acknowledge the basic screen, the awareness of aliveness. Acknowledge attention. Notice your own being here and now. Acknowledge the appearance if it comes up. Acknowledge the content of all the senses, including thinking, if attention goes there. Acknowledge the background. You are That — not a body or thought but rather the absence thereof...

A – Absence

Bob: This is not about accumulating anything, be it an understanding or hours of practice. It is about discarding what is false.

Your ego is already absent. See if you can find any 'me' anywhere. Absence of separation is all there is. Nothing has any substance or independent nature. Mental images have no absolute reality. You may view presence and absence as two sides of the same coin. You are the space or screen for both. They are not opposite, they are one.

Bob: It is not about gaining anything, achieving or becoming, but about discarding what is false. In absence of the falseness the truth lies.

Allow the abyss to swallow you!

A – Abyss

Bob: What is the worst that can happen if you make your fear of the unknown as big as you can? You may think you will faint, but that is just mind bluffing. Find out for yourself and be amazed!

This is the gateless gate. Stay there one moment longer than you think is possible and face that fear of annihilation. Amplify it, make it worse. Fall into the abyss. Allow yourself to faint or fall unconscious for a minute or two if you think that is what you're facing. It won't kill the body. Energy cannot be destroyed. You are and you'll always be. Always means the timeless now. To find the abyss, still the mind. To make it sweet, focus on the heart. You may find it amazing!

119

A – Amazing

Bob: *The whole manifestation is suffused with an amazing intelligence. Look at the brilliance of this human body! Look at the incredible capacities every pattern has. You can see the intelligence suffusing every particle of the appearance. If you look at the peacock egg, it is nothing special, yolk and white as in every other egg. But give it a little bit of warmth and love and see what comes out of it. Amazing intelligence makes all these colors on the bird's feathers.*

This amazing intelligence is suffusing every cell of your body also. The liver cell knows its job; it won't become or behave like a brain cell or heart cell. The same applies to galaxies, planets and changing seasons; look where you may; it is everywhere. Amazing! Affirm that!

A – Affirm

Affirm, acknowledge and appreciate the aliveness that animates your body right now. May the word 'affirm' always bring out the recognition of the natural state, the feeling of empathy and joy. To affirm also means to validate, confirm, assert, declare and endorse. Enjoy that beautiful energy of ascertaining your own existence. Assure that!

A – Assure

Direct your attention to its source and assure yourself of that pre-sensory certainty of your own existence. It cannot be denied. Let this word 'assurance' remind you about the only certainty one can ever have: You are. Don't go with any wrong assumptions!

A – Assumptions

Bob: If you have to go with any assumption at all, take this: you are already That. You are aware, awake and alive. There is nothing more to get or to become because there is no-one to get it and become it.

If that is assumed, evidence may start appearing to support it. And soon the obviousness of it will eradicate any need for evidence. Actualize it now!

A – Actualize

Self-actualisation or self-transcendence is viewed as a goal in psychology. But it really is a synonym to realizing. Actualizing self-love is realizing no-self. If that word moves you, let it serve! May life take such an attitude now!

A – Attitude

Attitude is a manner, disposition, feeling or stand-point with regard to a person or thing; tendency or orientation, especially of the mind. Openness and receptivity is a required attitude while listening to the pointers. Curiosity is an attitude in contemplation and investigation. Upon truth-realization, when resistance is seen through, attitude naturally shifts in the direction of joy, appreciation and gratitude. ...And what also shifts is spontaneous altruism!

A – Altruism

Being selfless suggests altruism, defined as the disinterested concern for the well-being of others. It is often valued and rewarded as the supreme, admirable attitude. In nature, altruistic behavior helps the survival of individuals through reciprocity. It builds trust and binds communities. The motivation for such selflessness seems quite selfish.

In zoology, it points to the behaviour of an animal that benefits another at its own expense. The survival of the species (or its youngsters) may be instinctively prioritized, as if identification as a whole race was there.

But we (as humans) live and learn through stories. We add narratives which further popularize, romanticize and propagate the altruistic attitude conceptually. We are in love with the love that we project as underlying altruistic action — and often rightfully so! It is such a beautiful, inspiring frequency! The heart says 'yes' whenever it is recognized. The heart knows when action is impure, imposed or faked for personal reward.

If I truly have no 'myself', and when I don't believe judgmental thoughts, what is in front of me is pure perfection. It is there to be appreciated. It is to be served without any selfish agenda.

A – Agenda

As members of society, we are told to play various roles, to set goals for ourselves, and to achieve them. We are told to have purpose, meaning and agenda at all times. These goals and agendas are the content of thought. Simple living in the present does not mean that thoughts of goals and achievements stop arising. It only means that the narrative, the stories of their importance, are not being believed anymore.

> **Bob:** *Commentary may still exist but it loses its sting.*

Living spontaneously and cruising through life in an effortless way doesn't require any verbalized agenda. It also doesn't need an absence of one. Efforts and agendas, when required, arise just as everything else does. So does the alarmed state.

A – Alarm

Bob: There is no need to stay alarmed and keep strenuous watch all the time. Natural vigilance is part of the body, even in the dream. When someone calls your name loudly while you're in deep sleep, you will wake up. There is no need to be on guard.

Who would it be, this alarmed observer? Wouldn't it be just another imagined location of imagined individual entity? Who would you anticipate to find there?

A – Anticipate

A very common obstacle to the realization of natural knowing — which is always and ever present here and now — is anticipation. We imagine some super-natural state of mind; a state of constant pleasure or love. Unless this is experienced, our intellect will maintain that we are not awakened or enlightened. Comparison between anticipated and present experience goes on. It overlooks and rejects the natural state.

Looking through these subtle beliefs is a shortcut to liberation from the slavery of thinking. You can call it 'spiritual by-pass' or street-smart intelligence.

Anticipation of spectacular experience or the gaining of super-natural powers is the grandiosity of ego. Imagining that anything will become different is an activity of the mind. The mind is designed to distract us from what is, so we miss out on natural, already present awake-ness.

Jesus was known to say: "Be ye like little children to enter the kingdom". Little children do not anticipate. Very little children are not identified as 'I' yet. They are pure intelligence energy functioning: timeless and ageless.

A – Ageing, ageless

Ageing is a great reminder of the transience of forms, and agelessness is a great reminder of their immovable background. The body is ageing, but the sense of presence is not. Both when you were a kid and when you were a teenager, you had a different body. You have also had a different self-image; different thoughts and feelings.

But the existence that you are is always the same. It doesn't change. You knew back then it was you. How do you know that?

Kids sometimes ask if they would still be themselves if they had different parents. They sense that even though they would have a different body, different face; their presence would not change. It doesn't change. It doesn't age. This ageless presence Bob likes to call Intelligence Energy.

I – Sa-I-Ior Bob

I – Intelligence energy

Bob: *Everything is energy. I like to call it intelligence energy, which means an activity of knowing. Energy is an activity. That activity is known. Knowing is an intelligence. I don't like to call it 'God' because people get confused with that word.*

And it is an amazing intelligence. When I'm pointing to it, I'm not talking about your intellect. You may be a lot smarter than I am, you may be not as smart. But that intelligence brought you into existence in the form you have now.

It suffused the sperm and ovum, which were grown in your parents by the energy of food and prana. Look at this microscopic cell called sperm. It can swim, and it knows where to swim to. It knows to find the ovum and penetrate its walls. So, it is suffused with innate intelligence to be able to do it. And the ovum knows what to do also: it attaches itself to the wall of uterus. Then, intelligence in them knows how to use the code, the genes — doubling and redoubling to form the body you use today.

It (the Intelligence Energy) also grows the seeds in the acorn. And each one of these seeds has the potential to cover the whole earth with trees. And it gives each life form unique qualities and patterns to help them survive and camouflage. Look at the stripes on the tiger. When he walks in savannah, the shadows of

125

trees makes him invisible. Or the panther or leopard mingling with the leaves on the tree. Doesn't it imply immeasurable intelligence?

Everything is an emanation of this infinite intelligence. Everything is an expression of that activity of knowing — Intelligence energy. Call it awareness, emptiness or whatever you like. I like intelligence, which is knowing, and activity, meaning energy.

For this amazing intelligence or life to experience itself as something other, form is required. What goes with it in the human package is an identification with the image or form.

I – Identification, image

Bob: *The 'me', this image that everything is relative to, is a total fiction. This dead image is not the livingness. It is based on yesterday. When the image is not there, the livingness shines forth in its fullness.*

Self-image is a mental construct made of ideas acquired in the past. 'I' is just a collection of memories. It is what we know through past learning. We add to it what we know about ourselves, what has happened to us and what it meant. This is to solidify that fleeting phantom, to make it more substantial.

But no amount of past images added to the 'me' alleviates the sense of incompleteness or uncertainty of 'who am I'. There is an uneasy feeling of being fake, inauthentic and void inside. Discontentment, dissatisfaction or even an anxiety often accompanies it. There may also be a blurred existential dread — a dim sentiment about the human condition or the state of the world — viewed from a personalized standpoint.

However, awareness just is. Being all there is, it has no reference point — neither in time nor in space. It can't be aware of itself because it doesn't have a self. It can't experience its form because it is formless. It doesn't have senses, so it can't experience anything at all. Being No-Thing, not being a thing, having no identity, it neither exists nor does not.

So it dreams itself a form...

In that open field of pure intelligence, every form is known to have a being. But who/what knows that? There is a being prior to the known existence of things. Being of an object known through the senses is secondary to direct, pre-sensory un-located being-knowing.

But with differentiating the object comes naming and identifying with the subject... Every creature is equipped with a particular set of skills and capacities. The human creature can reason. It can also imagine. A by-product of this amazing capacity to name and evaluate everything is the naming and evaluation of experiencer. An identification with it is its most direct consequence.

As far as we can tell, the question of identification with form doesn't arise in the planet, cell, cat or tree. This matter seems to require well-developed symbolic language.

> **Bob:** It tells you in the Bible that Adam and Eve ate from the tree of Knowledge of good and evil. That way they lost paradise, innocence. They started discriminating: "this is good, and this is not".

> *According to who? Me. So, relating it to themselves: "I like it, I don't like it", they allowed the 'I' to come into existence. They called it "I, Adam", or "Me, Eve, human being..."*

Identification with form is like a virus in the system. THAT (pure being-knowing-joy, life energy) now seemingly identifies and dreams to become the other, a thing, a separate 'I'. It is not possible for anything to be separated or independent from That. Separation can only be believed, imagined, dreamt. It is always and ever the One. Water can only dream to be rain or a wave but it is always and ever H_2O.

Yet, without that virus of identity, without this unquestioned belief, there would be no awakening. Without the prior dream of being a form, formlessness cannot be appreciated. Without a cage of identification, there is no freedom. Without seeming duality, there would be no appearance.

Recognize this pattern of identifying as a mental image and marvel at it. Let it be. You can't really drop the identification as a separate self because there is no 'you' or anyone else there to do so. It can only be recognized. Such recognition is neither personal, nor conceptual, nor logical.

This seemingly separate self dissolves in recognition, like darkness ends in light. It has never existed. Just like an imaginary monster under the bed or Santa Claus, so is the self-image only an illusion. Our conceptual images of others are all equally 'not so'.

> **Bob:** *They told me, I'm Bob, an Australian, a good bloke having a bad trot, or 'a sailor', or whatever else they made me identify with. These are all concepts. You are not this 'I' thought. You are not a concept.*

128

You are not a voice in your head telling you this, that or the other. Investigate and it will be very clear.

I – Investigation

Bob: *The false cannot stand up to investigation.*

Investigation is a blessing, a spontaneous grace arising from the same source as everything else arises. There is no doer or ego or mind performing it. Yet it may seem like an intellectual process to start with. This is only seemingly so. Intellectual activity is as spontaneous as breathing. Only language demands we say, 'I do it'.

Bob: *Nobody can teach you anything or tell you anything because there is nobody here. There are just different forms and patterns of THAT. How can another pattern tell you anything? You need to investigate and see it for yourself.*

How do we go about it? There are many ways. For example, this: you are seeing right now. Seeing is happening, but you tell yourself 'I am seeing'. You take credit for it. Seeing happens spontaneously and thought comes and claims it. But thought cannot see! Are you the thought? You are not. The same applies to thinking, speaking and functioning.

You gladly give up this I-thought when you go to sleep every night and nothing bad happens because of this. You are not it, otherwise you'd never lose sight of it. You'd be afraid to go to sleep.

> *When someone calls your name loudly while you're in deep sleep, awareness is not far away. You don't cease to exist when the I-thought is gone.*

So who are you? What are you? Who is I? What is I, me? You have to look and see if you can find anything anywhere that you could call 'me'. Where is it located? What are its limits? What does 'it' look like? How does 'it' feel? Who is watching 'it'? Wouldn't it be another 'me'? Where does 'it' appear?

Another way to do the investigation is to pause the thought and see what is left without any concept. Is there any limited individual there without the thought? Have a look. The limited individual is an idea, a thought. Boundaries have to be thought of. ...And yet, there is an existence. It is unlimited; it is without conceptual frame or any assumed shape or form.

Fruitful investigation leaves no doubt in the absence of an investigator. The answer to the question "What is 'I'?" is the absence of an 'I'; an absence of a questioner; and, therefore, the absence of a question.

I cannot say who or what I am. There is no one home who knows or wants to know that. There is no interest in finding out because the belief in 'I' is gone.

Yet, I am. *Presence is.*

I – I AM

Bob: *There is a story in the Bible (the Old Testament) on how Moses went on the mountain and got the Ten Commandments. He was looking after his people and needed to guide them how to live more harmoniously.*

So, when the idea of the Commandments dawned on him (he heard a "still, small voice"), he wondered, "When I go back, who shall I say sent me?" The 'voice' came to him again and said "Tell them that 'I AM' sent you. My name is I AM.'"

It was then that Moses realized in an instant, "I am that I AM".

What Moses realized is available to anyone, anytime, right now. It is 'I Am' communicating with 'I Am', only and ever in the now. There is only being, separated with labels, but inherently one. I Am.

Bob: *Do you believe that you are or do you know it for certain? Is it a belief or a fact? Even without the thought, you exist, don't you?*

Pause the thought for a moment and see if you disappeared. See if the sense of being present is still experienced.

What you are is a different question. ...Or *who* you are. Without the thought, there is no answer to it. With thought, any answer is limited. Every thought has its opposite, so you would have to be this but not that — not a totality. Not to mention, we assume there is a 'you'.

It is easier and wiser to explore and discard what you are not. You are not what you can objectify. You can see the body, you can hear the thoughts. They all change; you don't.

Bob: *So you are awake, aware. You know it. You are experiencing it. It is not a belief. Can anything else be known with that level of certainty? Can anything else be known without relying on second-hand information? It cannot.*

131

'I am' is an ultimate reality. The rest is a belief.

Nisargadatta used to say, "What you are is prior even to I am". Yes. You are prior to the concept 'I am', prior to all the concepts. Prior to existence and non-existence, prior to all pairs of opposites, prior to all the appearance. 'Prior', as used in this pointer, has nothing to do with linear time or space.

> **Bob:** *'I am' is the primary thought. That sense of presence expresses as that thought 'I am'. The mind can't grasp 'I am' because it is nothing. It is just a few letters. To give it some seeming substance, the mind adds the concept "I am so and so", or "I am confused". Now you have got a picture of what that 'I am' is. You see what it has done? It has added a label.*

Inquiry into this pre-sense is the way to see through it.

I – Inquiry – E X E R C I S E

To begin self-inquiry, sit quietly and allow the mind to settle naturally. Don't attempt to focus your mind or manipulate your experience; just rest as awareness itself.

You are that pure presence, existence. You are the experiencing of it. Rest in that.

Now, without taking a thought, as this pure awareness of presence, do you have any shape, form or colour? Without any mental image, can you experience your size? Without a concept, can you say, you are small or big? And yet you know that you are.

But can you know what you are without taking on a belief?

Scan the consciousness for sensations and inquire: Who is aware of this sensation? There may be a vibration somewhere, don't label it (don't call it tension or pain or cold, don't call location as a limb or stomach). Just inquire, who is experiencing that sensation? When thought appears, inquire: who is having that thought?

> **Bob:** *In any situation — particularly one of resistance or upset — ask yourself, "Who is this happening to?" The obvious answer would be: 'to me'. But wait a minute, "This guy was saying there is no 'me'; is he right or wrong? I saw it before; there wasn't any 'me' there. Let me look again".*

There are other versions of the "Who am I" question as well. I used to prefer "What is 'I'?" "Who is the 'me'?" or "What is 'me'?"

We will also look at the "Where am I?" or "Where is I?" options during the location exercise.

One Zen sangha (Kwan Um) which I used to sit with, suggests inquiry with the added answer: "I don't know". Sitting with the not-knowing mind is quite an adventure as well. There is a knowing, non-conceptual innate knowing about the not-knowing mind. The mind that doesn't know is close to the no-mind. Interpretation services are suspended. There is no individual I.

I – Individual I, interpreter

Bob: The 'I' or the mind is just an interpreter, a translator of what is coming up. I like to use the old Buddhist analogy of putting a piece of iron in the fire. It will get red like fire. It will get hot like fire. Pick it up, and it will burn you like fire. So, it has taken on the qualities of the fire. If it could speak, it would say "Look at me! Look what I can do, I'm red, I'm hot, I can burn! I'm the fire!" But take it out of the fire, and what can it do? It can't do any of those things.

It is the same with the sense of 'I', which exists only in thinking. Thinking is so closely aligned with that pure intelligence that it feels like it is the intelligence itself. It feels, "I choose, I have got free will" or "I can do this" or "I'm not good enough". But all thought really does, when you look at it closely, is translate the spontaneous urge.

There is a spontaneous activity of thinking (fire) and 'I' claiming it is doing it (iron bar). There is being and 'I' claiming it. It may feel like the sense of 'I' hijacks the being, awareness of presence. It says, 'My presence' rather than I-presence. Now, instead of pure being, there is 'I' having it. Instead of pure hotness and redness we have an iron bar having them.

This is only so in the language. Beyond the mind, such duality doesn't exist. Being without the thought (of who and how and where) is singular; limitless; free.

Bob: When you question it and look at it, you can see that of itself it (interpreter, individual) hasn't got any power. It hasn't got any substance or any independent nature. In seeing that and realizing that, what does the mind do? It just aligns itself with that intelligence. It just translates from That, instead of taking the belief that it has some power or some sense of entity and separateness to itself.

Mind viewed this way (as I) either simply interprets to communicate what it is that Life experiences and expresses, or it acts to substantiate the subject and take credit. Mind is either the servant or the self-proclaimed master. It is either clear or confused. It may oscillate between the two.

Bob: *That sense of presence that you are — not the body or thinking but the being — it translates through the mind as the thought 'I am'. You are not that thought, but what it represents.*

Life, Awareness shining through with clarity, without the cloud, filter or veil of identification calls itself 'I'. Life or Awareness hidden in the confused mind or ego, also labels itself 'I'.

Bob: *Society teaches us to value individuality, uniqueness and independence. But what do these words mean in common language and what could they really point to? Individual means undivided. One. The Whole. The whole content and whatever appears on/in it, indivisible. Individual equals undivided. Understand this word in that way and it won't bind you. Doesn't 'I' even look like a figure 1?*

The word 'I' is convenient in communication. 'I' in truth represents One. One Life. It doesn't have any separate existence apart from it, it *is* it. 'I' is Life. I am Life. Life is reading this book, breathing the body, seeing and feeling, being.

> **Bob:** *What are you? Let your heart tell you, not the thought (mind). Are you an individual identity or Life?*

And yes, there is a uniqueness to each individual expression. You are like none other. It signifies the pattern, which nature never repeats, even in snowflakes or blades of grass. Yet, every pattern is just a vibration of one energy. Is there such a thing as independence in nature? Can anything be independent of the elements it consists of? Can anything be independent from its environment?

I – Independent identity?

In common language, independence may exist only as autonomy from some factors but never from all of them. A young adult can become financially independent from his parents but he cannot be unconditionally independent from earth, water, fire, air and space.

Every individual body-mind unit gets a label, name and identity for ease of communication. Yet every unit is just a pattern, which that intelligence uses to express itself. It is a costume that emptiness wears. With the body-mind it can see, hear, walk and think.

The individual holds many identities. Some of these are related to race, sex, group memberships (including family, religion and nation) and various other transient roles and temporary functions. Association with characteristics or particular values is equally unstable and unreliable. The individual identity is transient, unreal, dependent on thought processes.

> **Bob:** *What were you before the thought of identification came about? Who are you when you wake up in the morning before you download from memory all the data of where, when and what you were told you are?*

You are. You are akin to Still, Silent Space or Absolute, Awake Awareness. Intelligence Energy. Life. Emptiness. Freedom. Totality. You are No-Thing, Undivided. Indivisible. You are not the word but what it points to.

This is not to say that role playing should not or will not happen. Animals are mates, parents, seniors and guardians, hunters, hunted, captured or free. So it is according to the after-story, because they do not form any such concepts.

Human bodies wear various costumes as well. Freedom doesn't deprive you of the ability to freely shift between various positions required by life. Life may play to be a controller at times, or a sceptic, a fixer, a pleasure seeker, truth seeker, finder, lover, god... But without the story it just spontaneously responding to the environment.

> *Bob: Words are merely labels. What you are is beyond words. They are all concepts pointing to the non-conceptual. You are none of these concepts...*

...But you Are.

Is-ness.

Being-ness.

Experiencing.

Some of these concepts may touch your heart... Some of them may ring the bell, strike home, influence, inspire...

I – Inspiration, influence

Bob: *Inspire means in-spirit. When you get a new idea, you inspire, meaning you take a breath. Let the thought ride on the breath, breathe it out (expire) and take in fresh and new one (inspire).*

Being inspired is like being in touch with subtle wisdom and greatness. There is a sudden surge of energy in the body when inspiration happens. Beauty inspires. Pointers are meant to inspire. They are given to put you back in touch with the heart of the essence.

Inspiration is a word that by-passes the doership. When Bob tells you to drop thought, it is an invitation to get inspired by the idea. Breathe it in. If pure consciousness resonates and responds to this inspiration, dropping happens. You didn't do it. There is no you to do anything at all. Inspiration creates a movement; it motivates the activity. It provides the energy.

We tend to project our own intentions onto nature. We anthropomorphize it. We say that the sunflower loves the Sun because it is turning to follow it. We say that the dog is offended or guilty. We even say that IT is raining. But we do understand that a sunflower doesn't have a heart. We know that we only project our interpretation on a dog whose behaviour is governed by instincts and not reason. We know there is no IT doing the rain. But there is no other way to communicate.

Particularly in terms of nonduality, the practicality of language makes it almost impossible to speak in precise terms. The idea of inspiration seems to translate into commands and advice what is merely impersonal happening.

There is no one to relax or pause thinking. There is no-one to do investigation. There seems to be, but there is not. These words are used to inspire spontaneous recognition to arise. They are like a feather tickling the nose to trigger a sneeze. With that sneeze, all clouds are dispersed.

Identifying as an individual is only an old habit. It has been created in early childhood and practised by no-one, religiously for a lifetime. There is an intrinsic innocence about it.

I – Intrinsic innocence

There is a tendency in some spiritual circles to judge and condemn identification as an individual. There is an urge to hate the ego, and a desire to destroy it. It is there, regardless of the obvious fact that it would only be an ego (thought) killing the ego, and ego would always remain. Yet, there is an urge to do something...

This comes from misunderstanding and wrong assumption that things could or should be different from what they are. As they are seems not good enough; there seems to be something wrong with me and the world. There is a fear of some sort of sin somewhere, that the 'I' (the ego) is all that is bad, selfish and deserving of condemnation.

From realizing the inevitability of what is (as it is) comes innocence and relief from great burden. Identification has happened innocently. There was no choice but to adopt this habit. Everyone who we could model or imitate had it well-developed. Without prior identification, freedom from it could not be known and appreciated. It would be taken for granted, as it is by other creatures in nature.

How does it happen? As the child learns words to label things, it slowly starts to create mental representations (images) of them. Once it can use symbols to talk about things out of sight, it moves into the conceptual realm of existence. It doesn't see things as they are anymore; it sees reflections of what it knows about them.

> **Bob:** *So he learns, "I'm little Johnny, a good boy" (...or "not so good") and "This is a wooden chair. It is to sit on".*

The mystery is now covered up with labels. Now, because of this wondrous reasoning, memorizing and learning capacity, little Johnny starts differentiating, organizing and judging. He also ate of the Tree of Good and Evil and lost Paradise. "This apple is good, that chair is bad". "This movie is fun, that person is evil"...

Now it is him, little Johnny, who wants more of the pleasure, and less of the pain. Before identification, there was a natural attraction and repulsion, but now it has become his desire and his aversion. Now it is personal. Pull and push are born. Conceptual resistance to the way things are right now is born. Psychological suffering arrives.

Little Johnny is only little and is insecure and vulnerable. He wants to grow up and become big, strong and safe. He needs attention, approval, appreciation; ...but no matter how much he gets, he is hungry for more.

Prior to words, he just WAS. There was no limiting idea of what or who he was. Now he thinks of himself as only little, and imagines that when he grows up he will only be big, strong and safe. He will never be totality again unless he is moved to question the appearance of things.

Prior to words, he was THAT, the Absolute, the Totality; unbound, limitless presence awareness. Now, though, no measure of strength or stature will ever make him feel complete, fulfilled and free.

> **Bob:** *He will go about and gather, accumulate, amass and hopelessly try to add to himself wealth, relationships, experiences, name and fame to get back to what he once was but now he believes he lost...*

But has he lost it?

There is an intrinsic innocence about the human condition.

We imitate, model our parents, teachers and leaders and our identification with the human form solidifies. We repeat the lie daily so it becomes an unquestionable premise. It couldn't happen any other way; and it didn't. It doesn't need to. It shouldn't.

How could anyone awake if nobody fell asleep?

Yet, one who awakens wakes up from the dream of being individual. It is a consciousness, not an 'I', that experiences clarity when the veil of 'I' disperses. Me, little Johnny or

141

anyone else who continues to identify with the body-mind, will never wake up or get it. "I, little Johnny" is the veil, the cloud, a figment of imagination.

I – Imagination

> **Bob:** *Nisargadatta tells you, "Nothing can trouble you except in your own imagination". Now, look at this word 'imagination'. The word 'imagine' you can break down to 'image-in'. It points to creating mental images.*

It is really a big claim that Nisargadatta puts in, that all problems are imagined. So, please put it into the test! What problem can you ever have without thought?

To be troubled is to indulge in imagination. We create stories, contexts. We introduce time and we project a future. This is imagination. We imagine our enemies, our gods and, most of all, ourselves. We imagine ourselves into existence. We imagine an entity with free will and the power to control. Using memories, we also 'image-in' our past. We imagine history.

Our magnificent reasoning capacity is based in our capacity to 'image-in' — imagine. Symbolic language is the result of operating in response to mental representations of things.

We imagine things as separate, with independent nature. We imagine a world filled in with things which can stand on their own. ('We' meaning Life filtered through body-minds.) As much as it is practical in daily life, it is completely impossible for anything to be independent of its environment. Even the interpreting service that the human brain provides is completely dependent on imagined content in order to be contextualized and given meaning.

Everything is interdependent.

I – Interdependent arising

We have learned at school about the law of cause and effect, which helps us understand the world around us better. It made us look for reasons behind everything and to constantly ask WHY. It brought research into existence and great good came out of this. We understood that Earth is not flat, therefore we can sail and fly around it. We know a lot about various things and causality makes our daily life functional. We can predict certain behaviours of things; we know what will break when dropped or how certain deeds will make us feel.

We seem to make choices and can trace back the reasons for certain consequences. We seem to learn from mistakes. Cause and effect seems logical, observable and unquestionable. But is that description precise enough, or is this model oversimplified for its practicality?

Is karma real? Cause-effect? Action-reaction?

I drop the cup of tea, the cup breaks and tea spills all over the place. I dropped it because I was tired, inattentive. I didn't sleep well. I had to work a night shift and that's the cause of the situation. End of story. All explained; well understood.

143

Really though?

Would the cup have broken had I dropped it over a soft carpet? How about if I had been using a steel cup? What if I really slept enough but only think I didn't? I've had nightshifts before without breaking any cups. How come the cup even exists to break?

The cause for the cup breaking wasn't just inattention due to a bad night's sleep. The cause of the cup breaking also includes the gravity of this planet. There is also the fact that the cup was made of clay (and not steel). There is the functionality of my hand. There are innumerable other factors involved, including my reasons for taking extra work. In fact, all of these, every single one of them, contributes to the occurrence of the cup breaking; together with the infamous butterfly in Chicago whose wing beats helped stir a hurricane in Tokyo.

The broken cup can also be partially blamed on rice farmers in China. Why? Because the factory worker who produced the teacup would not have had enough to eat without that rice. The water and sun which supported the growth of rice cannot be excluded. And neither can insects that pollinated it, nor chemicals that kept it from pests. Then there are feelings and hormones of all the mothers who influenced the personalities of clay-worker, rice farmer and my own; plus those who dressed us, fed us and provided all other services.

There is a music we liked or hated and those who played it. Plus hopes, desires and dreams; influences of the weather, electromagnetic noise, food coloring and more. And there are countless variables involved in our conception, including everyone's grandparents and their ancestors going back all the way to before the first living organisms!

There are the sources of building materials, earth, water, fire, air, space. Everything is included. Nothing is excluded; nothing is exempt. Nothing is separate. Everything is one, interdependent.

Any singular cause of anything is an illusion.

I – Illusion

> **Bob:** *They call it Maya or Illusion. This is a manifestation made of phenomena, meaning: "Made of that which only appears to be". Put a powerful enough microscope on any object and all you'll find is empty space.*

And yet, everything appears right in front of our eyes. Amazing! And even more appears when we dream at night, or when we take substances that excite the brain. Other quite different worlds appear in front of a vulture, puma or bee. Things appear solid, even though we know they are subatomic particles moving very, very fast. Earth appears flat even though we know it is spherical.

> **Bob:** *When you look at the helicopter blades rotating, they appear solid. Don't put your hand there, or you may experience that seeming solidity even more.*
>
> *You know what an illusion is. Mirage is an illusion. When you drive on a hot day, you may see a pool of water on the road. You come closer and it disappears. When was there ever water there? Or the snake in a*

145

rope. Or a Rainbow. It appears to be: it is only seemingly so.

Calling Life an illusion may feel unfair. Life in all its diversity and magnificence, in all its sentience — feels so very real! Illusion suggests something misguiding, misleading or misinterpreted. Optical illusion is a deceptive appearance. A false idea is called illusion as well. ...But the whole world?

To say it is an illusion is not to diminish its wondrousness. It is only to point out that — how it appears is not how it is. We do not say that world doesn't exist. We don't say that it does. It is akin to a dream, reflection in the mirror or memory.

Any logical explanation must fail for it can't be understood with the intellect. But 'real' means changeless, and all we think or perceive is impermanent.

I – Impermanence

Bob: *Someone said, "Cemeteries are full on indispensable people".*

Impermanence is the state or fact of lasting for only a limited period of time, says the dictionary. It is one of the essential doctrines of Buddhism, which asserts that all of conditioned existence, without exception, is transient, evanescent and inconstant.

Bob: *Everything we like and want to keep, will change. Everything we are attached to will move on. People we love will betray us, leave us or die.*

Beauty will fade; sharp intellect will decline; cute babies will grow into rebellious teenagers; health will turn into sickness and sickness will end, too; day will change into night; our tastes and opinions will be updated. Religions and empires will fall, new ones will arrive. There will be new technology, new solutions, new customs, new words, new people and new thoughts.

There is nothing in the manifested world which one could rely on to stay put. Even continents are moving; mountains and pyramids are eroding; air and water change their chemical and electrical structures. Species of animals, plants and insects are disappearing from the face of the earth. New viruses and bacteria are mutating. New evolutionary adjustments are made to the ever changing environment.

> **Bob:** *Just take a look at this: Christ was supposed to have raised Lazarus from the dead. Where is Lazarus now? What was the point? How about the blind man who received his sight back? Where is he now? We can heal or patch things up but everything is temporary, transient — just like the rest of the manifestation. How long has anyone been healed for? That is what impermanence is. But the essence of what you are was never born and can never die. It belongs to a different order of things.*

Bob saw all of his family go, one by one. His younger brother passed away a few months ago; his older sister last year. People he loved and trusted betrayed him. New caring friends have appeared. His body has changed and continues to change. The world he grew up in has transformed completely but his heart is with reality: that which never changes.

I can't help but see great beauty in the impermanence. My dearest, most beautiful friend, who was by far the best

147

reflection of me at the time, I lost to suicide. She had the same kind of personality, the same values and the same passions — but she was also better looking, more loving, smarter and more talented. Her marriage was better than mine at the time and her self-love brighter. I loved her as a reflection — like no one before — and we were transparently open and grateful for each other.

Yet, one day she took a taxi to the promenade and jumped off into the icy cold Baltic Sea to end debilitating tooth pain and sleeplessness which had lasted for 2 months. But 'she' didn't do it. She didn't choose her thoughts. She didn't shape her reaction patterns or her personality. Life was the only doer. Life created this beautiful, intricate and colourful sand mandala (her name was Dorota) which lasted for 35 years. Life filled it with such perfection and such greatness, and Life also blew it into the sea.

As I type this, my gorgeous friend is here as a thought, image and feeling — in just the same way as she was when she was alive. When she was still alive and I thought of her when we weren't together; she wasn't physically there then and she isn't here now, either. She was a thought then and she is a thought now. But how permanent can any thought ever be? Poof: she is gone, replaced by another daydream. It's a mystery. One too deep for the human intellect.

I – Intelligence and intellect

Bob: *When I talk about Intelligence energy, I don't mean your intellect. If you go back to when you were a little child, before you could reason, that knowing that you are was there. You were aware then, just the* *same as you are aware now. That is intelligence, not the intellect.*

Excessive attachment to one's intellect may be an obstacle in the investigation. There are people who have spent years studying ancient scriptures, and they feel that with another book or talk they might get it. They have invested so much; they are not willing to "empty the cup". They feel that they have already resolved and understood a lot and only a few pieces are missing. Others feel that they have only intellectually understood it all...

> **Bob:** *You put on the label: "I understand intellectually" and you sabotage your own knowing this way! Then you think there is some other way that it needs to be understood, and you are back in the trap of the mind. Seeing it is seeing it. Two and two is four. Is that intellectual or is there a knowing of it? In the seeing of it, nobody can convince you otherwise. What is intellectual in recognizing the bare fact of your own existence?*

People argue, "Intellectually I get that there is no 'me', but... but it feels like there is one". They also say, "I agree with you, I believe you, but I don't experience it".

'Me' has been believed into being and it feels real. It is so because its essence is real. The sense of presence (pure intelligence) is very real. It is the only reality. Now this real presence in the fictitious limiting costume of 'me' wants to experience its own absence. It can't happen. Experiencing the absence of presence is not on the menu!

Experiencing the absence of the costume (me) is ongoing in the non-conceptual space of awareness. No thought equals no 'me'. Naked presence is already so right now. Just recognize it, tune in to core of the essence; tune out of the chatter. The heart (pure intelligence) knows. It has no words; it has no word 'me'. Intellect is mind, intelligence is no-mind. Reality can't be grasped by the intellect and it is clear and obvious in the pure intelligence which moves this universe.

There is the fact of non-conceptual knowing of existence (intelligence); and there is the belief that a particular intellectual experience should accompany enlightenment or the natural state. There is the natural awareness of presence; and the intellectual expectation or anticipation of particular states or sensations. There is obviousness of being in the here and now; and there is imagination of a future in which the 'I' attains it. There is natural intelligence; and then there is the intellect, the mind.

> *Bob: It is not about gaining understanding (intellectual or other); it is about discarding confusion (intellectual clouds).*

Intellect is just not the right tool for the job. It can't comprehend what is beyond the mind. For the intellect it is incomprehensible.

I – Incomprehensible

The world neither exists nor does it not exist. It is neither real nor it is unreal. There is only one, but this one is in fact less than one; it is no-thing. But it isn't a nothing either. It is neither one nor not one. It is everything, infinity, zero. It is neither and both.

Separation is real and unreal simultaneously as well. There is nothing that can be truthfully said about it. It isn't even it, it is I, you, IS-ness. But not the 'you' that appears, but the 'you' which underlays all appearances.

> **Bob:** *It's just like the images in the mirror: they are visible; we can say they are there. But go and try to grab one. You can't. So they are not there at the same time. Just quit trying to grasp it with the mind. The answer is not there.*

IT is incomprehensible because mind operates on objects and symbols and THIS is not a thing. IT is incomprehensible because mind is an activity, a movement, and it can't comprehend stillness. Cessation of the activity of comprehending is stillness. There is nothing to grasp and no-one to do so.

IT is incomprehensible because mind is the noise. Noise can never grasp the silence. Singularity is just too simple for dualistic comprehension. Stop trying. It is not because it is so hard to comprehend but because comprehension of it is impossible.

I – Impossible

It is impossible for duality to understand nonduality. It is impossible for the ego to get rid of the ego. It is impossible for the movie to be the screen. It is impossible for the dream character to know the waking world.

It is impossible to understand the simplicity of One using the dualistic tool of reasoning. It is impossible not because it is too difficult but because it is way too simple.

Nothing is impossible for that great intelligence but there are still rules to the game in the appearance. There is a thousand years old question: "Can God create a stone that would be too heavy for Him to lift?" So, can he? God can do anything and everything, but in this example one of the rules has to be broken.

Can spirit know matter? Only if it forgets itself. Therefore the answer is both 'yes' and 'no'. The answer is beyond logic. The answer is impossible to grasp with the intellect. So, there is an answer and there isn't one.

Paradoxes serve an important role in pointing because they have the capacity to collapse the mind, to overload the system, so it stops. Impossibility of the task invites the mind to give up. *A Course in Miracles* says, "It is impossible, therefore it is certain". How well said! See it immediately: it is here, right in this instant.

I – Instant, immediacy

This instant is all there is. Past and future are mere concepts appearing in this present instant. They are just thoughts and images — nothing else. They are daydreams.

This moment is an eternity. It is timeless. It is all there is. You are That. You are this present moment, this "holy instant".

> **Bob:** *What you are looking for is right where you are right now, in this immediacy, this moment or this instant. It is bodiless, mindless, timeless, spaceless; beyond birth and death; beyond where, when, how or why. The (Bhagavad) Gita says, "The sword can't cut it, the wind can't dry it, the fire can't burn it, and the water can't drown it..." And yet it contains all things.*

Immediacy is defined in the dictionary as the quality of bringing one into direct and instant involvement with something, giving rise to a sense of urgency or excitement. An instant refers to an infinitesimal moment in time; a moment whose passage is instantaneous. It points out that it is alive and that it is beyond measure.

> **Bob:** *The seeing is happening in the immediacy of the moment before the mind comes into it to label or split it into seer and seen. That is what they talk about when they say "prior to the mind". When does this instant 'now' begin? It begins now. And as it begins it is already ending. So it is timeless. It is now. That's where illumination is.*

I – Ian's illumination – E X A M P L E

Ian is a Swedish, recently retired medical doctor, who sailed half the world in a 30 feet long wooden self-sufficient sailboat. The ocean made him feel small, almost non-existent, in the vastness of space. His long hours in solitude under the sky became a sacred contemplative retreat. It was the perfect remedy for his crisis.

The crisis came in his mid-sixties, after his youngest son left home and his wife found a younger lover. Ian wanted to die. He secretly hoped he would when he took up his solitary boat trip...

Yet Life had it otherwise: Life brought him to Bob, instead!

When Ian came to our home, he looked old and scary. He was a big bald guy with a brown, sun-burned face and red, exhausted eyes, visibly unhappy. He was roughly familiar with Bob's teachings through books and videos over the preceding three years but he needed more guidance in the investigation. Ian's brief moments of relief from the self were soon interrupted by the return of the painful narrative, which tortured him mercilessly.

Illumination came unexpectedly about an hour into his one-on-one session with Bob. He said it was as though all the lights in the world lit up, but not to blind him. It was like a gentle light that makes everything crystal clear. Suddenly all concepts started dancing around, completely benign, laughable — and soon faded back into the nothingness.

When Ian attempted to describe the realization the next day, he said he saw that everything wasn't happening *to him* anymore, but that "it was just a happening in spaceless space of now". He was and he wasn't, at the same time — and it didn't concern him at all.

There was a light of consciousness: a simple knowing that was aware of itself as both knower and known. But this known content wasn't important anymore. It had very little meaning and became completely impersonal. It was like someone else's story. In it, there was a solitary trip through the ocean and a divorce.

New insight shown that Inka, his soon-to-be-ex-wife, didn't betray him. She just fell in love with somebody else. It wasn't about Ian. Nothing was about Ian. There was no him and there was no her, either. No one had done anything at all.

Ian stayed in Melbourne a few more days before he returned to the ocean. He visited Bob every day and gratefully expressed many insights following his shift. Everything was both the same and different. Thoughts were there, but they were impersonal. Attention naturally engaged more with sensory experiences. The world of scenes, sounds and other impressions became brighter, more lovable.

The self-referential narrative did not return. The 'poor me' was disbelieved, so it dissolved. Natural joy replaced the suffering. It is about four years later that I type these words and Ian's understanding remains stable. He knows what he is not. There is no imagined 'him' anymore to wonder who or what he is. Life is. Nothing else is important.

I – Importance

Whatever we give importance to, we become a slave of. If money or power is important, we obsess about it. If family is important, we dread losing it. If spiritual awakening is important, we seek it and miss out on its immediate presence. Nothing has ultimate importance. Nothing matters. No-thing. Only that no-thing.

This is not to say that survival and success are irrelevant. They may draw attention and grow. It is a part of normal functioning. Animals also mate and look after their young; this is nature. They compete for status and territory as well, which often involves money in the human realm. Nothing is unnatural.

However, when the sense of importance enters the narrative, it often grows disproportionate. This is when self-enslavement starts. It comes about through learning from and modelling others — through imitation. It applies to the importance given to external things but also to the sense of self-importance.

> **Bob:** *As you touch your face, you wipe out a few million little life forms. You have killed them mercilessly. Some of them may still be alive and suffering. Some of them may be crippled. But you couldn't care less. We think we are so important but we are only small in the scheme of things. From the perspective of this galaxy what would you be? You would be even less than a microbe on someone's face! Yet, because we are here, we give ourselves so much importance. In the scheme of things, life is continually living on life. Life appears in all sorts of forms and shapes. But it is still the same life, the same intelligence-energy. And you are that life.*

Please consider using the sense of importance as a reminder — a red flag or flashing light calling you to investigate. What is really important? Is it being right? Is it the momentary pleasure of instant gratification? Is there anything bigger? Look into it!

I – In E X E R C I S E

Bob: *Nisargadatta used to ask us to contemplate upon: "What was first? The consciousness or the body? Is consciousness in the body or is the body in consciousness?"*

Before I met Bob, I first heard similar sets of questions from Sirshree, my guru in Pune, India. They would take me home every time I'd sit with them. These may do it for you now! Please, close your eyes and experience yourself fully inside the body. Experience the aliveness and experience the knowing of it.

Now contemplate and compare which one of the following two statements is more correct in your direct experience:

1. I am the body

2. I am in the body

Once you are clear that the second statement describes your experience more accurately, consider another two statements:

1. I am the consciousness inside the body

2. I am the consciousness inside and outside the body

When you recognize that as consciousness you are both, inside and outside (since you know the sounds outside, external temperature etc.) – try these two:

1. I am the consciousness inside and outside the body

2. I am the consciousness and the body is inside of me

Savour your realization. When forgotten, repeat the steps. Direct experience is the only reliable guide.

If you chose, "I am the body" at the first step, please contemplate how you came to know that. This is not a feeling or sense, this is a belief. Adopt a mental attitude of "I don't know" and try again. Look for a feeling, a sense, not the logic. For the logical mind, it is ineffable, inexpressible.

I – In addition on I

I – Inexpressible, ineffable

What we are pointing to is beyond words. There is no accurate way to express it. We often use paradoxes and contradictory statements to stop the mind or to highlight some seeming aspect.

We may say that everything is alive and that it is all Life itself. In almost the same breath, we say that the habit patterns are mechanical or dead but also that everything is patterns of energy. So, is everything dead, alive, neither or both? Are some things dead and others alive? We also say there is no death. Can you follow?

You can't. Please don't follow the line of thinking. The answer is not in thinking. The answer is where thinking stops — in the Inexpressible. Mental, conceptual representation is not it. It cannot be imitated by the mind, as there is nothing to imitate.

I – Imitation

Imitation or copying is an advanced behaviour amongst animals, whereby one individual replicates another's action.

158

Imitation is also a form of social learning which leads to the development of traditions and culture. It allows for the transfer of information down through generations through a process of non-genetic inheritance. It also highlights the complete innocence of that process.

> **Bob:** *Your parents, your school, your society (almost everyone you know) believed in separation and behaved this way. You had no other chance but to learn that through imitation. Especially when you admire or idolize those you imitate.*

I – Idol

An Idol is an image or representation of a god that is used as an object of worship. It can also mean a person or thing that is greatly admired, loved or revered. Either way, a belief in separation is a prerequisite for any form of relationship with it. The social benefit of worship comes from humility. The personal pay-off is in the sweetness of surrender.

Nonduality is pointing to the recognition that every form, shape and pattern, every human and object is within you: it is yours and it is you. Consider that you are already in possession of all that you so greatly admire. Even if it is thick hair when your head is bald or health or wealth that you do not have in your seemingly individual life. Who you are in essence has it all. If not in one body, then in another.

> **Bob:** *Muktananda used to say to us, "Kneel to yourself, bow to yourself, honor and worship your own being. God dwells within you as you". You are that immense, infinite That-ness.*

I – Immense, infinite

Immense means marked by greatness, supremely good or transcending ordinary means of measurement. It is a beautiful, poetic pointer to immeasurability of this basic screen, which is your essence. It is often used to describe the universe as endless, infinite. Infinity means boundlessness. Infinity can't be embraced by imagination. THAT is infinitely greater than anything that could ever be comprehended. You know it innately once you stop thinking.

I – Innate, inherent, intrinsic

These synonyms are used to direct the attention towards the key aspect of THAT. Innate means existing in something as a permanent, essential characteristic. Inherent means inborn. Intrinsic means belonging naturally. Innate wisdom, inherent knowing, intrinsic understanding. You do innately, intrinsically, inherently know your true nature or natural state. You may just think you don't. That is why pointers are intended to resonate, not to teach. Recognition is required, not a replacement of beliefs.

> **Bob:** *That innate intelligence is the essence of everything that appears and disappears but to the mind it is no thing. It is not any kind of thing whatsoever. That intelligence, that innate, intrinsic intelligence, which pulsates through this body, is registering everything right here, right now, just as it is.*

Your heart knows. It was unobscured before you learned language and started an inner dialog (the narrative).

> **Bob:** *...But even the learnings of a lifetime can't stop that bell from ringing. The knowing, the intrinsic,*

innate knowing of it is always present, indestructible.
Mind is immune but the heart knows it.

I – Immune

Immune means resistant to particular influences, protected or exempt. Initially, thinking habits are still quite strong when understanding first dawns on you. With maturation and re-wiring (deconditioning) immunity to the seduction of stories grows.

> **Bob:** *When Nisargadatta told me I wasn't the body or the mind I heard him right from the first time. I said, "I will never be caught up in the mind again". But I walked out the door and I was caught in it again. But it wasn't the same. Once you see through the false, you can never fully believe it again. I was growing immune to it. And so can you. Just make the recognition an imperative.*

I – Imperative

As we said, nothing has absolute importance, and yet, if suffering is acute, investigation is an imperative.

> **Bob:** *Get into it. It doesn't matter whether you consider yourself a body, a mind or awareness. These are just words. Life is the only doer. Do it! Investigate and see for yourself.*

Seeing for yourself is transformational. It has profound influence or at least makes an impact.

I – Impression, impact, influence

An impression is an idea, feeling or opinion about something or someone. Sensations are also sometimes called impressions. To make an impression is to impact, to influence.

161

To use these words as pointers, we link them with momentary, passing phenomena. Even if an impression is lasting, even if its impact is profound, it is ultimately transient. Everything that has a beginning has an end. Everything influences everything. Life moves to evolve, improvise and improve.

I – Improvement

Who you are in essence is Pure Perfection, the Absolute. It can't be improved and it needs no improvement. Yet, if the tendency in the body-mind is to gain skills and enhance qualities, it will continue to be a part of the happening, just as a young eagle becomes better at flying and hunting over time.

Just overlook or quit the narrative, if you can, about the pitiful little 'me' not being good enough and needing to deserve things. Simply recognize the habit and laugh. Life will move you to do great things without the egoic drive for immortality.

I – Immortality

The "Immortality Dream" is a well-known phenomenon that motivates individuals to take extraordinary measures to leave a legacy. Immortality is also a promise in many belief-systems and religions. The fear of death and annihilation (non-existence) is considered to be the strongest human fear. It is said that all other fears stem from this one, including the fear of being unworthy of love and the fear of failure (of which both could mean death by exile in some early human societies).

Yet, neither immortality nor non-existence can be adequately represented by language. They can't be imagined. Just as zero and eternity are concepts in mathematics that have no real life counterparts, immortality and death are only theoretical ideas.

Who you truly are is unborn, so it can't die. Space or stillness is not a thing that is mortal or immortal. By a stretch of the imagination, one could say that if immortality is a goal or dream, then it is already realized in this timeless immediacy.

The idea of the immortality of the soul is often supported with stories of near death experiences or past life memories. Seen with the clear mind they prove nothing but the amazing capacity of human mind to improvise.

I – Improvising

It has been widely researched and demonstrated how people come up with justifications for random actions while under hypnosis or after lobotomy (incision into the prefrontal lobe of the brain, which severs communication between cerebral hemispheres).

Mind is an extraordinary improviser! It perfectly reflects every movement of this great intelligence. Evolution itself seems to be a great improviser. Still, this doesn't disprove incredible stories about children seemingly born with fluency in a foreign language or specific memories from deceased people. In my eyes, it only adds to their great beauty!

> **Bob:** *Life is a mystery and everything is valid in the appearance. Everything is included. It is all happening. The -ING on it makes it immediate.*

I – -ING

Being is happening. In this field of singular being, content appears and is registered through the sensory organs. This immediate be-ING in sensory fields turns into see-ING, touch-ING, breath-ING, eat-ing etc. The immediate -ing is converted by the sense faculties into think-ing, walk-ing and function-ing.

We are pointing at the fact that all sensing is always immediate; it always transpires in the here and now. Whatever is, is simply happen-ING.

So we just looked at imitating, improving, idolizing, imagining, inquiring, investigating, influencing, impacting, inspiring, interpreting and more. Let's include including and involving!

I – Including, involving

One effective way to inquire is through negation. It points out that whatever I'm aware of is an object in awareness, and not awareness itself. I'm aware of my body, thoughts, feelings, impressions... Am I aware of awareness? Who is aware? If there is anything, discard it and stay left with no-one and no-thing.

Another way is through inclusion. Instead of "not this, not that", we look around and say "this too, that too". Everything is That. Everything is a reflection of That. Form is emptiness and this I am too, that I am too. Universe is my body, the costume I wear to experience 'I Am'. There is nothing outside of that 'I Am'. 'I Am' is in the sensing and everything within that activity is part of it, part of the 'I Am'. There is no seer and seen without seeing. They are all within me.

I Am the consciousness and everything is within me. It manifests, appears and disappears, within that consciousness that I am. Body is within me, thinking, seeing, sensing; every instinct and impulse is within me.

I – Impulse, instinct, impetus

Impulse is a sudden strong and unreflective urge or desire to act, like impetus. Instinct is an innate, typically fixed pattern of behaviour in response to certain stimuli.

164

The brilliance in using these words as pointers and reminders lies in their involuntary nature. They point to the innocence and non-doership. These things simply happen to us, just like sweating or salivating. Reacting to a sudden, unexpected noise is equally involuntary, and so is the fight-or-flight response, and so is the story-telling urge, and so is the intuition.

I – Intuition

Very close to the impulse and instinct lies intuition, which is like a "still, small voice". The dictionary defines intuition as the ability to understand something instinctively, without need for conscious reasoning.

> **Bob:** *Intuition means in-tuit or into-it. Some also break it to 'in-tuition', like in the process of learning. It is an innate knowing. Intuition is like a muscle. It is constantly there but if it is not used it atrophies. If you listen and hear this still, small voice, intuition will strengthen until it becomes just as normal as your other senses. Insights will flow freely.*

I – Insight

> **Bob:** *You have had glimpses of That all along — little insights or 'a-ha' moments. They come to the quiet mind; they never stop. ...But let them go as they go, so fresh and new ones can come up. Don't hold onto them.*

They spring out of nowhere, like the kiss of eternity. But there is no point chasing after them. What has a beginning has an end, and so it is a fleeting experience. No matter how enlightening and poetic, it is ephemeral. If you can put it into words, music or painting, great. If you can't, that's great too. Receive them and appreciate them. That's enough.

165

Insight is defined as the capacity to gain an accurate and deep understanding of someone or something. It is like a miracle, a sudden shift enabling a glimpse of what is beyond understanding. It is delightful to indulge while it lasts.

I – Indulge instead

Indulging implies excessive compliance and weakness in gratifying another's or one's own desires. To indulge is to let yourself do or have something that you enjoy, especially something that is considered bad for you. It may be a result of natural instinctual wiring for seeking pleasure and avoiding pain, but it may also be accompanied by the narrative. Narrative may induce suffering, which in turn will invoke the need for sedation. Addiction may follow, induce more suffering and close the evil circle.

Indulge in the deliciousness of pure being instead! Fall in love with Emptiness from which seeing starts! Indulge in awareness of aliveness instead. Love and bliss springs out of here. We knew it during infancy.

I – Infancy

> **Bob:** *When we were born, we had no words. As infants, we were free of any sense of separation. This is why we all know the natural state innately. Each and every one of us have lived quite well for the first couple of years of our life without words, in that non-conceptual ever fresh presence-awareness.*

May it serve as a reminder here: because you were an infant once, that you already know the natural state innately. It hasn't been lost. It just got covered up with the overlay of mental projection and interpretation.

I – Interpretation

The brain interprets input from sensory receptors as perception. It means that to see and understand the world, certain computing has to happen in the brain. The computing capacity of neuronal networks is great but finite. The amount of data that the brain can process within a period of time is limited — both at the conscious and unconscious levels.

Our interpretation of sensory input is the world as we know it. The world is constructed through interpretation and the automatic assignment of meanings to what is being perceived. That meaning is like a filter, a result of projection, conditioning. The personal filter has been created through the interactions of infinite factors.

A certain amount of interpretation can be altered by inspiration, investigation and introspection.

> **Bob:** You say, "I love her, I love her, but she did this to me, the bitch". This is how quickly it changes. Concepts you have about people, their motives, and the world you see are only interpretations. And they are interpreted in relation to yourself. They can't be trusted. Watch your thoughts: introspect and you will see.

I – Introspection

Introspection is an examination or observation of one's own mental and emotional processes. It is self-examination, analysing oneself, looking at one's personality patterns and actions, and considering our own motivations.

> **Bob:** Watch the mind and see how it operates. It is either future or past, good or bad, black or white and

everything between these pairs of opposites. See if it
can work in any other way.

When you are watching your mind, who are you? Where are you located? Silence is only known because of sound (it is its absence); day is possible only because there is a night. They are interrelated.

I – Interrelation

Interrelated pairs of opposites which constitute the boundaries of the known world are in fact one phenomenon. Interrelationship between black and white is in fact their interdependence. There is either duality or there is nothing at all.

If everything were white, there would be no white and there would be no thing. If there were no perceived fluctuation in hearing, there would be no hearing, which means no sound, no silence. Appearance depends on defining dualistic boundaries. Only intensity varies.

I – Intensity

The natural bias towards pleasure and away from pain may lead to obsession. Seeking power, seeking sexual fulfilment or seeking enlightenment are all forms of chasing intensity in variety. Wanting more control, more of recognition or more bliss are all desires of the bored mind. It is about the stimulation, about the entertainment.

As the sensitivity diminishes, more intense stimuli are required. Sweeter candies show up; more perverted porn; more exciting shopping experiences and scarier news. However, there is no ultimate fulfilment in increasing the volume, magnitude or quantity of experiences.

Pleasant spiritual experiences, such as Kundalini movement and the development of siddhis (extraordinary powers) may distract from the sense of incompleteness for few moments, but no lasting fulfilment depends on anything unreal (transient).

Still, with the lessening of the intensity of distractions, natural joy and love of being springs forth. With diminished intensity of cloud cover, the sky becomes clearer. That is an introduction to recognizing the natural state.

I – Introduction

> **Bob:** *That intelligence is registering everything as it is, without need for any label. Look around without labelling and realize that you are seeing as well as hearing at the same time: my words and the traffic outside or whatever is going on. Realize it is all being registered. The labelling is being registered also. That is a direct introduction to your own natural awareness that is registering everything just as it is. That is the pure intelligence that is cognizing everything. When you put the label on it, it is re-cognized from memory. You know it already, very intimately.*

I – Intimate

It is said that your true nature is closer than your breath, more intimate than your face or your heart.

Intimacy in everyday language means familiarity, but it can also mean 'private and personal'. Being intimate means being open and vulnerable.

We say that what you are is so intimately close, so intimately familiar that once seen clearly it comes with a shock that it could ever have been overlooked. Intimacy of being is simultaneously very private and completely impersonal. It is here now. It is the dearest, sweetest, most cherished and completely taken for granted, therefore invisible. It is pre-sensory but it can't be denied. Be interested in it and it will reveal itself.

I – Interest

Interest is a feeling of wanting to know or learn about something or someone. It excites the curiosity or attention towards an object of interest. Interest in philosophy or spirituality may develop into self-inquiry.

Every human pattern has different interests but there is always the same one life behind it. There is no need to evoke spiritual interest or manipulate others to self-inquiry. No one hobby is superior to the other. Collectively, all appearance is covered with curious attention.

Chasing a football, building financial empires, raising children and producing food are equal to chasing enlightenment, building a sangha or producing books. Don't convert anyone. Mind your own intentions.

I – Intention

Some common synonyms of the word 'intention' are: aim, design, goal, intent, objective and purpose.

To take up an intention is to be a doer, to have free will and to choose. If there isn't anyone inside the body-mind to do so, the choice or free will is out of the question. Yet, intentions do show up, just like decisions and choices. Just like judgements show up, opinions and mental images. Just like narrative, just like everything. They may be inspired outwardly, induced or intuited.

Intentions aren't good or bad unless the narrative comes and relates them and interprets them. Projections of intentions and motives of others happen the same way, in commentary only. They are often triggered by insecurity.

I – Insecurity

Insecurity is an uncertainty or anxiety about oneself; a lack of confidence. It is also the state of being open to danger or threat, meaning that there is a lack of protection. Identity-based insecurity can be questioned, seen through and discarded. If there is no separate self to claim vulnerability, only instinctual insecurity is left. That motivates the fight-or-flight response, which supports survival.

> **Bob:** *If I believe that I am an individual, a person, then I am insecure. When I have a warm and loving family, I'll feel more secure for some time. For the same reason, families form into tribes and tribes form into nations. Nations go to war with nations over that same self-centeredness or insecurity, division and separateness.*

Sense of insecurity or incompleteness are invitations to inquiry. They are deep rooted inclinations of an identified self.

I – Inclination

Inclination is a person's natural urge to act or feel in a particular way; it is a disposition or tendency. It is a part of the makeup of the individual body-mind unit. Animals share this characteristic as well. Inclinations result from interactions between an infinite amount of environmental factors, and so they point to the inherent innocence of the process.

Inclinations are neutral in essence. Through a societal lens, though, they may be considered desirable or undesirable.

171

Some may result in talents and skills; others may lead to damaging addictions. Really, though, there is no-one to have them. They belong to the body-mind unit, which belongs to Life itself, not to imagined individual owners with their inner talk.

I – Internal monologue, inner speech

Internal monologue is also known as *inner* speech, self-talk, *inner* discourse or *internal* discourse. It is a person's *inner voice* which provides a running monologue of thoughts while they are conscious. It is usually tied to a person's sense of self. I like to call it a narrative or commentary, as it may at times be also conducted as a dialog.

It is vital to watch this pattern to see how mechanical it is. There is no need to strive to silence or alter this voice.

And it is not to say that if life moves us to experiment with the volume, tone and tune of it, we shouldn't. It may be fun. Let life change its location, authorship or content. There is no doer. Life plays as it pleases. The inner critic or judge can speak from our big toe if life moves us to try it. It may speak with the voice of a cartoon character if inspiration comes up to play this way.

Just remember that the credit for this play must go to Life and not the ego. There is no imagined 'me' speaking these words. It is just speak-ING, language-ING.

L – Sai-L-or Bob

L – Language

According to the philosophy of the ancient Buddhist Yogachara school (traceable back to Vasubandhu and Asanga in the 5th century CE), the three interpenetrating natures of the world are: *constructed, interdependent* and *realized.*

We have learned to interpret perceived objects using memory and to express ourselves using language. In this way we *construct* an overlay of a personalized world comprising subjective meanings and values. This is the constructed nature of the world.

In fact, everything is only as it is. It is the interplay of elements without any separation. This is the *interdependent* nature of the world. To know the realized nature of the world is to *realize* inherent emptiness of the appearance.

This pointer is not only theoretical! Contemplation reveals its practicality. Language is the key, as it is the singular factor differentiating us from animals.

> **Bob:** *You can argue that animals communicate using certain forms of language. There will be a different call for danger or for a mate, but it is always based in present functioning.*

Language is responsible for the whole projection of mental constructs and images. Language is the root of the narrative self (an imagined 'me' which exists only in the memory, in the inner commentary). The world filtered through and interpreted by "the languaging centre of the human brain"

(Default Mode Network or the 'self-ing' part) is the constructed, personalized map of reality. Underneath it there is a world as it is; not a map but a territory, the world reported on presently by five senses.

Waking up **from** the dream of being a separate self is waking up **to** the dream of being the interdependent, non-separate world as a whole. It is waking up from the belief in the narrative self (inner dialog, commentary) to the dream of impersonal present happening.

Nonduality could be seen as transcending (rising above) the language, liberation from seeming slavery to a belief.

> **Bob:** *In Hsin-hsin Ming, the third Zen patriarch told us, "The way is beyond language, for in it there is no yesterday, no tomorrow and no today". It shows us that past, present and future are mind. Timeline is also a construct of language.*

For British people, 'time' is linear, moving from left to right, but Chinese think of the idea of time in terms of 'over' and 'under'. In the case of the Greeks, time has size, so it can be 'large' or 'small'. The Hopi language is considered timeless, so everything is translated to present tense (instead of saying "a week ago", they'd say "on the seventh day").

They are tribes (like the Pirahã) who do not have numbers or any words for 'one', or 'two', but instead they use words like 'small', 'somewhat larger' and 'many'.

Similarly 'space' is also a construct. According to research, in some of Aboriginal languages (Guugu Yimithirr) there are no words for relative direction, like left or right, but only cardinal words like north, east, etc. They describe everything geocentrically rather than egocentrically, which influences their conceptualization of space and perception of the world.

Many languages, including my own mother-tongue, Polish, assign masculinity or femininity to inanimate objects, which can shape the different feelings for, and associations with, these objects. (For example German speakers associate a bridge with typical 'feminine' adjectives like pretty, elegant, peaceful and slender. In contrast to that, Polish speakers use typical 'masculine' adjectives to describe a bridge like grand, tall, massive and powerful).

Various languages focus our perception, attention and thought on specific aspects of the world. They will have more vocabulary around what is valued amongst their users. Thus, language is also used to transmit values, laws and cultural norms, including taboos and censorship.

Language, since it expresses and reinforces culture, influences and shapes personal identity and creates boundaries of behaviour. The usage of words and phrases significantly impacts individual thought and character/personal identity.

> **Bob:** *If you focus on regurgitating the painful past or scare yourself thinking of what could happen — if you are negative in your inner dialogue — you need to recognize that pattern.*

The whole world around us is organized and made sense of through language. We are told by physics and quantum mechanics that the mere fact of observation narrows down the field of infinite possibilities for the manifested world. Our language narrows it further to the sum total of objects with various meanings, typically imposed by society.

> **Bob:** *To feel more complete I add concepts to that 'I', so now I'm Christian or Muslim, white or black, Australian, middle class etc. and my tribe, my God is better than yours.*

There are/were languages (for example, Hopi) which define words as 'collection of actions' rather than objects. It was about verbs rather than nouns. Nonduality pointers also attempt to show the processes instead of artificial division into subject and object. We say there is a seeing, which is much truer that saying that there is a seer and seen. There is thinking, not there is thinker and thought. In the same way, labelling is a part of an automatic functioning.

> **Bob:** *When you come to my home, leave all your concepts outside the door, where you leave your shoes. Come here empty and receptive. Nothing can be poured into a full cup.*

Let's be mindful about the limitations of language and the impossibility of precise pointing. Let's feel into it, so we won't crash on illogical phrases. We won't waste time rubbishing imperfect pointers but will use these which resonate and ignore those which don't.

When we hear that "emptiness is prior to form" or that "perception underlies label", we'll know that 'prior' doesn't mean 'before' in linear time, and 'underlying' is not a special order. There is no linear time and there is no objective space. They are labelled out of pure potentiality, which isn't a thing.

L – Label

Bob: All the mind (a thought) can do is make a concept, an image, a label. It can't even understand or grasp anything. All the thought does is translate what is coming from that intelligence, puts it into words. The thought is just a process of labelling or translating what is happening in that pure intelligence.

We tend to assume that we know things when we label them. We put the label 'brain' on it and we think we know what this incredibly sophisticated organ is. We think it is separate from its environment, even though we know it can't function on its own. But the label suggests it is separate; it is surrounded by 'no-brain' things.

As far as we can observe, the sense of separation comes only from using language. One landscape becomes buildings, trees, chairs and people. They are on the background of fields and sky, but only when labelled so. Without labelling, everything is just as it is. There are sounds of various volume, including no volume. There are scenes of various intensity of light.

Bob: Are you seeing right now? Look around. You are not labelling everything you see, you can label only a few things. But you are still seeing everything, and you know what it is even without the labels. If there is no label on it, you can't say it is this or that. All it is then is just what it is, appearing as such and such. Intelligence knows what everything is immediately and directly. To be able to express it through the mind, it needs a label.

Labelling is just an overlay of narration. Labelling is a convenient tool for communication and as such it is to be greatly appreciated. It helps memorising. It also enables us to learn from one another and through generations. It has delivered lots of ways in which we can connect, find similarities, common ground, which in turn enabled grand and dominating civilisations to be formed. So, even though labelling may lead to psychological suffering, it is not to be condemned as bad. It is not to be avoided, but recognized and utilized.

Bob: *Well, if you are not labelling it, you are really seeing it for what it is. It is just pure intelligence energy. When you put the label on it, you have a concept of what you believe it to be. We get so involved in the labels... Just be aware of that. Prior to the label is that KNOWING.*

*Labels may come up. You call yourself a human being, you call God the Supreme Being. Take the label 'human' off, take the label 'supreme' off and now, try and separate the **Being** without the label.*

The word is not the real. You can say the word 'water' for the rest of your life, but you can't drink the word. The word 'water' won't quench your thirst. The word 'fire' won't burn your mouth as you speak it. The word 'me' is not what you are, it is just the word.

When you look around the room, without labelling anything, you realize everything is being registered just as it is without a label. In that instant you are prior to the mind. Look around quickly and back again. How much could you label? 15-20 things maybe. But you saw everything, didn't you? You can't deny that you saw it.

It is always quite enlightening to look at nature. Animals don't have symbolic language so they don't label things. Yet they function efficiently. They navigate through their lives without language or labels, so they don't create narrative commenting on everything that is happening. They don't label themselves as doers of deeds and they don't dwell in the past or imagine the future. Yet, they instinctually prepare for the change of seasons if necessary. They learn from their actions.

Certain brain damage may produce similar effect in humans, and that is rather undesirable! Nonduality is not about regressing below the language or discarding it! It is rather about transcending the slavery it may create. Recognition is the key. This pointer is to show the tendency, the mechanisms of functioning, so it is known in consciousness. When known as an object, it doesn't hijack the whole stream of attention anymore. Part of attention is released to maintain awareness of the thought-stream. Not just labelling and inner talk, but listening takes place.

L – Listen

When you look around, names of things (labels) may spontaneously come up in the narrative. Who is doing it? Who is naming or speaking? Who is listening to it? If there was just one entity, speaking wouldn't be necessary because it would know already. So who is informing who? Is there two of you? One? Or maybe there is no-one there, just automatic functioning? Have a look.

Who hears the inner voice or voices of commentary? Is there a physical ear that listens to it or is there some kind of inner knowing of this silent inner voice? How about outer sounds? Who is listening to these? Is there a different knowing or just one knowing?

> **Bob:** *Is your ear telling you, "Listen to this, listen to that?" My ear doesn't say anything. It is an instrument through which hearing is happening. But the thought comes up and translates it into 'I hear'. But the thought 'I hear' can't hear. Block your ears off and prove it to yourself.*

Hearing is happening. In this field of hearing, sounds appear and are registered through the ear. We are pointing at the capacity or ability of hearing; the potential of hearing or simply hear-ING. ING makes it an immediate process, right now.

Listening, however, means paying attention to sound, hearing something with thoughtful attention and giving it consideration. Listening requires concentration so that your brain processes meaning from words and sentences. Listening can be appreciative, empathic, comprehensive or critical. Discriminative listening is the most basic type of listening. In discriminative listening, the listener interprets the differences and nuances of sounds and body language. The listener is sensitive to attributes including rate, volume, pitch and emphasis in speaking.

How do you listen to somebody you don't like? ...Or to somebody you disagree with — a parent, maybe, or a politician you've labelled as 'stupid'? How do you listen to annoying noise? How do you listen to self-judgment in your own head or judgment of others? How do you listen to this sense of incompleteness and the fear of failure?

Your attitude is paramount. Staying open is paramount.

> **Bob:** The Big Book says, "Some of us have tried to hold onto our old ideas and the results were nil, until we let go absolutely". So, if you come here to listen with your old ideas, concepts and reference points of: "They say the same in Buddhism", or "I got it in Christianity", or in similar teachings like Hinduism or Islam, then you are hanging onto your old ideas and beliefs. Walk in here with a clean slate. Just drop all your old ideas, concepts and images. Just be a little bit open in "letting go absolutely". Listen with the heart.

L – Listening with Love, to Love

> **Bob:** The way you need to listen to this, is not head to head but 'heart to heart'. Everybody knows what 'heart to heart' means. When somebody shares a sad story and you say, "My heart went out to them", this is 'heart to heart'. Listening from the heart does not mean listening from your physical heart. It is listening from the core of your being, from the very essence of existence.

How is the listening experience with beautiful music, or listening to your beloved? How is the listening when there is a whisper that you really want to hear, one that matters to you? What is the quality of attention then? Aren't you all ears? Haven't you 'disappeared' in the experiencing?

If not, do you still filter what you hear through your judgements about it? Do you compare new ideas with your old data-base? Do you fit it with what you have known or heard before? Do you judge whether it sounds familiar or reasonable? Do you evaluate it using logic? Do you agree or disagree with that?

There's nothing wrong with common sense or healthy scepticism. It might have kept you away from dangerous cults or from making a fool of yourself. It is to be honoured. But remember, it can "throw the baby out with the bathwater". There is a time to listen with your head and there is a time to listen to love. Life navigates this. Stay open. Adopt the attitude of receptivity.

> **Bob:** *Listening with the mind to what is beyond the mind will take you nowhere. It can't happen.*

Initially we don't know any better. Your first hundred times hearing the nondual message may trigger various reactions or simply put you to sleep. However, persistent exposure to this unique frequency of pointing usually builds up receptivity; and love for the truth wakes up.

> **Bob:** *We need to listen in a relaxed manner, overlooking the meanings and simply resonate. IT can't ever be grasped with the mind. How could mind understand that what it appears on? Mind reduces everything into concepts and we are all about non-conceptual awareness.*

Thought patterns form in childhood. There are survival strategies, habitual objects of focus, particular preferences... And they become filters through which we view the world. So, when we listen with the mind, we translate everything we hear to match our strategies, habits and preferences. We reinforce the individual. This is not pure listening anymore. It

182

is filtered, translated, adjusted and interpreted. It is useful, but not here, not to see through thinking.

Yet, even the naughty narrative can be heard with the heart! Even harsh inner commentary can be recognized and serve as a reminder about the natural state! It can be listened to with love and love can be recognized as the energy underlying every statement.

When inner judgement tells me I'm a failure, I feel the depths of loving care underlying this statement. Something in there seems to warn or punish me because it wants me to succeed! When the inner voice blames others, I see how it values my own innocence. Comparison happens to raise my standards, only because it cares — because this too, is Love in disguise.

L – Loving to be

Bob: Everything is One, so why not call it Love? Nisargadatta says: "Life is love and love is life. What keeps the body together but love? What is desire, but love of the self? What is fear but the urge to protect? And what is knowledge but the love of truth?"

Does it mean that the sense of lack, incompleteness or inferiority is also love? Is my self-hatred also love? Is the ego, the limited self-image, also an expression of love? How about the Holocaust? How about acute selfishness and inconsideration of others?

Nisargadatta explains further: "The means and forms may be wrong, but the motive behind is always love: love of the 'me' and of the 'mine'. The 'me' and the 'mine' may be small, or may explode and embrace the universe, but love remains".

So, the answer is YES. Everything is already That, and it is the inseparable One, which means there is nothing outside of Love. Only That. Light is love and darkness (absence of light) is love also. Recognized or in disguise, it is always the One, Love.

> **Bob:** *The ancients are pointing to Sat-Chit-Ananda, which is Being, Knowing and Loving to Be. These three are just three aspects of the One. Love is an aspect of Being. Knowing is an aspect of Being. Everything is because it loves to be.*

Being is evidence of Love. Everything exists because it loves to be. Every living form is equipped with some or the other life-protection mechanism. Thought also loves to be; it demands attention (life essence) and it seeks survival and replication. Looking from that angle, if it didn't love to be, it wouldn't exist. Existence is an expression of 'loving to be', Ananda. It is a field of unconditional love. It is Love that allows everything to be. It allows both good and bad, pleasure and pain. It allows unconditionally. It loves unconditionally. It is unconditional love-ing.

This love of being or loving to be may not be very obvious in our habitual way of looking. To survive, we learned to look out for dangers, to look what is wrong and to fix it. As we learn to use mental representations of things — words — we cover the reality with added meanings and relations. We label. We look through clouds of interpretation and clarity gets obscured. Love of being is buried under concepts and images.

> **Bob:** *There is loving nature but not 'your' loving nature. That loving being is what is expressing and displaying through you, as you. That is the essence of*

life. Life is energy. Energy is light. Light is love. That is
your true nature, that loving to be.

Loving to be — Ananda — is like the sky. It shines forth when
the clouds of concepts disperse. It never disappears, even
when overcast. You are that Sky already, regardless of your
current belief. Your heartfelt appreciation for existence is
close, maybe just one thought away.

Once recognized and realized, thoughts cannot obscure it
anymore in any lasting way. It is there simultaneously with
them. Self-obsessed commentary, which was once hurtful,
may now point out the beauty and love. It may evoke
spontaneous gratitude instead of constant complaints. The
narrative, if any is there at all, changes from 'me, me, me' to
wonderment and awe.

Bob: *Both Nisargadatta and Muktananda used to say,*
"Love yourself". What did they mean? We know what
that means. It means, "Be warm towards yourself,
give yourself a little wink, a hug; appreciate yourself!"

It is often said that Love is who we are. Being is who we are.
Awareness, which is Knowing, is who we are. And we are
because we love to be. If we didn't love to be, we wouldn't be.
And it doesn't matter at this point who we consider ourselves
to be; the mental image, the body or the Love, the Life, The
Absolute. We are. It is. There is is-ness.

Bob: *People want to be more loving. That only means*
you have a concept of what loving is. You can't live up
to that concept because it is an erroneous concept
from the start. The natural being-ness is a loving-
ness. Life is love.

Loving into being means also loving someone or something into existence. Love sustains the dream. Loving to be applies to every form.

In absence of the recognition of its imminent presence, there is a deep heart felt longing for love...

L – Longing for Love

Longing for Love is one of the sweetest memories from 'my past' life as a seeker. It was less than six years ago, so I still remember it pretty well. Tears of devotion towards IT, melting in surrender, wanting it so badly and so deeply that this very emotion would catapult me to temporary dissolution in the blissful love I was longing for. I was ready to die for IT. In that readiness it died, I died: there was a short glimpse of death of separation.

It is only too obvious that to long for something I need to know it. I have to know what I want, what I'm longing for. So, it is a re-connection, a recognition. Because the manifested world is dualistic, it seems like there is an 'I' and an 'It'. It means that an overlay of imagination obscures the singular, energetic process of longing. In the pinnacle of longing for love, there is nobody and nothing outside of this immediate -ING. In this surrender, the devotee and the object of worship disappear, collapse, unite.

If an illusion of an individual reappears and is believed again into seeming reality, it may again want to surrender to IT (or to Him, the Lord; or her, the Mother Nature). This is a hide-and-seek play of Love. That Presence never leaves you. The

Lord (the Breath of Life) is always with you. You are the Nature. Recognize that and rejoice.

Longing has other faces too, but all of this is the movement of Love.

The human condition is defined by suffering, says the first noble truth of Buddha. It is due to identification as an individual, a body, a limited entity. With this comes a resistance of the never-good-enough costume; wanting things to be different. With this comes longing for safety, for appreciation and for recognition. Part of the experience is also the longing for fun, for connection and for beauty.

Why, if not because of love? Why do we want to give ourselves and others all that is precious, valued, pleasant and dear? Why do we want to take away from others and add to ourselves?

Everything is Love or longing for love, which is a flip side of the same coin — a singularity.

Forgetting who we are is Love. Identifying as an individual is Love. Trying to get rid of the ego (which is always attempted by the very same illusion of ego) is Love. Beliefs are Love. Freedom from beliefs is Love. Suffering is Love. Freedom from suffering is Love. Longing for love is love. Because there is only One. Nondual One.

Please, rejoice and savour this unique flavour of longing for love if you still can! Appreciate it with all your heart! Once it is clear there is no one to long and nothing to long for, there will only be a fleeting memory and reflection of that beautiful energy in others. You may never experience it directly anymore.

Kahlil Gibran said, "Your children are not your children, they are life longing for itself". The whole manifestation, trees, clouds, thoughts, are children of life. They are life longing for itself, can you see it? Experience and expression are Life longing for itself.

> **Bob:** *Once you see that everything is one (call it love if you like) there is nothing left to do but laugh. It really is all laughable.*

L – Laughable

Upon seeing though the dream, laughter is the most common response. Many call it a cosmic joke. What is being sought has never been lost. There is nothing to be found. The one who is seeking has no real existence; it is a phantom, a fantasy. He/she can't find the answer because there is no answer; and there is no seeker either, no questioner, no question. Yet, the obviousness of existence is staring in the face of the faceless. How brilliant! It is closer than your breath, never hidden, never obscured. Isn't that amazing?

Once this is clear, there is nothing left to do but laugh, wholeheartedly, at the genius of this cosmic joke.

A popular quote from *A Course in Miracles* illustrates it in a similar way: *"Into eternity, where all is one, there crept a tiny, mad idea, at which the Son of God remembered not to laugh. In his forgetting did the thought become a serious idea.... Together, we can laugh them both away.... It is a joke to think that time can come to circumvent eternity, which means there is no time".* ACIM Text, Ch.27 v6.

> **Bob:** *You say, "Yeah, I get it now BUT when I get out there..." There is no THERE! When you are so-called*

'there' it will actually be 'here'. Yes, we can laugh, but let's not miss that wherever it is, it will always be HERE and NOW. Or Now-Here if you like, No-Where.

You may be just one idea away from that heartfelt laughter! Also, laughter is the best exorcist! Laugh your fears away! Laugh lovingly at your own seriousness! Very young children think less, have accumulated much less information, so they laugh much more. Life is lighter, less serious and abundant in natural curiosity. In some cases "ignorance is bliss". You can't worry about things that are "out of sight, out of mind".

Socrates' insight, "I know that I don't know" inspires natural humility and awe. It expresses the understanding that parroted knowledge is not a wisdom. It offers seeing through the conditioned interpretation of perceptions. It penetrates through the collective belief system called science.

Nonduality pointers are to help you see through the brilliance of Leela (divine play). They point to the roots of myth, superstition and prejudice. They bring an appreciation of the ability that simple thought has: to convince, to steal the show, to take you for a ride. This is the best joke ever! It is laughable indeed!

Bob: *You have got the mask on and you're playing the role. In essence, you are the star of the show, the Academy Award winner.*

The punch line of the cosmic joke is that nothing has ever happened.

Learn life's lessons and laugh!

L – Lessons of Lorna – E X A M P L E

Lorna is a very slim, very tall, very Dutch woman who, for the past 15+ years has spent most of her summers in Australia. She is a lesbian, has never married, has never parented a child and has been single since 2012, when her much younger girlfriend left her to return to the same cult they met each other in years prior. Lorna couldn't stop her or save her. Three years later, in June 2015, the ex-girlfriend committed suicide. Lorna is in her early 70s now. She is fit and healthy, with short, straight, thick white hair, blue eyes and very wide smile with really big, white teeth.

That is now. Bob saw that smile coming up very slowly, very gradually over the last 10 years. Lorna had a tough life in the outskirts of Rotterdam. Her birth family had disowned her and her desk job behind a computer had nearly drained her. She had a lot to let go of. She had a lot of lessons to learn, she would say. Lorna considered herself a slow learner. That assumed identity had always served her as a self-fulfilling prophecy.

She was guru-shopping and learning other languages of pointing. At times, she would get really confused with the vocabulary. Her collection of books and films and her participation in various discussion groups had made her a walking encyclopaedia but the knowledge was superficial and shallow. The simplicity of experiencing wasn't recognized.

The first little lesson for Lorna was to empty the cup!

> *"What do you know for certain?"* **Bob** *would ask. "What do you know experientially and not from books, teachers or parents?"*

Discarding all accumulated ideas and beliefs wasn't an easy road, but she took it anyway. Discarding, discarding, discarding... Without assuming that she knows what anything is, she was left, more and more, with non-conceptual being-knowing.

She would keep coming back to that basic experiencing, staying with that sense of presence as much as she could. From there, little insights would guide her further, towards greater clarity.

One of her little lessons revealed that every experience is really happening here, where she is, now. Experiences of Africa, or the moon, or her deceased ex — all here, in consciousness. From there, she would realize that even the most immediate experiences, like pain or hunger, colours and sounds, were also here, in consciousness. In fact, they are nothing but consciousness itself.

This realization would make itself known in many different ways. Sometimes the movement of the wind in sea-grass would stop the mind and flash a little lesson. At other times it would be a scent or sound. Little shifts would dawn without any seeming triggers as well. Hundreds of fleeting moments, sometimes hardly noticed. It is akin to seeing through the dream. It is continuing to this day.

Further understanding has glimpsed that noticing is a movement of consciousness, and that so is its subject and all seeming objects. There is nothing that is not it. There is nothing that is not her perceiving. The dream continues and living continues but the world is not solid or something outside anymore. Everything is made of impressions: everything is sensing; it is consciousness dancing; changing images in stillness.

Today happily single, missing nothing and retired, with a sense of completeness and joy, Lorna is free from the bondage of self. She is free even when self still seems apparent. There is a knowing. Consciousness is free because Lorna is just a label of the vehicle.

She has never had a particular breakthrough moment from which she could say she was done (or undone). Instead, she had many small insights that continued to deepen and are deepening still. The deepening never ends. It is alive.

There are emotionally charged thoughts at times, running their course for minutes or even an hour, but she knows not to claim them as her own. When habitual claiming comes up, she makes nothing of it. When doubting thoughts creep in, she knows to laugh at the attempts for the identifying software to re-establish itself.

She can't say if this is 'IT' — she doesn't claim to be enlightened or 'awake'. She knows that seeking and claiming are just other ways in which consciousness dances, and that remembering and forgetting are also a part of it. That part is not active anymore. Life has become an effortless adventure. There is a celebration of livingness.

L – Life, livingness

Bob: You're being lived. Life lives you. You can call it life force, life energy or life essence, if you like. It animates your body, it enables you to think, to see, it breathes you.

The body is being lived. The mind is being used. Senses are being utilized. Life does it all. Life is the only doer. Life is the only force responsible for everything that is happening. Life animates a tsunami. Life creates tyrants and injustice. Life creates religions and life dreams about the separation. Life is seeing through the eyes of the body. Life is the cells which constitute the eyes of the body. Life is clarity and life is clouds. There is only life.

> **Bob:** *Have a look, and you will see that life continually lives on life. There is no death at all. As you breathe and bring fuel of food into this body, integration is happening. It continually builds new cells and keeps growing it. At some point it turns around, goes the opposite direction, and disintegration starts. You call it death but in the breaking down of that body, there is only more life.*
>
> *There are enzymes, maggots, worms and bacteria — all life. It is giving life to millions of them. They break it down back to the elements. If it goes back into the earth, it becomes a fertilizer. Out of that comes more life. Seeds may sprout in the soil. Something will come along and eat those. That something will be eaten by something else. So, life continually lives on life. There is ONLY life.*

There is an innocent habit of taking credit for the actions of Life. It has been learned through imitation. We say, "I did this, I didn't do that". With it goes the guilt for wasting your potential or your life. With it comes the sense of responsibility; the tension of never being good enough; the need for more time. With it comes fear and hope for an eternal life of punishment or reward. With it comes past and future lives as explanation and redemption. But Life is now. Only now. Nobody lives Life. Life is.

> **Bob:** *Some believe they will have another life, never realizing that there is only now: never looking to see what it is that is going to have this other life; never investigating what it is that has got this life now.*
>
> *This, now, is the livingness. You can never live this moment again, this moment, right now. If that intelligence-energy, that life force, that livingness wasn't there, how many thoughts could you have? Could you even be self-aware? And could you lift a finger if that animating essence wasn't there? Life is like the ocean, ever changing but never changing.*

There, here, everywhere, nowhere, where? Try to locate it!

L – Location - E X E R C I S E

Please relax into your being, stabilizing in that sense of 'I am here'. Where is the centre of this 'here'? In other words: where are you? Where is that sense of 'me' located? Where is the 'I'?

Notice the movement of attention, the checking...

Body has a location, but how about you? A costume, car or house also have a location. But do you? Where is the centre of the spirit? Are you scanning your head? Your chest? Throat? Gut? Can you narrow it down to a point? Maybe you can only locate it vaguely? Perhaps behind the eyes or around the heart or solar plexus? How big is the area? Is it the size a pin point, a fist, a basket-ball?

You can also start by discarding areas you know the 'I' doesn't reside. Start from your left foot. Do you feel it is where the centre of your being (your 'soul') resides? No? How about the whole leg? Back side? Hand? Any chakras? Which ones? If you compare between locations, which is the winner? In which point can you sense that aliveness the strongest? Where are you?

As you see, in this exercise we overlay mental projections (mental images of bodily parts) on the 'spaceless here'. We will temporarily use these projections to transcend all the images.

Once you have located (even if only vaguely) the 'I', please verify where you were looking at it FROM. To say it is, for example, a thumb-sized dense but transparent point in the area of the head or grey tennis ball shaped vibration around the heart, you must have been sensing it from somewhere. Where did you look from?

Please locate the area from which you were observing, witnessing the sense of 'I'. Where was it watched from? Was it from outside the body somewhere — in front of it, behind it or maybe above it or to one side? Or maybe it was from inside the body? Where was it located in relation to the observed 'I'? Can you narrow it down to a certain point in space or is it a rather vague area? How big of an area do you feel it is?

Once you have located the area from which you were looking at the sense of 'I', please verify how did you know it was this particular area. Where were you looking at this from?

If, for example, the sense of I (located behind your eyes, thumb sized) is being observed from another location (let's say, the size of a balloon, a half cubic meter of air floating close above and in front of the body), where did you observe this observation point from? How do you know the observing area is where it is? Where is the knowing of this located?

The obvious insight is that the 'I' observing is more intimately 'me' than the object observed. Please, notice how this sense of 'I' travels as you keep inquiring. The witness position shifts to describe the object of observation.

Coming back to the I-locating game: can you roughly define the area of knowing from which you located the observing (half cubic air balloon) of the sense of 'I' (thumb size behind your eyes)?

Is that knowing even more vague and hard to pin-point in space? Is it more like the size of a room? How do you know that? Which one is the true you after all? Location one, two, three? Neither? Who/what knows all these locations? Isn't that (knowing/consciousness) the truth of who you are rather than the temporary viewpoints?

If you give it enough time to contemplate and locate the sense appropriately, every proceeding step of knowing the location of witnessing will be more spacious, larger, and harder to define; until it is undefinable. You may need to step back two, three or four times before awareness becomes space-like. Please don't rush it to avoid the mental loop.

Space-like awareness contains all locations; the whole world appears in you. You/Awareness contains the whole sphere of seeing and everything in it. You are the world and you are the space in which the world vibrates and changes. You can't go beyond the world to see it. You can't observe, understand what you are. You can't be located but you also can't deny your being.

Please repeat it as often as you like (it takes seconds!): to remind yourself that un-locatable knowing is what you are. Obviously you are not this sense of 'I', since 'you' are aware of this sense from somewhere else. By locating any observation point you are proving that it is not the observer, but object in the field of knowing.

As you can see, who you are cannot be truly located because in order to locate it, you would have to leave it, and then it is not you anymore, but 'it'. Who you are is all knowing limitless pure consciousness without any location. Just look!

L – Look

Bob: Look, investigate and you'll see the falseness of the so-called person. Get yourself out of the road. Look and see the falseness and continue to see it.

Look who is looking! Look where looking is happening from! Where does the looking start? There is a seeming sense of location. The location is 'here'. Through this particular set of eyes, as through the lens of a camera, looking is located. Pure looking, like through the lens of a device, contains no judgement. A camera doesn't like or dislike what it registers.

A camera has its angle; it usually doesn't see 360 degrees at once.

So, the looking or the seeing has its peripheries and blind areas. But what is it that looks? Does it have any shape or form? Is the eye looking or is the eye merely an instrument through which looking happens? Who uses the instrument?

Who or what is looking through the eye? Please, have a look who is looking! Anybody there? How does it feel? What is sensing the space behind the eyes from which looking starts? Is there anything to grasp about this unknown abyss?

Could this be the space-like Awareness, the Being, the Knowing, the Loving to Be? Maybe No-thing is looking. No-one is looking, yet there is seeing, an activity without the subject credited for it... Maybe unbound Life, Pure Intelligence or God Energy is seeing through this instrument of the eyes...

If there was an entity there, we would have found it. We would have known that this entity is merely another object in Awareness and not the one who is looking. The one who (which) is looking can't be looked at. Even the instrument, the eye, can only see its reflection, not itself. The reflection is not it. Please, look and see for yourself, so it is yours.

This particular pointer was real fun for me for a while straight after seeing through the no-self. Placing curious attention just behind the eyes for a moment while walking, sipping my tea, even chatting or writing. It would drop into the bottomless pit and dissolve in joy.

The same thing happens when one listens.

L – Listen – E X E R C I S E

Please sit with your eyes closed for five to ten minutes. Focus your attention on listening, exclusively. From the immediate environment pick four to five sounds (or more if you can hold them all in your field of attention). It can be from outside traffic, the sound of your own breath, a clock ticking, footsteps, birds chirping, a fan or a heater, a computer, distant conversations...

The important thing is to focus not on meanings, or what words you hear, but on pure sounds. Suspend or push aside your judgment and all likes/dislikes. Register them the same way a voice recorder would do.

You may repeat this exercise while in nature. Choose four to five (or more if you can focus that well) different birds in different directions and at various distances (volume). Try also doing it when in a crowd of people, in the train station or on a bus or tram. Pick homogenous humming from various directions, of various volumes. Don't try to understand it, just hear the sound.

Once these four to five sounds are established and held in consciousness for a minute, acknowledge the location of these sounds in space. How do you know they are there? What is that knowing? Is it because as awareness, you also are there?

It is beautiful to repeat this exercise in a musical concert, choir or symphonic orchestra, holding in attention as many separate musical instruments and voices as you can. Notice the nature of hearing, its origin; check whether you can ascribe any attributes to it.

Enjoy the space-less vastness of your own un-located, un-locatable consciousness. You are everywhere, indeed! 'Here' has no location, no boundaries and no end.

Did you notice that when the attention is busy holding onto these sounds there isn't much of it left for personal drama? Thinking has stopped. The more sounds you can hold in awareness, the more they'll blow your mind! What a learning!

L – Learning

There is nothing you need to learn to see through the illusion of self. It is unlearning that helps the seeming process. It is about questioning and doubting any absolute statements, including those from science.

Everything that has been learned is to be reviewed and recognized as mere information, which need not be believed in or taken as reality. It may be useful in the appearance, treasured as a romantic idea (and nothing else), or discarded as limitation.

> **Bob:** *If you acted on this gut feeling, before it is referred to the 'me' of past memory, your life would probably be a lot more effortless and easy; but we have learned to disregard that spontaneous functioning and refer it to the 'me' of memory.*

Learning is great fun and it is crucial in this dream called life. It may enrich the experiencing — when you perfect some skills or develop talents. But the attitude "I know, I've learned it" is irrelevant to the recognition and may actually impede it.

We learned to measure time and it is a useful tool in the daily life but blindly believing in time means missing eternity. We learned names of things but to take the label for what it represents is to miss the thing itself. We learned social skills and we learned to take credit. It ups the game but it means missing out on its mystery.

What we learned, we do not really know. We only think we know it. We really know only what we know innately, which is the certainty of our own existence. The world we see is constructed by a habitual perception/interpretation of it. It won't stop being constructed when the process is recognized. People and places which are not within your gaze will still potentially exist in the constructed reality.

You have learned the rules of this game. Things are for you as you say they are. There is no game without rules. The agreed-upon reality with its forces, gravity, conspiracies and laws of attraction is as defined. Limits are defined. Other cultures have different definitions and they experience different agreed-upon realities. These rules need not be unlearned.

Other rules can be established, too. Special powers may be obtained, but there is no need for this. Special powers often prove to be just another distraction from the basic recognition.

Unlearning or questioning some rigid rules is only to take away the seriousness and fanaticism of the belief. What we think or believe we know, we do not really know. When the thought is stopped, that type of knowledge (acquired, second hand) is truly put to the test and fails.

Instead of questioning everything, unlearn to identify as a form. The rest will follow. For this, unlearn the belief in time, so you won't associate as a collection of your past memories anymore. Unlearn trusting your thoughts because they are just thoughts. Recognize non-conceptual existence beyond thinking. Fall in love with 'I don't know'.

The paradox is that the non-knowing, thought-free mind is a mind that is open to learn. Some call it no-mind. It is pure mind, curious about everything. Life shows itself to itself through clear, open mind. It reflects itself in such a mind. Thought-free mind is the mind in which thoughts are free to arise and pass without fixation of attention.

Bob and I are in learning mode more or less all the time. We don't project the future; we let life show us what comes. When we guide people, we ask questions first to learn their particular language so we can serve them best. We listen and learn.

> **Bob:** *From the time you started to reason, everything you know has been acquired or learned, picked up along the way. Even the thought 'I am' is acquired. You didn't have that thought prior to that. You didn't have a name or a label for anything. Then we start learning, and we are acquiring everything from then on. But the functioning, the primal activity, is what is living you and breathing you: beating your heart, growing your fingernails and even doing the thinking. But all the activity is happening by itself.*

We learn labels, including the word 'me'. All they are - are sounds or a line of letters.

L – Line of Letters

Powerful drama in the head, which fuels distressful emotions and unreasonable actions, often becomes just a line of letters when written down. The 'demon' loses his power when seen clearly. Scary images reduced to letters are benign. Writing words as letters slows the thinking. Journaling may be the way out of hell. It often was for me.

Lines of letters or written text is just the content of the page. Movie and movie characters are just the content of the screen. Smells, sensations, thoughts, images — all are the content of that consciousness, Cognizing Emptiness. They are within your experiencing, your being-knowing. You are that page, screen, consciousness.

Do any of those words touch your heart? Any amongst presented letters S, A, I, L, so far? May they serve you well! Those pointers which do not resonate now may open up for you later. Or maybe some new ones will bug the dream.

The word 'emptiness' is a concept, a line of letters. So is the 'ego', 'I' or 'me'. You are not the concept. Collection of sounds or letters constituting words Awareness, That, God, Love, Intelligence, Self, Sat-Chit-Ananda, Sky etc., are not your essential nature. You are none of these concepts. You are not a collection of sounds or letters. What you are is pure subjectivity, but not the letters constituting the word 'subjectivity'. It is the Being that cannot be made into a thing; it cannot be appropriately represented by words.

But every word, being a simple collection of letters, could be a reminder. Every time you see words — letters on a page or screen — they may remind you of the background they couldn't exist without. On which background does the whole process of you seeing them happen? Where does the page, the screen, the consciousness arise?

The letters in your name, or any other letters you ever see or read, could serve as a reminder about the screen: the page or poster on which they appear. That, in turn, can point to the awareness on which posters, bodies and the movement of attention in consciousness — appear. There is always a bigger picture to step back to.

If you anchor that reminder, you will acknowledge the background every time you see the letters in words. You will acknowledge your true nature both in movement (form) and in stillness (the formless). Being lucid about it, you will see the content as a dream; the lucid dream.

L – Lucid dreaming

Lucid means expressed clearly, easy to understand, bright or luminous. But in spiritual circles this word is usually an adjective followed by the noun 'dream' or 'dreaming'.

The analogy of a dream is often used to point out several colorful aspects of the play of life. This particular one — lucid dreaming — is a very potent pointer. It reminds you that the dream goes on but now you know you are dreaming. Now there is a knowing, which is not owned by the 'me'.

> **Bob:** As Nisargadatta says, "You dream the dream called life. Stop looking for the way out. The dream is not your concern. Your concern is that you love one part of it and not another. Love all of it or none of it and the rest will be done for you by the same life that brought you into existence".

When the dream becomes lucid, you know you are dreaming but you do not wake up and you do not wish to. Why would you? (The same as knowing you are watching a great movie doesn't make you switch it off!) That would spoil it! You keep dreaming. You enjoy it much more this way, because scary things are not scary anymore but pleasant things are still pleasant. What a great deal! Lucid dreaming is, indeed, great fun.

Once you discover you are dreaming, a lot of limitations may just drop off. I would fly in my lucid dreams or exercise special powers, move objects, manifest things, change seasons... In my (infrequent) lucid dreams I'm a mighty doer, but a doer without any self-concept. I'm simply not bothered by defining myself; I'm too busy having fun.

There is not much self-definition in ordinary, non-lucid dreams at night as well, but on top of that, there is no knowledge of the dream being a dream. I hardly ever know anything at all about the role I play or who I am as a character. I have no past and no recollection of how I ended up where I find myself to be. When I happen to see my own reflection (very rarely), it looks unfamiliar. It can have different skin color, opposite sex, a different age, an unknown face. It is not alarming. Critical thinking is off. When I don't see a mirror, I assume upon waking up I was who I am in daily life. I improvise the resemblance to memory of places and people when I write down the glimpses of the dream in my journal. It is a non-essential fun habit allowing a lot more of the juicy experiencing to be recalled.

> **Bob:** *Consciousness stirs in deep sleep and you start to dream at night. In this dream you create a world and you see yourself taking an active part in it. It might be in a town, a city, a room or out in the country. You can dream of all sorts of things. There could be other people there also. There could be cars, animals or anything, and you are participating in all this.*
>
> *Yet, that body of yours has not moved from the bed. Your eyes remained closed and no word was spoken by your lips. All of this seeming world has been taking place in that little space between your ears.*

I worked as a ship's officer for 17 years of my life, always surrounded by a vastness of blue (or grey during the day, black at night) in every way: blue ocean, blue sky and nothing else. It was then that I learned to find variety in the many vivid dreams I had every night, which I also practiced remembering. To date, I still enjoy having a close look at this phenomenon and also love using this old analogy as a tool.

If you remember any of your dreams, even from the distant past, please see if the same applies. There is a world in the dream: an environment. There are activities and situations which need responding to. Responding happens through the main character (you). The character is engaging in physical or verbal activities. Usually, you can't see its (your) face. You most often don't know your age, and you may not remember much about your background, education, spouse or kids (unless requested to describe them during the course of dream-activity). Science would say, it is normal, it is related to limited frontal lobe activity, but our direct experience is a most reliable guide.

Even less questioning and doubting is applied to what is happening and where we are in the regular dream. Weird or impossible things may be well-accepted without much resistance. The almost non-existent narrative is rarely used — only to silence any doubts about the reality of the dream. There isn't much self-ing (obsessing about self) going on. There is no 'poor me' story or sense of incompleteness. If there is fear, anger or anxiety, it produces action, even if that action is to freeze up. Emotions are untamed, raw, basic, very strong and honest, not representative of anything else.

> **Bob:** *If you continued to dream every night and the dream continued on from the night before just as it appears to do in the waking state, could you tell the difference between the dream state and the waking state at all? Zhuangzi said, "Once upon a time I*

*dreamt I was a butterfly, unaware that I was myself.
Soon I awakend, and there I was, veritably myself
again. Now I do not know whether I was then a man
dreaming I was a butterfly, or whether I am now a
butterfly, dreaming I am a man".*

Who wakes up from a lucid dream and to what? Where does
the dream go? Who wakes up from the non-lucid dream at
night and to what? Where does the dream character go? Who
wakes up from the daydream or fantasizing? What wakes up
from the 'me'?

Awakening is only FROM the 'me', NOT FOR the 'me'. 'Me'
doesn't wake up because it is not real. The mask, the costume,
doesn't wake up. Consciousness wakes up from the dream of
being a 'me'. If you still believe that you (the identified
self/mind/ego) can get that, wake up! Please wake up from
this idea. It is false. The dream character is what Life wakes up
from.

Upon recognition, not the 'I' but consciousness dreams the
lucid dream. It wakes up from the 'me' TO the dream of
duality. The dream goes on. Waking up FROM the dream of
duality occurs when consciousness is no more. But even the
elegant lucid dream analogy can be deceiving. Every pointer
has limitations.

L – Limitations of Pointers

Every pointer, every analogy, has its limitations. Dream
analogies are limited in a few ways. From the dream at night,
awakening is inevitable but it causes the disappearance of
both the dream character and the dream. The vague idea that

it was 'I' dreaming, the same 'I' that is awake now, will fade with the world it belongs to. The world is gone, the hero is gone — and soon to be forgotten.

In a lucid dream, the character can become lucid without disappearing and the dream goes on. It can even have dreams within it! However, the character is free from many rules of the game and may discover having super powers (like manifesting things or flying). The illusion of control is super strong. In fact, it is grandiose, enchanting!

Upon self-realization, the character doesn't become lucid but it is recognized as a conceptual costume, utterly unreal. It is the naked consciousness (without the mask now), without any need for self-definition, which is awake; it is not the character. Upon realization the personality structure of the body-mind continues to filter perception. However, that filter is impersonal now. The illusion of control, free will and doership is seen through.

The simulation game analogy has its limitations as well. In the computer game, a fictitious character is created and called 'me'. It has one life or a few lives, it goes through challenges, grows, learns and transforms. The player identifies with the avatar, but also remains a player (God). In a very good game he/she may forget having a physical body-mind outside of the virtual reality, but a very strong illusion of control and doership remains.

The player is indeed like a god: she/he can take and give life and often kills without hesitation. It happens even if it isn't in the player's nature to hurt others outside the game. The player may 'run' a few characters and identify with each one of them in turns. The game may illustrate how irrelevant it is whether every character in these artificial worlds survives and wakes up or not.

When the forgetting of oneself in the game is over, the shift from the avatar to the player can be used as a good analogy for the shift from ego-identification to pure consciousness.

A similar shift can be experienced when you put down a novel or finish watching great movie. As long as you are empathizing with the character in the story, and have believed yourself into being that character, there is no way out. The character in the novel stays in the novel. It can never get out of the novel. But how did he get there? How real is his existence? How did you become him? Did you?

If a character on the cinema screen were to dream about liberation from the screen, how could he attain it? Could he? The film is already in the can. Nothing can be done. The character can't transform or leave the screen. The screen is his world. He can't stop being himself to become the viewer. He can't do anything at all.

It is only ever the one who watches the film recognizing, recalling that he/she is already free (and always was) from being the screen hero. If it doesn't happen while watching the movie, it will certainly happen when it ends or the projector is off. Transcendence of a character is 'the shedding of his skin' by cessation of imagining wearing it. It is non-action, only cessation of active imagination.

It is stopping to wear the mask, the costume; like an actor who has finished the performance and is ready to go home. He likely won't take his role to the dinner table.

If you were to write the novel yourself, how would you go about it? Is your personal story much different? Are you trapped in the role of a character or are you free to watch the unfolding? If you were to act in the screen-play and be good at that, wouldn't you invest your full attention in identifying as a character?

The limitation of these analogies lies in the fact that realization of no-self does NOT take you to a different, more real or authentic role. There is no-one to play the role once the illusion of self is seen through. There is no transcendence of hero to become a witness, author or God, the creator. Life unfolds for no-one. Everything is known by no-one. The character may or may not show up: no-one cares.

Another beautiful way to illustrate the oneness is the analogy of the ocean and the wave. It points to the fact that everything is already that one, ocean or water. The wave is to recognize that it need not seek and try to become what it already is. The ocean creates waves of itself to experience separation, height, shape and form (and even some foam on the height of that form).

A similar picture is that of gold and gold ornaments. Ornaments are already gold; it is a matter of recognition. The ornament is an expression only.

The limitation of these images lies is fact, that even to illustrate oneness there needs to be two. If there was only ocean and no air (space) above it, waves wouldn't be possible and the label 'ocean' would be unnecessary (for there would be nothing to differentiate it as anything). If there was only gold and no space in which it could be labeled gold or admired as an ornament, it would be nothing. For anything to exist, a background of its opposite is required. If everything were gold, there would be no gold: there would be no appearance at all.

God (Life) creates of itself. Everything is the body of God, and nothing is not it. So, there really is nothing; it only appears to be something through tricks of contrast.

Bob: I like the analogy of the mirror. Look at the mirror. It is full of reflections but they are neither there nor are they not there. You see them, so you say they are there, but go and try to grab one. You can't. The limitation of this analogy is that the mirror needs something outside of itself to be reflected in it. Awareness does not.

One could almost say that to stumble upon these metaphors is pure luck!

L – Luck

The diamond of great fortune Nisargadatta called staying with the I-am-ness to the exclusion of everything else. Holding onto this diamond of great fortune facilitated his recognition of ultimate truth. Gratitude for great fortune is often a part of loving to be.

Being truly lucky was often the story of my young adult life. It was also a spiritual name given to me in Truc Lam, a Vietnamese Zen Monastery in Da Lat. Disasters which Life made me avoid — near misses that resulted in learning rather than loss — and scary incidents which were rather mild compared to what might have been, were all evidence of that luck. Even the darkest times, the scariest situations and the deepest wounds and abuses — viewed in hindsight — brought me here, to the place of current joy.

There were also times when the story of my life was that of a victim, or a warrior or a worthless nothing. In these stories, I was ungrateful and unloved. The fact that Life was somehow always looking after this body-mind was overlooked.

Before we use the word 'luck' as a pointer, though, let's look at its dictionary definition. Luck is a success (or failure) apparently brought by chance rather than through one's own actions.

What in life is really the result of one's own actions? Not a thing! It was a diamond of good fortune for Nisargadatta to meet Siddharameshwar, his guru. It was Life's doing for Bob to meet and hear Nisargadatta correctly from the outset. How lucky it was that he was able to visit him for a few days every couple of weeks, for 12 months, so that a great bond and real friendship could be formed between them! What great fortune!

What were the odds that I would meet and marry Sailor Bob, a man twice my age and living on the opposite side of the planet to where I used to live? What were the odds that we would find each other to have relatable personal backgrounds, upbringings, family histories and careers at sea? Wasn't this luck?

One day, I had the sudden idea that I should study navigation in the really tough five-year-long militarized Maritime Academy to become a ship's officer in Poland. I had never met a ship's officer in my life, and had never read, watched, or heard anything about this profession. It was also against the post-communistic rules and laws for women in Poland, but action followed my intensely charged thoughts nevertheless.

There was very little hope for success and therefore almost complete detachment from results. Yet, there was also the energy of complete commitment to do everything I could to make it happen. There were many meetings with various officials, Including from the Ministry; many petitions and letters; and even some TV and radio interviews. It took a year. Finally, the gate was opened for the first time to just two females. I became a hero to many of my girlfriends. A few newspapers and magazines featured me as an example of determination in following one's dreams.

But did I really do it? Did I make this decision to change the law? Did I make these synapses fire in my brain in a particular manner to create this particular vision of a career? I did not! It was luck indeed! There was no method, no application of the law of attraction, no affirmations or prayers. The desire was strong and irresistible, and the emotion was pure, but I did not evoke it. It just came up, inspired by nothing more than the sight of the ocean and sky.

I knew all along that the results of my actions were uncertain and that it was all just blind luck: the right person in the right mood handing paperwork over to someone else in the right mood; the evacuation of the Ministry building upon my arrival due to some teenager's prank bomb threat; sunny winter weather on the right day; the apparently charming effect of my shyness. Across all these coordinated instances, the universe acted as one.

Life is the only doer. It acts using all available means, including our own brain, hands and sweat. But it is Life that has given us these hands, brain and breath. Seeing the brilliance of life leaves us speechless. It is a great fortune to be able to see the life story as a story of luck. Where does such an attitude lead?

L – Little more on L

L – Leader, Leading

It seems like the leader or guru has something to teach or point out. It may feel that it is essential to follow, to look where he or she is pointing. It is not completely unreasonable, but watch out: there is an important disclaimer! You are both equal as the same essence, even though your body-mind costume may lack some skills that the guru seems to have. Your mind may appear to be clouded by believed concepts in a way that the guru's experience is not.

In olden days people believed that to be Christian meant to behave like Jesus — to parrot his deeds. This was not what he was pointing to, though. "Find the kingdom first and greater miracles you will perform than I do", he promised. (Maybe there is no need for another Jesus since life hasn't provided it.) If your calling is to be a true Christian, will you behave like him once you see what he saw? Well, let's find out!

May every great leader with his or her beautiful strengths and qualities serve as a reminder that equally great talents may express through you! Peaceful, ordinary life is as precious as the most outstanding performance. You are all of it. Every pattern is you. Life expresses through you, in you and as you.

Likewise, let every bad leader, including every tyrant or bully, remind you that same Life is running blood in their veins. The same Life is in the process of changing them even now. Nothing lasts.

L – Lasting

Just like the concept of impermanence, the word 'lasting' cannot apply to things. Nothing lasts. Only No-Thing can actually be lasting.

Every time you wonder if something is to last, remember the No-Thing. Food from few a days ago, old clothes, ancient cities and changing seasons can all serve as anchors for this pointer. Only No-Thing lasts. Nothing else lasts. This is a good thing to realize! It's liberating!

L – Liberation

You are already free. Simply recognize that it is so. Liberation from karmic chains, from satanic forces, ego — or even liberation from illusion — are all beautiful romantic stories. Liberation from the illusory self is not required because the self is illusory!

The dictionary says that liberation is the action of setting someone free from imprisonment, slavery or oppression. It's release. It can also mean freedom from limits of thought or behaviour. Viewed from that perspective, slavery to the mind, believing in thinking, can be broken. The spell is broken by simple recognition, which is either spontaneous (often surprising) or the result of investigation (the origin of which is spontaneous as well).

Either way, the word can be anchored as a pointer. Liberation (freedom) is already present and only needs to be acknowledged. Liberation is had by breaking the spell of imagination and disbelieving self-concepts.

> **Bob:** There is an ancient text titled "Self-Liberation through Seeing with Naked Awareness". It describes non-conceptual awareness as "naked awareness"

215

and this is a great way to put it. It is also called Love or Light.

L – Light

Bob: What is light if not just energy? Some like to call it the Light of Love, Light of Consciousness, enlightenment...

The word 'enlightenment' has light in its structure. En-lighten-ment is akin to brilliance, brightness, but also lightness, weightlessness. I like to joke that falling for dark, rigid belief is 'endarkenment' but seeing through it is enlightenment. Falling for some heavy story is 'enheaviment'; letting it go — enlightenment.

It is life itself that falls for it and sees through it, not any limited entity. Heavy clouds of thoughts obscure the Sun and it is dark; when they disperse, everything is enlightened.

Also, to be enlightened about something is to have clarity about it. There was the historical period we refer to as the Enlightenment, which was roughly one century of glorifying reason while questioning superstitions and prejudices.

For the mind, to be in light is to be translucent and clear. Expectations of seeing visible light upon recognition or realization are born of imagination. The metaphor of physical light may be misguiding when taken literally. Visible light is so often used as analogy because darkness is merely its absence: light dimmed to zero. Light is all there is, only its intensity varies in the appearance.

Bob: Love is another term for light. Christ says, "I am the light of the world". (He is not talking about himself as a 'person'.) It is that 'I am' — that sense of

216

presence which is the light of the world. By what light do you see the world?

Also, to be enlightened is to travel lighter, it is to put down the heavy burden of self. Pure being is light, it is weightless. Heaviness and darkness come from added weight of dense conceptual framework in which things are being viewed and given meaning. Clarity and weightlessness characterize awareness. Limitlessness does too.

L – Limitless

Limitlessness is a quality of space. This is who you are.

Unlimited means that nobody has set limits as yet, but limitless means boundless, infinite, endless, everlasting, cosmic, untold, immeasurable, bottomless, fathomless, immense, vast, huge, great or extensive. It is utterly beyond imagination.

Can you conceive of a limitation that wouldn't be just a concept? That on which every concept/limitation appears is the limitless screen.

If you were to describe something as limitless, you would mean that there is or appears to be so much of it that it will never be exhausted. There is no such thing in this world, where time changes and ends all things. Let this word remind you of what is true and real: the limitlessness of No-Thing or the Source. Concepts only seemingly restrict it. Take, for example, the concept of lineage...

L – Lineage

It is a popular concept in formal schools and it is occasionally used as a colorful story to lend credibility to a speaker or guide. This is just a story. There is nothing to be had, given, taken or transmitted in the lineage. Nisargadatta has given no-thing to Bob, Bob has transmitted no-thing to me.

There often is a natural gratitude to Life for the mentor, for the love and patience exercised, so to acknowledge the lineage may mean to just highlight this part of the story about the past. In more formal teachings of various sects of Buddhism, lineage is stressed for other reasons explained in their scriptures. There is some logic in it, too.

L – Logic

Logic is the part of reasoning capacity that provides us with linear proofs, sees patterns and writes equations. It is a reasoning conducted or assessed according to strict principles of validity. It is the mother of science and philosophy. It is usually quite simple and elegant. It is to be greatly appreciated, for it opens the door to creativity and allows amazing inventions!

...But it cannot contain or grasp the No-Thing. It will not provide the answer to ultimate questions about life and the nature of existence. Logic is just the wrong tool for this. Logic belongs to duality and is useful there only. Logic needs to be transcended, recognized as a thinking pattern emergent from the Absolute and appreciated as such. If you want the ultimate answer to life and everything in it, don't swear loyalty to your logic.

L – Loyalty

The most common synonyms of 'loyalty' are allegiance, devotion, fidelity and piety. This beautiful value or quality is another part of the play — part of the dualistic dance of Shakti. It is neither good nor bad. It just is.

Bob's loyalty to his first Guru Muktananda made him decline a few invitations to see Nisargadatta at first. One could call loyalty 'bad' in this context because it seems to have impeded the journey! However, Life, which instilled Bob's innate loyalty, also resolved it when needed. Life conspired a number of coincidences to push Bob towards Nisargadatta. After a few pokes from a few directions, the synchronicities couldn't be ignored anymore.

This inbuilt loyalty, as a personality pattern in the dualistic human adventure, made Bob a beautiful man, a loving husband and my dearest friend.

My loyalty was to awakening, not to any particular messenger. Because of that, I entertained my mind by listening to many speakers (and had a few favorites). One day, someone challenged me to focus for a few weeks or months on one talk from one speaker only. The point was to replace my relatively shallow, entertainment-level engagement — with real devotion and loyalty to the truth being spoken.

So, I listened to the same one of Bob's spiel every day between my shifts at the ship's control desk for a few weeks. All the subtle aspects and nuances of it started opening up and deepening. Soon, I didn't need to listen to messages from any sources outside myself.

I still experience surges of gratitude towards Bob for the influence of his words, even though it was only life playing with life. Today, I don't go for 'nonduality entertainment' at all, so as to avoid affecting my inner clarity. I used to love it but now I can't even say that I like it anymore.

L – Like, Don't Like

The Buddha's teachings suggest that attachment is the source of suffering. Personalization of life, adding meaning and judging things as good or bad (in relation to 'me') enhances engagement, seriousness and the need to defend your position.

> **Bob:** *There is no such thing as a personal self. There is only one Self and that is the empty, open field of awareness-being-joy. Nothing can ever be personal if there is no person. Your desires, aversions, likes and dislikes are all impersonal patterns in One Self. Look at the little baby, spontaneously driven by attraction or repulsion — all natural.*

There is a natural inclination in every animal, including the human animal, towards and against certain things, particular colours, sounds, smells and tastes. These are harmless and need no defence. In fact, they are crucial for survival! Deprivation from following preferences causes discomfort, but not psychological suffering. That can only exist in the narrative.

In the narrative, natural liking becomes 'my' liking, something 'I' don't want to lose, something important, an attachment. Like-ING becomes 'I like it'.

Fortunately, the body is equipped with brilliant feedback mechanisms to distinguish between natural inclinations and attachment. The sense of seriousness has a distinguishable flavour. The need to convince others to like what I like is also something very easily detected. Animals do not seem to have any need to defend their preferences.

Watch out for that uneasy feeling of inner tension and you will make great use of the like-dislike pointer. In seeing this tendency, letting go happens.

L – Letting Go

This pointer is not meant to suggest that there is somebody doing the letting go of something. It is rather the relaxation, like when you have your fist or jaw clenched. To keep them this way, force is applied. To stop applying this force is to let go.

> **Bob:** *You know what letting go is. When your bladder is full, you hold it and hold it until you go to the toilet and what do you do? You let go. This is the letting go we are talking about. Stopping holding, letting go, is natural.*

Holding onto unquestioned beliefs about a separate identity also requires applying force, just like clenching a fist. Remembering the conceptual image, holding onto opinions and judgements, and onto knowing and being right about things, is hard work — even if done on autopilot (completely involuntarily) — due to the inertia of lifelong habit.

All that stubbornness is to stop, to be let go of. Letting go is to stop doing, struggling mentally, trying to grasp. Letting go of the thoughts is to let them flow freely.

Letting go of resistance is the key to liberation. Resistance must be recognized to be let go of. It doesn't require effort. It stops the effort applied in the opposite direction. It restores oneness.

O – Sail-O-r B-O-b

O – Only One, Oneness

Bob: They call it "one without the second, not two". It is ONE which nothing follows. In fact, even the word 'one' implies that there is something other than one, but there isn't. It is not even ONE, but we have to use some words to speak about it.

All is ONE Essence, One Taste; One non-thing appearing and expressing itself as a multitude of things. Oceans, waves, rain, lakes, waterfalls, icebergs, snow, clouds and fog are all water. Vases, walls, pots, cups and bricks can all be made of the same clay. Thought, feeling, emotion, sensation and perception are all one energy of knowing (sensing).

Awareness is everything. It is ONE. All that exists is known, it is know-ing. Your experience of yourself and of the world is known as sensation appearing on the sense-less background, which is pre-sensory presence. The whole manifestation can be brought down to the being-knowing. Sensing is all there is. One.

Oneness also means Wholeness, Completeness. Being at One with everything is often glimpsed when mind is transcended, when there is no thought activity, no chatter. But it is not about the joining of separate parts; it is not that the one is uniting with the rest. There are no parts. It is all Oneness — a holographic dance of light creating a 3D image of apparent depth in which each seeming part is a reflection of the totality. All is one inseparable and space-like no-thing, vibrating into patterns, shapes, forms and colours.

Bob: It is all the One. The mind and the body are also that one: the one essence on which and of which everything is appearing. It just needs to be looked into and seen that they are all the one substance or the one taste. So, there is really nothing that needs to be purified. It's like the mirror which has never been contaminated by anything that has appeared in it.

Oneness means totality and wholeness, not just eternal bliss. It includes every seeming thing without separating anything conceptually. It includes the human form with its personality, its identification with ego and its dark nights of the soul. It also includes the commentary in the head, with its divisions of good and bad.

It allows light and dark, day and night equally. It allows bliss and suffering and it transcends bliss and suffering at the same time. It is not half-ness but one-ness, whole-ness. It is not the sum total of fragments. There are no separate fragments, apart from the labels put upon the One. Recognition of oneness is the recognition of the unifying principle of life (or consciousness, the being-knowing). Every form is equally empty of self-nature; everything is no-thing. One — or, rather, not one and not zero, either.

This is who or what you are. You are Oneness, God and the Source. You are the Consciousness, the Emptiness that is enlightened, realized and awake while portraying itself as lost, identified and condemned. You are both limitless and confined; both free and in bondage; both nothing and everything. These things are all one. There isn't any 'all', just One. There is only one. You are That. You are: as magnificent and as ordinary as you are.

O – Ordinary

> **Bob:** *There is this simple beautiful ancient text by Padmasambhava titled Self-Liberation through Seeing with Naked Awareness. He brings up all the names by which they call it. He says, some call it Mind, Atman, Self, absence of self, Tathagata and many other Sanskrit names and as the last one he says, "And some simply call it by the name 'ordinary awareness'".*

"Ordinary awareness" — really? How disappointing! I, too, was looking for a bliss that would usurp my desire for sensory pleasures! Who wants ordinary? Boring! I wanted ecstasy!

I wouldn't have bothered practising meditation and all the sadhanas; reading, watching or listening to — let alone travelling to all these monasteries and ashrams to get 'ordinary'. I was reaching for the pinnacle of human evolution that I imagined enlightenment to be. I wanted super special!

I refused to hear it for many years. My mind would switch off and skip that part while listening to pointers. It simply couldn't be so. All these places of worship, amazing statues, temples, pyramids, devotional songs, carvings and paintings couldn't be there to honour ordinary every day awareness. It made no sense.

And yet, they say everything has Buddha Nature. Truth is that which never changes. The lord is with you as your presence, ordinary and changeless. It is nothing special or superb. Yet, it is no less miraculous, mind-blowing or amazing for its ordinariness! On the contrary, ordinary being-knowing-joy is pure completeness, fulfilment and absence of lack. "There is nothing wrong anymore", Nisargadatta would say.

Bob: All you need is to sit with that ordinary wakefulness. It is there. It is immediate. It is with you right now, without any conceptualisation on it. It is just pure ordinary, commonplace, everyday awareness. We try to grasp it with the mind instead of simply sitting with it.

Because it is ordinary, because it is normal, transparent and subtle, we take it for granted and miss its significance. It is commonplace, everyday wakefulness: everyone is already That. It is indeed ordinary but it is also extraordinary in its omnipresence, omnipotence and omniscience.

O – Omnipresence, Omnipotence, Omniscience

Bob: In Christianity they call it Omnipresence, Omnipotence and Omniscience. It means total presence, total power and total intelligence. Omnipresence doesn't mean my presence or your presence, but total presence. All-being.

It is Presence in every form and in the emptiness. If you like the word God or Lord, it is he who is always and ever present, and there is nowhere where he is not. He is looking out of your eyes, beating your heart. His presence is in all beings, in the blade of grass and in the distant star. In other words, there is only God: there is nothing other. It's not that the Lord is always with you in the sense of one alongside another; it's that the Lord is what you take yourself to be. The Lord is expressing through you as you. There is only God and it is God's presence, not yours. See whether there is any you which exists apart from that presence.

Bob: *Omnipresent also means timeless. It is always present, ever present. It is only now-ness or presence. If you understand that, you will see that any search for it is futile. You will not find anything at any future time because there is no future time. Have a look and you will see it clearly. You have some memory which is seemingly the past. You may have some anticipation or imagination which relates to the future. But what memory have you got right now if you are not thinking about it? And when you remember something, isn't it now anyway? That's omnipresence: always now.*

Omnipotence is all potency or all power. The heat and gravity of black holes is That. The energy released through the clashing of continental shelves is That. The fury of volcanic eruptions; the power of storms: all are That. The destructive power of viruses and the creative power of human imagination are That. The life-giving and life-taking potency of the Sun are That. The potency of soft music or a light breeze are That. Energy expanded to filter your blood and move it around in the veins is That; and energy used to filter and interpret reality is That. Fury, hatred, empathy, love – it is all that omnipotence in action.

Omniscience is all that is ever known, every piece of wisdom. It is the know-ING activity or intelligence energy. It is God's knowing, direct or through the instrument of consciousness in all its vessels – bodies. You are not separate; you are a not a part. All knowing is your knowing. It is your universe. Knowing that some piece of information may be missing in some dream character is included.

Bob: *All the traditions somewhere along the line will tell you, when speaking about reality that*

Omniscience means pure and total knowing, or all-knowing. Omnipotence means pure and total power, or all-power. 'All' means that it doesn't leave room for me, you or anything else. It is all that. That is why we say that what you are seeking you already are. It reveals itself once you open up.

O – Openness

'Openness to experience' is one of the domains which is used to describe human personality in the Five Factor Model. Openness involves six aspects, including active imagination, aesthetic sensitivity, attentiveness to feelings, preference for variety and intellectual curiosity. Adding variety in daily choices may help bring out the openness-to-experience side of personality.

Being open is being child-like. To be open-minded is to be willing to consider ideas and opinions that are new or different to your own. It is a readiness and willingness to question your beliefs. It means also to wait until you know all the facts before forming an opinion or making a judgment. It means using less filters, less comparison with what is known, less of being right and less rejection.

To have an open mind means to be willing to consider, entertain and implement new and diverse concepts. Being open-minded involves being receptive to a wide variety of viewpoints, information and ideas. It means being flexible and adaptive, able to step out of your comfort zone and consider other ideas and perspectives.

It may take courage and vulnerability at first. In agreeing to have an open-minded view of the world, you're admitting you don't know everything and that there are possibilities you may not have considered. Open-mindedness is the willingness to search actively for evidence against one's favoured beliefs, plans or goals and to weigh such evidence fairly when it is available.

> **Bob:** *When I was in Muktananda's Ashram, I read ancient scriptures a bit. The first one that sort of opened me up was the Avadhuta Gita. I knew there was something in it but couldn't quite grasp it. My mind was opening to it but not quite ready yet. Then, after Nisargadatta, I re-read it and it was very clear.*

Shift from body-mind identification to no-identification is often referred as opening of the mind or opening in the mind. Zen calls the open mind "beginner's mind". Open mind is also called the "not-knowing mind", "the unborn mind" or "no-mind".

The mind which knows things is a closed mind; it can grow to be a dangerously fanatical mind at times.

This pointer can also be used as a reminder to keep your eyes open (beautiful things can be spotted all around!) and to have your ears opened to all sounds. It is also great to be open to new tastes, subtle smells and to bodily sensations, such as touch, breath, balance and temperature.

When a certain strong idea hijacks the attention, openness is a reminder of inclusion. If the idea is too strong to be dropped, open up to include its opposite. Open up to include "I don't really know". Open up to "What is wrong with right now unless I think about it?" and open your senses.

Bob: Just be utterly awake with five senses wide open, with un-fixated awareness. When you are open, you may hear something that you would otherwise miss out and it may take you somewhere else where you are better off being. The opposite of an open mind would be a mind that is obsessed.

O – On obsession – E X E R C I S E

Obsession is compulsive preoccupation with a fixed idea or an unwanted feeling or emotion, often accompanied by symptoms of anxiety. It is a persistent, disturbing, compulsive, often unreasonable attachment to an idea or emotion. Obsession is defined as the act of letting a thought or action rule your thoughts or actions. It is a focus on one thing with little interest in anything else.

Obsession in romantic love often means being possessive. It generally goes with selfishness. Indifference is the opposite of obsession.

Please spend as much time on this exercise as you feel you can. Learn about your preoccupation. Is it a body? Is it food? Coffee? Is it your relationship or relationships at home, at work, at school? Or maybe particular obsessive images or fantasies? It could be an emotion of sadness, anger or anxiety. It could be future or past. It could be truth.

Bob: Watch your mind to see how it functions! It always vibrates into thoughts, concepts and images that are defined by the labels you put on them.

229

Now recognize how your obsessions are always related to the 'me'. Even if you obsess about your child or partner, it is because they are 'yours'. Even if you obsess about the house, the dog — it is also through association with the 'me and mine'. Every problem is a problem of the body-mind, called 'me' or 'I'.

Seen from this angle, every obsession can be narrowed down to self-obsession. Obsession about the truth, enlightenment or liberation is also for the 'me'.

To exercise a shift out of obsession is to just plainly observe it without any judgements. If judgement comes up, it can also be plainly observed as another pattern of thought. Going throughout the day, notice any predominant thought. See how it relates to the 'me'. Observe how often it comes up and how long it stays, on average. Notice the feelings and images associated with the thought.

Let's look at the example of the 'fashionable' thought "My partner is narcissistic". Observe the feeling and emotion associated with the arising of the thought. It may be a feeling of slight irritation at times; and anxiety or strong anger at other times. See how personal it is for you, even though it seems to be about your partner. Observe how that thought and feeling engages the mind. Don't follow its logic, just notice the tendency to justify, explain and defend your position.

Example: "My partner is narcissistic because she said this and has done that". The thought came up during breakfast and stayed for 12 minutes. Obsession was on a scale of four out of five — meaning pretty strong, engaging and emotionally-charged, felt in the body. It came again on the way to point A, it was a background feeling, charged one to two out of five, meaning weak. The narrative would go away for a while but then return later. During 20 minutes of commuting, it came up three to four times and stayed for 10-15 seconds each time.

Second obsessive thought: "I need to lose weight". The thought came up in the morning as well as for few seconds before and after every snack, accompanied by a strong feeling of inadequacy, charged four out of five. I had a small snack five times apart from usual meals.

No need to write it down, but it may be a helpful learning tool if life moves you to do so. This exercise brings consciousness to otherwise mechanical, unconscious thought patterns. It brings the light of impersonal, non-judgemental attention to the narrative which causes suffering. It uses difficult patterns to our advantage.

> **Bob:** *The so called 'me' is the cause of all your problems! It is only 'me' that can feel depressed or ashamed or full of self-pity. Keep looking for it: there will be an opening!*

O – Opening of Oscar – E X A M P L E

Oscar was a very young man, not yet 23, when we first met him back in 2018. He is a good looking Aussie with brown hair and light brown eyes. He lives in Perth and visits Melbourne twice a year for couple of weeks. When he came to an individual session with Bob, he was greatly disturbed and very anxious with visible posttraumatic stress symptoms. He didn't even tell Bob what caused it, fearing rejection, which he didn't think he could take at this point in life. He stayed for a group meeting after the one on one session.

After many text messages he told me over the phone about his dark LSD trip eight months prior, in which he reached what seemed to be the core, source of all things. It was cold, dark and terrifyingly scary. It wasn't a cheerful joke, it was a cruel inferno. Under the psychedelic influence, his mind was completely receptive, brain activity widely enhanced, so the experience was more vivid, realistic and believable than anything he has ever experienced before and after in his entire life. The seemingly safe daily dream-overlay didn't fool him anymore. He knew the drastic, dark secret of the universe and was all alone with it.

Life brought Oscar here. Gentle pointing back to the neutral screen on which both darkness and light play brought him moments of respite but the peace never lasted long. The scary narrative would always return soon after the session had ended. So, Life led him to fully immerse himself in a months-long intensive program of regular pointing, individual and group meetings with Bob.

No single pointer ever resulted in an epiphany for Oscar; his understanding deepened slowly and gradually. The clouds of confusion dispersed a little more, every single time. A couple of friendships Oscar made while here also contributed significantly toward the rebuilding of his trust in life.

Finally the day came when he shared with us that he had not entertained a single anxious idea for quite some time. In this stable peace that he recognized and called "That I Am", clouds of thought came and went freely. He would engage with them a bit here and there but not overly, and not for long.

He didn't seek anything anymore. He didn't feel that life or Oscar himself needed to change, or that there was anything to be had other than witnessing the miracle unfolding right in front of him moment to moment. Anxiety, inferiority and incompleteness were over. They were disbelieved out of the experiencing. Life became suffused with the joy of simply observing.

O – Observer

In many cases, when one's search begins, identification with the mind is total, complete. One feels, "I am my mind, there is nothing else". In this junction, the concept of an observer can initially be very useful. The observer of thinking helps recognize patterns in mental activity.

> **Bob:** Some will tell you to become an observer or the witness, I ask where are you observing the observer from?

The shift from the idea of being an observer to recognizing that observing is happening is the next step in disentanglement in identification. In the sphere of observing, both the observer and observed come up simultaneously and interdependently. With even one of them absent, there is no observing.

It appears that one static observer is watching all changing objects, but that is an illusion. The form of the observer changes also, even if the change is only very subtle. Only the essence of the overall situation — the fact of presence — doesn't change. Both the observer and the observed can be known as objects but then who is the observing subject?

The shift is not about changing identity from very limited to less limited or unlimited. It is about recognizing the tendency of assuming identity at all. It is not about being a wider, more spacious observer, nor about being something called no-thing, but about recognizing and observing all activities of mind without any identity whatsoever.

There is no-one home, no little man inside, no self or observer. Who is there to identify as anything at all? And yet knowing, cognizing emptiness goes on. Registering, observing goes on.

O – Observing E X E R C I S E

There is a simple experiment that helps to illustrate the observing principle. Mind is being witnessed. Who is observing the mind? Observe the observing. Be aware of the knowing, the noticing. Be aware of the awareness itself, the observing principle. Notice how there is no need for asserting your position or shape and form in order for observation to be noticed.

You can do this exercise while sitting or walking. I like both options, especially while in nature. If you decide to sit, you may initially close your eyes to avoid distraction. Pick out a sound or noise, hold it in alert attention and turn within to see where the observing originates. Is it within or without? How is that observed?

Now pick out a sensation in the body (or a couple of them at once). It may be the sense of touch where the body meets a surface, where the lips are brought together, where the fabric of clothing touches the skin. It may be internal bodily sensation, such as muscle tension (for example, around the eyes or in the shoulders) or tingling that seems to appear wherever you hold attention for long enough.

Holding onto these sensations, turn within and check who or what does the observing. Where is the observing process known from? How is it observed? What is observing the observing?

Now, look around and see how the looking is being known. Keep observing the process of observing. Turn within and try to observe the source of observing. See if it even is within or anywhere specific.

Now bring your attention back to all the hearing, sensing, seeing and observe the observing of it. Notice how the seeming observer (body) is within the observing, together with sounds, scenes and sensations. There is awareness (observe-ING) of the whole lot. Inside and outside doesn't apply anymore and relating to the 'me' drops off.

When the attention is overwhelmed with sensory inputs such as hearing, seeing, touching, not much left is available for thinking, comparing, analysing and creating psychological suffering. Attention that is busy with present experiencing doesn't fuel the false construct of the 'me'. Experiencing happens but it is not translated into a narrative about things happening to any entity. This is a sample of freedom.

The same experiment can also be performed with thoughts. Think of an object or image and see how the registering of it happens. You may hold three ideas or images in your mind, such as three issues that you are facing or three desires you have and see how you know they are there. Why a few and not one idea? It is easier to detach from the content if your attention is divided between two to three objects.

How is the knowing happening? Where is that knowing? Is it even yours? Is it inside? Is it outside? Does the division like that even apply? Who knows about it? How is the observing of it known?

If you are drawn to meditation practices, you may find it particularly difficult to hold/be neutral space for thoughts. They are sticky, attractive or distressing — distracting in any case. A good tip is to say to each passing thought, "next please", and then let it go, as though you were watching passing cars from the sidewalk. We will look at this deeper on R — Register exercise. I used to quite like this option.

O – Options

Options, we could say, either arise or are recognized as already present. Some options are more compelling than others. The potentiality or probability of being chosen is inherently present within the option in the immediacy. It is inseparable and it depends on the whole environment. As much as it seems like there is a choice-maker with free will to pick any option, it is not so. It seems like she/he is having a preference towards a certain option and is then acting out and selecting it. However, non-conceptual singular functioning is actually much simpler and more precise explanation.

Let's say there is a decision to be made on what to have for dinner. There are few options, each potentially having its own associated justifying story. There is seeming vacillation or hesitation before one of the options gets more of an emotional charge than others. That is how energy moves and how it is been interpreted.

Why pizza over salad tonight even though healthy options were winning for the past few days? The answer would have to include the whole environment, which is the whole universe. There may be a simple justifying story, like whim or caprice, free will, a memory from childhood or some advertisement, but this is not really the whole answer. There is no singular cause and effect because there is no separation. In the interconnectedness of all forms, every particle plays a role in the final outcome.

> **Bob:** *Options may arise, choices and preferences may be there, but there is no choice-maker. Decisions are made but there is no entity making them.*

Bob taught me to look out and find answers in nature to easily understand the redundancy of this fictitious entity. We have two fairly young cats at home, who are spoilt with food options, play options and sleep options. And they have preferences. As far as we know, they do not engage in narrative and do not take credit for any of the choices and decisions. They endure consequences nevertheless.

Although so called wrong decisions and incorrect choices may lead to dreadful consequences, nobody has taken them. Labelling them negatively in comparison to imagined alternatives is adding to the psychological suffering. Believing that we could have done otherwise is irrational. What would have happened if... cannot be foreseen, because of the infinite amount of data influencing the algorithm.

The instinctual setting for survival suggests that the best option is always followed in light of available resources. Thoughts and beliefs are resources as well, alongside with past experiences and conditioning. The narrative, however, only comments on the process, relates the outcome, and takes credit for the job. We will expound further on the topic under chapter R — Rationality.

There is an innocence to the whole process, which does not alleviate natural responsibility. Option-picking is singular, it is one of expressions of complex functioning. How complex? Let's face it: we are quite oblivious.

O – Oblivion

Oblivion is defined as unawareness or unconsciousness of what is happening around, or as the state of being completely forgotten or unknown to the public. We also use the word oblivion to point to deep sleep or death, complete annihilation, or extinction. Obscurity, non-existence, limbo, void, vacuum and nothingness are all synonyms of oblivion.

Antonyms of oblivion include awareness, consciousness, perception, sensibility.

The fear of oblivion is a fear of non-existence. It is one of the primordial fears which leads to psychological suffering. But is there such thing as non-existence to be feared? It seems absurd. It can't be imagined. Nevertheless, it seems real. We can imagine being reduced and impaired, but the lacking of any consciousness whatsoever is not a reality that can possibly be experienced. Deep contemplation of that fact can ease the fear of death.

Bob: *Because that 'me' is the separation, it fears the unknown. It would rather stay in the old way, no matter how painful it is. Take that step into the unknown, into the abyss and see! An old saying is, "Do the thing you fear and the death of fear is certain". Let the intuitive take over without the 'me' thinking it knows better. You may find out there is no death, but only life. Life cannot know death just like light cannot know the darkness.*

But how oblivious to the final answer can our cherished science be? Almost 100 years ago, the Austrian logician Kurt Gödel introduced Incompleteness Theorems which have destroyed any hope for a mathematical theory of everything. He proved that any set of axioms you could posit as a possible foundation for logic will inevitably be incomplete. And that applies even to heartless numbers, let alone to any other branch of science which defines its terms using its own specific language!

Additionally, nearly 100 years ago the German theoretical physicist Werner Heisenberg published his Uncertainty Principle showing that nothing can be known (measured) with absolute precision. This is our trusted source of wisdom admitting limits to its own omniscience.

Even earlier, 220 years ago, the British multidisciplinary scholar Tomas Young conducted the double slit experiment (in light interference), also known also as the Observer Effect. It demonstrates how conscious observation inevitably influences the outcome of any experiment.

Many other traditional branches of science, as well as some new disciplines (like memetics), have hit the wall in trying to find the answer in the mind.

In my eyes, one of the better ones a human has come up with is... 42! This is the answer to life and everything offered by the author Douglas Adams in his *Hitchhiker's Guide to the Galaxy*. A cosmic joke. As it happens, 42 is also the number of the closest tram stop to our place! (There is another tram than the one stopping at 42; with it you need to go to the end of the line! Nowhere further to go!)

No in-depth understanding of the manifested world is available in either science or religion. There are innumerable metaphors, analogies, theories and beliefs but, really, we stand oblivious in the face of mystery. We know that we do not know. Awareness can't be known and described as an object: it is the knowing principle.

As a pointer, the word 'oblivion' can be used as a reminder of the impossibility of experiencing death. The word 'oblivious' could be a humbling reminder of the mystery, which is beyond the conceptual understanding of the mind. This mystery is the home of the heart. It is obvious.

O – Obvious

The reason why the simple truth is so commonly missed is that it is too obvious. Obvious means easily perceived or understood; clear, self-evident or apparent, predictable and lacking in subtlety. It is so obvious that it attracts no attention. It seems unworthy of attention.

Who cares about the screen itself when going to the movies? It is too obvious; not interesting. Who cares about the canvas under the painting? Who reads the blank page instead of the text? Who pays attention to space when there are so many fascinating things around in it? We also don't notice temperature unless it is out of balance. We don't have neutral taste, only no-taste. When there is no sound, attention goes to another experience. The obviousness of the basic screen is thoroughly neglected. This happens without any guilt or blame on our side but re-discovery is the only path to full appreciation.

Bob: Who is it all happening to? The obvious answer is 'me'. But what is this me? Is there anything other than presence with concepts on it? When is all of this happening? The obvious answer is that it can only be happening presently. So, is it anything other than presence? It is too obvious, that is why we miss it.

We miss the obviousness of the unquestionable, immovable background and instead we think that our beliefs are obvious and certain. But are they? They need questioning. Almost everyone takes it for granted that they are the body. They also think that the existence of linear time is obvious. These things seem obvious because 'the creation' is a manifestation of pure perfection. It is indeed a perfect illusion.

Bob: Another obvious thing, have a look: without life, this body is a corpse. So, are you this body or are you the life force which animates it?

The obviousness of being-knowing is now here. It can't be denied. Even to deny it, being-knowing has to be here. Everything else can be questioned. Everything else changes. Yet this obviousness seems to get obscured...

O – Obscured

> **Bob:** *Once you have a taste of that essence that you are, you know that nothing could really obscure that presence awareness. That is why I'm telling you, start from the fact that you are already THAT. Now, see what comes up to argue with that simple fact.*

What often comes up is BUTs, IFs and WHYs. Thoughts. Doubts. Arguments. Non-conceptual awareness is underlying all these concepts and is not touched by any of them. They don't obscure the space of consciousness that you are. Lines of words or images and strong, charged questions and feelings appear and disappear but you remain throughout.

> **Bob:** *So, it really isn't obscured, is it? There is still hearing going on, there is still seeing. There is still cognizing going on. Everything is still being cognized. In the immediacy, that innate, intrinsic knowing is constantly with you. But then it gets seemingly obscured with all the thoughts and everything that comes up and appears in that knowingness.*

Obscuration is only seemingly so. Thoughts are being charged, believed. "Yes, but I don't feel I'm enlightened!" Of course 'I' doesn't feel it. 'I' is the very veil. It is imagined. 'I', and imagination of what should be felt and how, is precisely what (seemingly) obscures pure knowingness. What else can obscure it but movement of attention to thought or strong sensation?

> **Bob:** *This is our problem. We believe we are this entity. That is when this idea of self-awareness comes upon us. That is what obscures the primal awareness. The intelligence-energy that is growing the body and*

doing the livingness has always been there. It is happening right now; in the immediacy of right now.

Please see what is seemingly obscuring the obviousness of being for you now. See, investigate and discard. Watch temporary judgements and passing opinions.

O – Opinions

Opinion is a view or judgement formed about something, not necessarily based on fact or knowledge. It is a way of thinking about something. It justifies preference.

> **Bob:** *Hsin-hsin Ming tells you, "Hold no opinions for or against anything". The Third Chinese Zen Patriarch doesn't tell you to not have an opinion. Opinions will arise, same as preferences; but don't hold onto them. Let them come and go; don't make them yours.*
>
> *Everything is judged from a certain point of view. That becomes the self-centre or reference point, or the 'I' or the 'me'. So, here in this body-mind of Bob, there are no set beliefs and there are no set opinions. I can have opinions but they are not set in stone — just the same as I can say 'I' or 'me' and that is not set either. They move on.*

When I believe in something so deeply and hold it so dear in my heart that I need to defend it, fight for it or convert other people to 'my' world-view, I'm not free. It would be more appropriate to say, that the opinion has me, not that I have it.

I'm a slave to that viewpoint or opinion. But who is that 'me'? Attention is. Life is.

I (life) used to be a slave to many opinions on diet, politics, religion, sex, certain individuals and probably much more that I could not consciously observe. Some of them may still arise today but now they are impersonal; they lack importance. Some of them seem to belong to the body-mind for a short time and then move on. Others stay longer and are recognized as opinions or preferences.

There is no need to fix or suppress any tendency in the body in order for the truth to be recognized. Yet, with repeated realization of no self, attachment to personal opinions and beliefs naturally subsides. Judgements arise and move on. Nobody does them. Viewed as patterns or clouds, they become harmless. As patterns, presence or absence of opinion are equal. If opinion is there – good. If there is no opinion – that's equally good. Not one position is more desirable that the other. Freedom transcends both opposites.

O – Opposites

If not for the opposites, there would be no manifestation at all. If everything were bad, there would be no bad. There is no hot without cold; no up without down. Thin and thick are always relative, as are short and tall. If there were no me, there would be no you. There is either the duality of the manifested world or nothing at all.

> **Bob:** *It is the nature of this manifestation to be in pairs of opposites. Could there be silence without sound? Could there be stillness without movement? What can you compare them to, without their opposites? So, there is no day without night; no winter without summer. They are opposites but not in opposition. They never fight with each other; they take their turns. Each takes its turn. The opposites are continually functioning in nature.*

When that conceptual division is applied to the 'me', I'm fragmented. I may believe that I have a noble soul but an ugly ego, for example. I may have a good heart but a bad temper. In this way, some tendencies or behaviour patterns get rejected or denied. I will soon hate them in others! I may start carrying around guilt, shame and self-hatred. The sense of wholeness, completeness, is gone. Now I need saving, working on myself, finding myself or integrating parts which were defined only conceptually. I never ask who has these parts, bad temper, good heart, soul and ego.

> **Bob:** *The very same tendency to divide into interrelated pairs of opposites will now tell you that you are not good enough. And that is how mind functions. As long as you are embodied, you're going to have that mind. It is still going to think in the same way. It can't think in any other way than in the pairs of opposites. In understanding it, you are no longer bound by it.*

The noble desire to be only good and kind, never angry or sad; or to be utterly authentic, unrestrained, powerful or just, debunks this tendency to polarize. In knowing our blind-spots, we see the urges to supress and deny what is in contrast to an adopted belief system. That pattern maintains integrity of assumed identity but at a high cost.

> **Bob:** *Look at the mind and see how it functions. It constantly vibrates. Thought is a movement of energy, a vibration. Being a vibration, it can only function within the pairs of opposites, which is the past (memory) or the future (anticipation and imagination), happy or sad, pleasant or painful, loving or hating, good or bad, positive or negative (or somewhere in between) and so on. It functions within that range set up by words.*

If not for pain, pleasure would not be known and appreciated. If not for the dream and daydream, awakening could not be experienced. If not for our stories in time (past, future), mental commentary and noise, the bliss of being in silence would be taken for granted and not even acknowledged.

> **Bob:** *All you need to do is look at nature again. You'll see tides coming in and tides going out; seasons coming and going. ...But the opposites are not in opposition to each other. The incoming tide is not fighting with the outgoing tide. Winter is not fighting with summer.*
>
> *And look at your own body: the incoming breath is not struggling with the outgoing breath; they take turns. Expansion of your heart is not in conflict with its contraction. It is only in the mind that this conflict goes on.*

Recognition of the nature of the mind makes this seeming conflict laughable and light. There is no preference anymore for this phenomenon to cease. Let it be. Thoughts may play out and continue to appear as conflicted but there is no-one home who cares. These thoughts do not belong to anyone (me) anymore. There is no suffering without the 'me' — its cause and origin.

O – Origin

Because as humans we love stories, we have collectively created many fascinating myths about our origin. We look back in time (in mind) and project a past, some 'long time ago'. Cosmogenic myths have their functions in uniting societies and justifying rules. They also provide role models and values. Knowing and identifying with myths of origin supports a sense of belonging and creates opportunities for celebration.

Some of these stories are still alive and portray the origin of the known universe as explosion and following expansion. Others put life on earth and humanity down to extra-terrestrial intervention. There are beautiful tales of divine force intervention. Some old myths we can trace uncovering historical uses of animalistic totems and symbols. There are also theories by modern science, and traces of extinct beliefs in ancient or dying languages. All this only adds to the mystery of infinite creativity of that Immeasurable Intelligence Energy.

> **Bob:** *It is uncreated. No origination. It is ceaselessly arising but only seemingly so. It is no thing. Always and never. The Buddhists call it unborn, meaning un-originated. That means it has no origin, no beginning, has never been born. It is beginningless and endless. It is timeless. It is spaceless. It is bodiless. It is mindless. It is no thing. Yet, it is the essence in which*

247

*everything appears and disappears. That is what you
really are.*

Questioning our own origin myth is part of the investigation.
Each story may have hints or aspects which point to something
of value in them. For example, the Biblical idea of man being
made of clay points to the fact that the body belongs to
(Mother) Earth. Father Heaven (sky) infused it with the breath
of life. It also suggests that the first people were free...

> **Bob:** *The Bible will tell you that the first people lived
> in the Garden of Eden but they ate a forbidden apple
> and understood the difference between good and
> evil, and that's how they kicked themselves out of
> paradise. And that is what we have done also, by
> differentiating with words.*

Where do our night dreams originate? Where do our
daydreams and fantasies originate?

What is the origin of every dream, every form? When does it
take place? Where does everything appear?

> **Bob:** *Understand that the appearance is not the
> actual: it is illusion. It is an illusory manifestation and
> it is transitory. It means it is constantly changing. It
> has nothing static about it at all. They point out that
> there is no static thing in this universe and there is no
> self-nature to anything. In Buddhism they talk of non-
> conceptual awareness.*

Certain self-discipline which originates in love for the truth
makes the contemplation easier. Devotion may even evoke
obedience!

O – Obedient mind

Realization of the truth does not depend on the condition of the mind. It happens regardless. There have been people suffering from acute schizophrenia and other mental illnesses, including amongst Bob's students, who spoke with amazing clarity. Mind would still play its games at times, go on its trips, but there wouldn't be ownership and therefore no suffering. Mind antics would play in the open field of pure witnessing (knowing). There would be discomfort, but no self-pity or resistance stemming from the belief that things should be any different.

Nevertheless, an obedient mind is a noble mind; a well-trained mind that is organized and ready to serve. There is nothing wrong in mind training, just as there is nothing wrong in body training. A mind that can be single pointed on a mantra, or a mind with otherwise great concentration skills developed during meditation, is a beautiful mind. Any valuable skills can make this dream called life more attractive and more fun.

Only the notion that there is a requirement from the personal self to help omnipresent Consciousness is delusional. Omnipotence needs nothing, especially from the non-existent phantom.

So, please, keep your exercises and practices if Life has given you inspired thought and feeling to do so. Look after this body-mind as the Life guides you but, for the sake of clarity, disregard personal doership. Give all credit to Life. Disregard the story that such practices will give you enlightenment in some future time.

> **Bob:** *There is no such thing as enlightenment. There is no 'you' to attain it and there is no time, no future.*

And if you are moved to sit in quiet, by all means sit in quiet. Stay with 'I am' but don't put any expectations — don't create a meditator doing meditation. Quiet mind is no mind. In no mind there is no separate self and no other.

O – On and on, on O

O – Other

The moment I conceive of the other, 'me' comes into the picture. The moment I feel separate, other and others come into existence.

> **Bob:** *That 'I' thought is the separating factor. Mind functions in the pairs of opposites. As soon as that 'I' comes up, there has to arise something other than 'I': 'you' or 'the other'. The very idea of that 'I' thought immediately implies separation.*

Once primary separation is in place, the multiplicity and diversity of "ten thousand things" comes into being. It is not to say they do not exist for the little baby, cat or dog, or in the absence of the projector (body-mind), but it is not to say that they do exist, either. Like a pattern on the carpet, they belong to the carpet. It is a totality of One and Only.

O – Only

> **Bob:** *'Me' is only an idea, a thought. Thought is only a movement of energy. There is only one reality: "Thou art That".*

Body-mind is only an object in consciousness. The mental image of 'me' is only a pattern of energy expressing past knowledge and experiences. The world, which seems so real and diverse, is only an appearance — just like in a dream at night. Time is only in the mind. It is only duration. Space is only projected by sense-perception.

> *Bob: So, all this manifestation is really only that space-like awareness, vibrating into patterns, shapes and forms, but its essence is still space-like, sky-like; empty but alive. Pause the thought, only for an instant, and this will be very clear to you. All the so-called different things are in reality still only the display of awareness. Everything can only know its existence. That knowing is awareness. It knows itself as an awareness only.*

It is one and only. "One-ly", Bob sometimes says. It looks like a diversity and multitude but is ONLY seemingly so. Real ONLY now.

O – Out Of Now

> *Bob: They may tell you to stay in the now. I tell you, "Try and get out of the now". You can't. Even if you are recalling the past, you are doing it now. When you are imagining or anticipating the future, it is happening now. There is only now. There is no way out of the now.*

You cannot leave the present; you can only dream or daydream that you have. Who is the dreamer? It is only attention, life essence trapped in an enticing story for a moment. Once recognized, the recognizing principle is free. This principle is not an object.

251

O – Object

An object of perception can't be the perceiver. Being aware of the body is knowing it as an object. Noticing thinking is seeing objects. Grand ideas, models of reality and types of personality: they are all objects known in the sphere of consciousness.

Pure subjectivity cannot be objectified, so even speaking about it in the third person is wrong. It is not IT, That or God; it is not awareness; it is the 'I am'. Not my 'I am', but rather yours if we excuse the grammar again.

There seem to be innumerable objects all around. They happen in perception. They seem separate because of the angle of looking, hearing, or touching, but the perceiving in which subject and object both arise is one. This is a great mystery and miracle of appearance — and a great contemplation opportunity.

O – Offer or Opportunity

The ancients considered it great fortune when the body-mind becomes curious about Truth and the search begins. To meet a guide, a book or a school calls for gratitude and humility but it is not a prerequisite for consciousness. Nothing is.

There is a frequency on offer: please tune in if it rings true. It is an opportunity for guidance; an aid in investigation to be used once or on an ongoing basis.

O – Once-Off vs. Ongoing

Recognition is not once-off event that happens in time and lasts for the duration of the body. It is now. It is clear now or it is clouded by distractions. There is nobody who does recognize or who is too distracted. It seems like there is but this isn't so. There is only recognizing. ING means an activity. There is no doer or owner of it.

Calling it an ongoing process suggests the involvement of time but if we excuse the limitations of language, we can say it is always on. Life is never off. Sky is never absent and yet it is always an absence, empty space. When there is movement of attention, clarity is obscured. In stillness, there is no mind. There is present occurrence.

O – Occurrence

There are many awakening stories, even in this very book, showing it as an occurrence of immediate, momentary transformation. It seems to happen this way in some body-minds. Identification as 'me' gets obliterated in one single occurrence.

In others, clarity comes in many smaller occurrences or insights after which the self-referencing narrative may still re-establish itself. It creates an illusion of "I had it but I lost it" and brings much suffering. Investigating who had it may help to see through the cloud again. Clarity is when 'I' is not.

To wait for the occurrence, to prepare for it, to expect a particular experience is to dream. The more we dream, the more habitual dreaming becomes. All imagination is an activity of the mind. Recognizing this releases the energy trapped in the hope for an epiphany. This epiphany is nothing for the mind anyway. Mind hides gold in ornamental forms.

O – Ornament. Ocean

There is a popular analogy in Vedanta used for pointing. It compares the Life Essence or divinity to gold and all seemingly separate things to golden ornaments. You cannot have a golden ornament without gold. It is the gold that has all the value. The shine of gold, its indestructible nature, its malleability, and its relative scarcity made it an ideal material to embody divine qualities. It is still used to decorate temples, sanctuaries and churches.

Golden ornaments are forms of gold but they can also distract the observer from gold's inherent qualities. This analogy serves as a reminder to focus on the essence, not on how it expresses — to see the gold in the ornament.

The analogy of an Ocean and its waves also points to the same recognition. Ocean, or water, is essentially formless. Waves, icebergs, steam: these are all temporary forms through which formlessness expresses itself. But its eternal unchanging essence is beyond the momentary appearance of objects or organs.

O – Ovum. Organs

> **Bob:** *This little cell which has formed in your mother from the essence of food she has eaten and prana (the air she was breathing), is a grand demonstration of the unthinkable intelligence of life. It knew what it needed to do. It knew where to attach to and how to facilitate creation of a foetus when sperm penetrated it and division begun.*

If it doesn't make you marvel at the brilliance of Life, please look again. It is not just you — not only your body. Many life-forms operate in a similar way, creating eggs, cocoons and dividing original cells into intricate patterns of well-tuned bodily organs. It is deeply profound, don't gloss over it! See the magnificence!

> **Bob:** *A liver cell will not develop to be a brain cell. Each and every one has its specific instructions and*

functions; each and every organ is suffused with that innate intelligence which operates there.

O – Operate

Bob: *Look at the mind: see how it operates. Everything is good or bad or somewhere in between that range. What does it mean? It means that it can only operate dualistically. Mind is duality. Thinking is always happening somewhere in the range of interrelated opposites. It cannot happen any other way.*

To transcend duality you have to overlook thinking. Simply shift out of it; disregard it. You can't taste nonduality using the dualistic mind. In just the same way, you can't find the stillness by moving. The way mind operates is through movement, vibration. That is also how life is optimally organized.

O – Organized. Optimal

Life self-organizes. If you can only see the brilliance of self-organizing life, it will teach you, entertain you and tell you most magnificent stories of love and beauty. You will see greatness everywhere in the manifested world.

Body is organized in an exquisite way. Information is organized in the mind. Everything is always being used in the most optimal way. There are no mistakes or errors in nature. In every moment every available resource is used in order to organize optimally.

Each ecosystem is self-organizing. Evolution is the improvising of optimal solutions for adaptation. Bees, ants, sardines, monkeys, wolves, bacteria, cancers, humans, minerals, stars — all live in optimally organized clusters. It may not look like this for the judgemental mind (for example, seeing horrific exploitation or violence), but there is a greater order to everything. Just step back to see the bigger picture.

Organized religions, dark pages in human history, wars, famines, politics — there is order to all of it. Destruction is the flip side of creation, they are interdependent. The whole of the environment is an optimally organized system. Thought patterns of selfish beliefs, fear or greed — are part of an environment, and part of the self-organizing system. In the bigger picture there are social and spiritual functions served by these patterns, hence their inevitability in given circumstance.

This is not to justify abuse or to stop striving for perfection. This very striving is a part of the self-organisation towards optimal order. It is its outcome.

O – Outcome

Outcome has a meaning that is different from and more precise than that of consequence because it doesn't have to relate to a single cause. It is more general than a result; it is not borne of one particular thing or action. Still, it is a story, interpretation and meaning that is given, nevertheless. It is often viewed as optimistic or pessimistic.

O – Optimism

Optimism is an attitude (mostly pre-conditioned, but can also be learned) — reflecting a favourable view of events and conditions — and the expectation of a positive outcome. In philosophy it is the doctrine or idea that this world is the best of all possible worlds. 'Thy Will is done', Christianity would say. As a pointer, it could remind us of present serenity rather than speak of hopes for a non-existent future. What's here now is more of a reality...

R – Sailo-R Bob

R – Reality

Bob: *The definition of reality is "that which never changes". Since you were a child, your body has changed; thoughts and feelings have changed; the image you have of yourself has changed. But what hasn't changed? How do you know that child you once were is the same you as you are today?*

I vividly remember my first day at school. Mum dropped me off and then disappeared. I had no idea where I was supposed to be. I didn't know any of the other kids I would be going to school with for the next eight years and I was anxious and confused. I was not yet seven, had thick prism glasses and a small body — I was much smaller than the other kids around me — and it was cold.

On my first day in college, I was already a teenager and confident among the few girls I knew but still shy with most strangers. On my first day as a cadet in the Maritime Academy, I was too excited to be shy but still as invisible as I could be, embarking on a ship for an adventure training that would last the next six years.

For these three events, I know I was there. But what was there? Not one cell of the body was the same, not even those in my bones. My world view was drastically different. It has changed from a dark and dangerous Inferno to something liveable, and then to something actually exciting. My own self-image was changing daily or sometimes hourly depending on external approval, internal hormones and a thousand other things. Underlying shyness and inadequacy lingered through all three events, but not through my entire lifespan.

There were moments of bliss in all these years. There were moments of terror. When bliss or terror were absolute, there was no 'me' relating to it and there was no shyness. Many times throughout my life things would suddenly become clear, beautiful, intimately known and loved as an inseparable part of me. Many times I would face dread, the abyss: trauma of which I wouldn't speak or think of for a year or more.

But something makes these experiences 'mine'. What was there that never changed with the changes of the body, thoughts, beliefs and self-images? What knew all these different experiences? Realize that, for That is reality. That is what never changes. You are that changeless Reality.

The seeming realities of the movie, the dream, the drama you are telling yourself about in the narrative are not real. They change.

> **Bob:** *In reality, nothing has ever happened. Patterns come and go but that which never changes undeniably is. You are. The only reality you are absolutely certain of is the fact of your own being. Realize that.*

R – Realize

Here are some sentences copied from a couple of my earlier transcriptions where Bob organically uses the word 'realize'. I trust this will be refreshing reminder!

> **Bob:** *I came to realize I was being lived. I came to realize that my seeming journey was how it all panned out. The realization was that there is no centre, if I am that space-like awareness. I realized that there is no 'me', there is nothing there at all. I realized that everything I had believed in, I was not, and everything just dropped away.*
>
> *Realize there is only now! You can realize just how much takes place without the use of the mind. Realize that the functioning is happening effortlessly, without any 'me' involved. Realize that before anything can be wrong, there has to be thought.*
>
> *There is no relationship between apparent seeking and realization of liberation. In the dawning of that, you realize that any direction you go in will always be in the mind. What 'way out' of the mind is there? Full Stop! Realize that all that is happening is conceptualization.*
>
> *Realize that there is no personal doer of it. Realize there is no one to do it, and nothing to do and it will settle down of its own accord. Realize that which is ceaselessly and spontaneously arising, prior to any thought. You are beyond the mind. Realize that. You must realize that you have been lived.*

You may not realize that even when the thoughts are going on the silence is still there. You have realized that you don't have to get to the silence. There is more silence in this room than there is sound.

You realize there is not a thing you can say about it. But you can't deny the fact that it still is as it is. Realize you can't negate your being, you can't say, 'I am not'. Realize that prior to the mind there is always that pure intelligence or knowingness. Just come back to the sense of presence that you are, and realize that that is birth-less, deathless, timeless, spaceless, bodiless and mindless.

We are not realizing that we were whole from the start, that we never have been separate. When you realize that you never find an answer to it in the mind, what happens? But realize that thought has come up spontaneously, effortlessly and intuitively on that what you are.

You realize also that you can't cut space; you can't grasp space; you can't stir it up; you can't do anything with it. The same applies to this awareness. See that and realize that you are the emptiness itself, the no-thing-ness.

But realize that you were seeing before the thought 'I see' came up. Look again without labelling and realize that you are seeing as well as hearing at the same time. Realize that, before words and images came up, there was a registering of things. They are only being translated into words and images.

Don't you realize that there is never a time when it is not there?

Realize that there is not a past unless you think about it. And what future is there unless you think about it? From that, you see that mind itself is time.

When the mind realizes that it has no power of itself, just like the piece of iron in the fire, then it aligns itself with that intelligence.

Realizing that that intelligence is functioning, that's the 'razor's edge'. All you need is to recognize that it is already so.

R – Recognition

Bob: *Cognizing Emptiness is the emptiness with the capacity of cognizing. Re-cognizing or remembering is done by that emptiness, not the illusory entity, the 'me'. Realize that you are cognizing right now; everything is being registered.*

To re-cognize is to know again. It means to identify (someone or something) from having encountered them before. To realize is to understand clearly, to become fully aware of (something) as a fact.

What is it that has been known always and ever since and even before you can remember? What is that which can be known (realized) as a fact? Did you know you are a body or a person before you knew words? You did not. Is that a fact or just a belief? Is that learned or experienced? Did you know the world as separate from yourself before reasoning started? Did you know it (the world) or your own self as any-thing at all?

What was known? What was there that could be cognized again or re-remembered? What is and was a fact, even before any beliefs divided the experience?

Some pointers say that there is no such a thing as enlightenment and that there is nobody to be enlightened. Yes. You are that enlightened nobody already, and now it is all only about recognizing it. Nothing needs to be done — only recognition of what is already so.

> **Bob:** *Recognize that you have never left this moment now or at any time. It is effortless. Recognize that you are aware of being present right now. You recognize that you are awareness and that you have never moved away from awareness.*
>
> *Recognize that you are that which is aware of all these things. Recognize that livingness, that essence, that intelligence-energy or whatever you want to call it. As soon as I open my mouth I'm using concepts, but you must recognize that the livingness is there, too. Recognize repetitively.*

R – Repetition

> **Bob:** *We were hypnotized into believing that we are this 'I', a separate entity, an individual. It was reinforced over and over again, all of it, the name, the gender, the nationality, roles... It was learned by repetition. That is not going to die down overnight. The seeing of it is immediate but the old habit patterns will come up again and again because*

patterns are repetition. Unlearning has to happen the same way: repeated recognition.

Bob came back from India in early 1977 and started speaking to people. Meetings organically formed and the spiel grew over the years to constitute a bag of more than hundred potent pointers which he repeated over and over — to be questioned and contemplated upon in the group setting. Repetition was required to overwrite old beliefs, programs and habit patterns.

There were people who visited Bob some 20-30 years ago, heard the spiel a couple of times, and disappeared — only to return recently and say that it worked slowly within them, like a cotton bale smouldering after contact with a spark: slowly but surely. They grew to understand more and more pointers and appreciated the shifts that pointers seemed to produce.

Bob: *How many times were you told you were this body? The most effective learning is learning through repetition. Now you begin to see through but the whole world will try to pull you back into the illusion. Keep seeing through and — through repetition — it will stabilize in you. Now, instead of them pulling you out of clarity, you will pull them into it and it will reinforce it in yourself.*

R – Reinforcement

Just like the hypnosis of repetition, constant reinforcement stabilizes the world which we have projected out and labelled — believed — into seeming solidity. We have solidified emotions through reinforcement. We have reinforced self-image, identity, the roles we play, the things we perceive and the rules we obey.

> **Bob:** *The fresh and new sensation comes up; a vibration or pulsation or contraction appears and you label it 'fear'. How do you know it is fear? You had it before, in the past. What have you done now? You have loaded yourself down with all the past fears you've ever had. You have reinforced that feeling with the thought, the label.*

You can also reinforce the questioning. Once that strong sensation comes up, see it fresh and new, without any label or assumption. Reinforce the investigation of this plain movement of energy, this pulsation or throbbing. Reinforce recognition instead.

> **Bob:** *Think about what had to happen to make you believe that you are a separate entity. You did not just go along twice a week to a meeting to come to believe in separation. Every day, every hour of the day while you are awake, that idea of a separate entity is constantly reinforced not only by you but by all of society, our parents, our family and our schools. Everybody around you is confirming that idea that you are separate. It has become habitual and we have hypnotized ourselves with the belief in it.*

Instead, reinforce the understanding of your inherent innocence. Reinforcement means strengthening or supporting. That initially faint pattern of seeing through will brighten and patterns of hanging onto ideas with the energy of belief will weaken with spontaneously arisen investigation.

> **Bob:** *I may still experience a bad feeling coming up for a while but it doesn't hang around now as much as it*

used to — where before it would go on for days. As soon as that feeling was there, it kept getting reinforced with "I shouldn't have done it" or "This shouldn't have happened". Today it doesn't get reinforced. Nothing is needed for recognition, but initially all the reminders helped.

R – Reminders

The main intention of this book is to provide many simple reminders that can be easily recalled when needed. When everything in the appearance brings attention back to the source of the appearance, appearance will be perceived as what it is.

This is a trick of using reminder-thoughts to release attachment to other, sticky, personalized thoughts. It's not a spiritual by-pass but a short-cut, a 'smart-pass'. In memetics and Zen, 'Who am I' is a thought that eats away all the other thoughts. Ramana Maharishi called it a thorn used to remove other thorns.

Reminders, just like insights, are there to do a job, not to be collected. They may not produce the same shift twice. They may expire and need to be thrown away. It is good to know their limitations.

> **Bob:** *Jesus told you, "Be ye transformed by the renewing of your mind". What does it mean? It means re-mind. You need to remind yourself as often as you can to go back to that certainty of being.*

And this is not to say that there is a 'you' who needs to stress about remembering all the time. Quite the opposite! That seeming 'you' needs to relax its apparent boundaries and rest. The seeming you is a contraction, resistance.

Life itself will move you to pick up reminders to resonate with. Life itself may bring a reminder to look through the list of contents of this book or to hear Bob speak when needed. Life may move you to create your own set or to do nothing at all. Life may move you to recognize the resistance. Resistance is an excellent reminder!

R – Resistance. Resentment

Resistance is an excellent feedback mechanism with which this body-mind is equipped. It is an excellent aid to investigation. It announces loudly that mind is very active in sustaining the self-centre right now. It is an invitation to question. While it is still there, it can be perceived as a gift; a milestone to freedom and clarity.

> **Bob:** *Look at the mind. It is creating all sorts of stories just to perpetuate itself. Thought comes up and tries to modify what is. It says, "I like this, I don't like that; this is good, this is bad". Then there is a resistance to what is. If it is good or you like it, you will resist it from going. But no matter how much you love it, how much you want to keep it there, it will change. Everything is transient. It is bound to change. But you want to keep it there: you resist it from going — and you suffer.*

Youth and beauty are good examples here. The natural process of aging causes many people a lot of suffering. It is particularly painful and scary for those who associate their self-worth with physical attractiveness. The body is changing shape; hair may be falling out or going grey; skin gets thin, saggy and wrinkled; there is less strength in muscles; libido may go down; weight may go up... As aging progresses, some body parts may start wearing and causing discomfort. Some important systems may become compromised.

But that is the way of it. It doesn't have to cause distress. It need not be resisted. This is not to say that slowing down the process is wrong; by all means, if Life inspires you to eat better, exercise, buy a wig, wear mascara or put crowns on your teeth, you may just see action following these ideas.

Resisting all changes, wanting things to stay the same is a short but certain way to suffering. (For example, if you prevent your kids from leaving the nest, you may handicap them!)

Psychological resistance is a cause of stress. Stress causes diseases.

> **Bob:** *Resistance is uneasiness and uneasiness is disease. Look, you resist things you like from going and you resist what you don't like from coming. Either way, you are uneasy. You say, "This is bad, I don't want it", but it is there regardless of what you think or want.*

If you relax into it, accept it fully and open up, inspiration for right action may come. Instead of self-victimizing because of cold weather, you may put on an extra layer. Instead of resenting the pain, you may take a pill or schedule a doctor's visit. Energy trapped in resistance is an impediment to healing when the body is unwell.

The word 'resistance' has a positive meaning as well but only when there is no psychological resistance to the natural resistance. In other words, if there is a feeling of reservation or rebelliousness but no inner conflict because of it, then resistance is not being resisted. It is natural. Bodily resistance to cold and heat for example are part of a wondrous functioning.

Unhealthy, unnecessary resistance which causes stress and disease resides in the narrative, in the inner talk. This one can be released and be rid of.

> **Bob:** *You don't have to look very hard to see that any resistance is conflict. So, the idea that "I don't like this" is just an idea in the mind. What is it that I don't like? I don't like that shirt or that person.*
>
> *How do I know that it's a shirt or person? I was told or I named it from some previous experience. I don't see it fresh and new. The name I've given it is just another idea in the mind.*

"I don't like this shirt" is an idea. Within that whole idea is a presupposition that there is an 'I' who has some opinion or preference. But is there any 'I', really? 'The shirt' is only a label put on a fresh and new mystery, inseparable from the rest of the universe.

The presumption of 'I' is coming purely from the structure of language. Resistance and conflict exists only on the level of ideas! There are just thoughts wrestling with thoughts! In reality nothing has ever happened.

> **Bob:** *So, the mind is in conflict with itself, a seeming energy blockage, resentment, a resistance to what is. If it is just what is and there is no resistance to it, what*

is happening? There's no conflict there whatsoever and things just express as is. But if the resistance comes up, and "I don't like this", then that thought gets hold of it and builds it up until the energy will be such that it will come out as anger or violence, for example.

But how to end all psychological resistance? Who could do so in the absence of a presumed entity?

Recognition of resistance is enough for the pattern to start breaking. Recognition of the pattern comes from the place beyond this very pattern. It comes from the place of freedom, which is already so. Please, look out in nature and learn from nature. She is such a wise guide!

Bob: *Day doesn't resist night; winter doesn't resist summer. They are opposite but not in opposition. There is no resistance to them. One comes along and the other will take its place. With us, too, the opposites can continually function without resistance because we ARE that natural functioning.*

'I', the sense of 'me', is the cause of resistance in narrative. It is both the cause and the effect; the embodiment of psychological resistance itself. 'I' is resistance.

Bob: *We are the same microcosm as the macrocosm. But when the opposites come and we think, "This one is good; I want more of it", or "That one is bad; I don't want it", there is constant resistance to them. That resistance is conflict, and that is where we are uneasy. All our anxieties and fears come about that way.*

Psychological resistance is a by-product of language, which is a component of our capacity to reason.

R – Reasoning

> **Bob:** *We have reasoning capacity much more developed than that of other animals, birds and insects. Other creatures have other capacities more developed than those we have. Dogs have a sense of smell much better than you or me: they can smell drugs; find traces. Birds can fly, and we can't do it naturally. But through reasoning capacity we learned to build airplanes, balloons and helicopters which enable us to fly. Birds also have eyesight much better than we have, but through reasoning we built eye-glasses, microscopes and telescopes.*

Each and every capacity nature has designed is unique and beautiful, custom-made for the species, useful for their survival. Reasoning is one of them. It is like a sixth sense. It is a capacity for consciously making sense of things, applying logic, establishing and verifying facts, deducting, intuiting, etc. Reasoning is defined as a process of thinking that evaluates a situation considering past experiences, critical thinking abilities and emotions.

Self-realization (or realization of no-self) does not impact or change these abilities or skills. It merely abandons false ownership of it. However, with less investment in personal drama and lower psychological stress, natural creativity tends to spring up. When inner commentary decreases, some arrangements may be needed for an external memory device (much as in the case of normal aging).

If there are stories of fear that one's duties won't get fulfilled upon dismantling the illusion of self-centre, reasoning can be used to dispel these very stories. One could say that there were individuals in history who experienced disruptions in rational thinking upon awakening. That may be true. It may or may not have anything to do with the recognition of what is already so. The decision of such recognition is not in anybody's hands, though. Worrying about it is simply irrational.

> **Bob:** *It is a very useful capacity; it took us to the top of the food-chain. But it is also self-destructive when applied to oneself. The very same reasoning will tell you, you are the body, you are separate — and then it will make you compare yourself with others and deduct you are not good enough.*

Clarity, quality and speed of rational thinking varies between individuals and changes throughout the lifespan as well as on daily and hourly bases depending on environment (everything contributes, interdependently). We tend to think more rationally when in optimal health and in a neutral emotional state. Some are brightest in the morning, others before their last meal of the day or under mild stress of challenge. It is socially desirable and rewarded to be rational.

R – Rationality

Reasoning is the means by which rational individuals understand sensory information from their environments, or conceptualize abstracts such as seeming cause and effect, truth and falsehood, good or evil. Rational thinking, as a part of executive decision making, is closely identified with the ability to set goals, beliefs and attitudes and to form traditions and institutions. Therefore, it is also closely identified with the capacity for freedom and self-determination.

This, in turn, reinforces the illusion of free will and assumption of an executing entity called 'me', who this free will possesses. The 'me' was believed into existence without questioning. Instead of enabling easy communication, it often (if not always) leads to psychological suffering.

> **Bob:** *When you were a little child, before the reasoning started, you spoke about yourself in the third person. It wasn't "I do this or that", it was "Little Johnny does this". The little child (under two years of age) does not see himself as a separate entity. Then, after a while, he becomes 'I'. The thinking process seemingly forms the individual.*

After accumulating enough words, we start taking credit for actions, decisions and deductions that have spontaneously arisen. Little kids know better, and still they function and learn, without taking credit for thoughts that come up. This is because rational thinking simply comes up. There is no doer doing it.

Reasoning is different in dreams; things are justified more easily and questioned less. However, there is no doer there, either. Yet, the illusion is grand! It feels like 'I' made the choice or decision.

> **Bob:** There is always that question of free will coming up. But who is there to have or not have the so called free will? Things spontaneously arise, decisions, choices are made, but there is no choice maker or decision maker. If you think you can decide on your thoughts, why would you ever choose unhappy or miserable ones? Wouldn't you have only blissful thoughts or no thoughts at all?

This is something really worthy of pondering upon to embrace its full significance. A simple experiment will demonstrate: resolve to stop thinking for the duration of a day, a week, an hour. If you have free will and you can choose your thoughts, choose no thoughts for some time. Prove it to yourself that thoughts arise regardless of rational thinking (deciding), which also just arises.

One thought cannot control another thought. The 'me' is also just a thought. Without the energy of attention (belief) the thought is only a potential, less than a corpse, which has no power at all.

Let's look at one largely discussed, repeatedly verified and well-described discovery from early 1980s. American neurologist Benjamin Libet was investigating the role of consciousness in the generation of motor actions. Participants of his experiments were asked to perform a simple task such as pressing a button or flexing their wrist. Sitting in front of a timer, they were asked to note the moment at which they were consciously aware of the decision to move, while EEG electrodes attached to their head monitored their brain activity. Libet showed consistently that there was unconscious brain activity associated with the action — a change in EEG signals for an average of half a second before the participants were aware of the decision to move.

This experiment demonstrated that changes in brain chemistry and bodily responses (breathing, heartbeat, blood-flow etc.) happened regardless of the narrative (conscious decision), which was only reported after the fact. It shows that free will was an illusion created in the commentary after the decision is made.

Without the urge to take credit for it, decision is simply recognized as already present when it arrives. This fact, although it reinforces the innate innocence of all beings, does not take away so called personal responsibility for anti-social behaviours!

R – Responsibility

Bob: *Responsibility or response-ability means the ability to respond.*

Look at nature: animals look after their young, prepare for winter. People also have their duties and obligations which Life fulfills through them.

One of many excuses to avoid investigation is the fear of losing capacity to carry out responsibilities. The fact of the matter is that it can happen and sometimes does, regardless of recognition or its absence. Strokes, accidents, diet imbalance, depression and other calamities can debilitate certain capacities. It is not up to you if, what, how, and when something comes up.

Discovering that there is no doer carrying out any duties usually does not influence normal functioning. The immediate consequence of that discovery is the realization that there has never been a doer in the past, either, and there has never been any doer in any other individual. All deeds were done and they will continually be done with or without that clarity. The credit taking habit may break, as well as some other self-referencing habits present in the narrative. That's all.

However, Bob and I know the case when dropping of personal story did cause loss of interest in a job which was the main source of income. Our dear friend was a Vedic Astrologer, who stopped performing his art for few years because his heart wasn't in it anymore. It took a while for crowds of his followers to beg him to take it on again because they wanted it, they needed it and they loved it. There is no way of knowing, however, whether this temporary loss of interest would be absent if seeing through didn't take place.

We also know and dearly love a person, whose personal story did not drop because it could cause her not just a loss of income but unbearable identity crisis which she isn't equipped to face right now (obviously). Life has spared her from this calamity so far. Her cherished identity is 'a scapegoat', a victim. She believes she attracts and surrounds herself with psychopaths and narcissists. She works as a therapist and all her clients are also scapegoats surrounded by psychopaths and narcissists. How convenient! She lends them an empathetic ear and assures their innocence and victimhood (as well as the continuation of therapy). This is how Life plays it out for the good of everyone. Every role is precious in the greater scheme of things! As loving and supportive as she is for her fellow victims, she can be extremely hostile and dangerous towards imagined opponents. She didn't choose to be this way. She can't choose to recognize it. Recognition doesn't guarantee it will stop.

'I' also didn't choose anything in my life. I didn't choose my partner, the whole world did. I didn't choose my career, my holiday destination, my dinner. It was an outcome of the sum total contribution of all past experiences and present circumstances.

Please consider re-writing your own life story without credit and blame, but seeing clearly the contribution of innumerable factors. Name a few of them, just to open your mind. Look at every past decision and see how life lived you through that process. Please notice how the choice or conclusion appeared in the past and how it bore on the present. Notice how little you know about whatever momentary decisions you will make tomorrow.

From the absolute perspective, the perspective of Life, nobody has ever committed a crime; every particle in the manifested world contributed to that outcome. Yet, crimes are committed. Horrific deeds are being done and the prisons are filled with innocent people.

Perfection of this divine play is evident when no credit is taken for either the problem or the solution. They both organically arise in the awareness and they change, evolve or involve. Dangerous and harmful individuals are being isolated, even though they didn't choose the environment, parents and conditioning which made them so. Prison systems and rehabilitation movements are proposed, therapeutic techniques designed, all by the same Life expressing through available channels. All responses and reactions simply just happen.

R – Reaction vs. Response

Bob: I like to differentiate between reaction and response for the sake of pointing. Reaction is blind, unconscious — from the old habit pattern. Response is coming from presence and clarity.

Reactions are done on impulse, without putting much attention into it or considering what the end result may be. Responding can be defined as saying or doing something in reply. Response is more logical and compassionate. For example: little Johnny breaks a glass. You may immediately react by getting angry, yelling, upsetting the child and yourself, and therefore severing your bond with him.

Response may be taking a deep breath and allowing the initial emotional reaction to pass before addressing the situation in an adequate manner. You **respond to your reaction** first by noticing it in consciousness.

To learn responding appropriately is a great life skill to have. It is to take a moment or two to pause and breathe. It helps to recognize the unresolved emotions responsible for guiding (or misguiding) our automatic choices on a daily basis. It is essential to listen to the body, which always provides priceless feedback of uneasiness. This priceless feedback of uneasiness is an invitation to pause, notice and give attention where it is called for.

Bob: When there is a pain or tension in the body, it is a way to communicate that something is wrong in there. It needs attending to. But if there is a so-called lump in the throat or knot in the gut, you can't pin-point it; you know it is psychological.

277

Recognizing reaction as an old habit pattern means to dissociate or dis-identify with that habit. Recognition introduces distance, a space in which the object (reaction, behaviour) is known. In that pause, there is a new possibility born. Instead of perpetuating the habit, the light of conscious attention examines it. Instead of feeding the justifying story, attention goes to the present sensation.

An interesting and pleasurable way to deal with strong emotional reactions is to introduce curiosity in bodily responses to it. Bodily sensations are here-now, so attention invested there will not fuel the story.

Now, when the child breaks the glass I notice the blood rushing up to my face; my fists and jaw clenching; and my breath becoming short and shallow. I notice my heartbeat increase and feel a strong vibration in the solar plexus. Here-now.

I sit down and close my eyes. Life is rushing through the system and it is fascinating. In 2-3 seconds, alarm bells in the body stop and I'm ready to respond with love. Now I'm in tune, receptive.

R – Resonance. Receptivity

Listening to nonduality pointers may invoke warm feelings within. When you or hear something that "rings true", like a forgotten tune you once knew and held dear — this is resonance. You are on the same wavelength. You may feel this warm, intimate familiarity, like coming in from the cold; or it may be like a dawning 'a-ha' moment. It comes when you are in tune with the core of your being, the essence. You are "on the same page".

For the pointers to have that effect, receptivity is a must. Receptivity is an ability to receive; it is an openness with genuine curiosity.

> **Bob:** *People know what they are saying when they say "I had a heart to heart" with someone. It is when you really opened up to someone, they were receptive to you, and there was communication and resonance in that. You were in tune.*
>
> *You won't resonate with every pointer but as you hear them over and over and your receptivity increases, more of them will ring the bell and bring you home. They are all about One anyway, just different aspects.*

Some old scriptures promise a master's arrival only when the student is ready. They also talk about great fortune in having access to the word of truth at all, and especially from a living guide. In olden days, very few people who saw through the illusion managed to gather students to pass on the message. Some would express it in art, some would fall into the silence. In the information era, we can seemingly pick and choose which way of presenting the message resonates most.

However, it may be beneficial in some cases to initially focus on one source of pointing, purely because of the language. There is no (and there may never be) unified language to speak about what's beyond words. Different speakers define their terms differently and use similar analogies to demonstrate different aspects of the One. It causes confusion.

We are often asked to explain words of Ramana or Nisargadatta, which is fair enough because they can't speak for themselves anymore. But we are also requested to argue or defend terms like awareness or 'I am', which one or the other speaker approve or negate as it suits their style of guidance.

There are different approaches to pointing. There is for example the idea of gradual vs. instantaneous enlightenment. Fans of gradual recognition may believe that certain activities will take 'them' 'there' in the future. It can resonate strongly with the mind because mind is future-past oriented. Also promises of 'me' doing something to get something or go somewhere are very appealing.

If that is your case, relax. It is Life playing its game. Enjoy the ride. Certain disciplines and mind training may ease the suffering in the daily experiencing. It is Life that inspires practices. It is Life that writes the justifying story and elusive promises. Just relax the credit for it and enjoy doing whatever Life moves you to do! There is nothing wrong in repeating mantra or chanting, but it is Life that does it. Not you. There is no you. The purpose, reason and hopes behind the activity are just the interpreting commentary (which Life runs on autopilot). Disregard it. Stay empty, receptive, curious, not-knowing.

Gradual recognition may also be a valid after-story, a memoir of the seeming journey. The story of seeming progress, of where Life took you and how overcast (clouds of beliefs) was thinning may be beautiful and inspiring. Nothing is wrong or invalid in the appearance. Understanding seems to deepen; thought patterns seem to lessen over time. Stabilization in living, without adding meaning or believing the commentary, seems pretty gradual indeed!

Fans of instantaneous recognition are often waiting for the big bang to happen for 'them' now and feel crushed that this now is not The Now. If that is your case, see if you are unconscious or unaware right now. You are not. Wow! This is it! Instantaneous recognition. This Now. And Now. And Now.

Being aware is not a small thing! Just notice your presence. If there is a sense of contraction, doubt, disappointment and self-pity present as a content of that awareness of being conscious, so be it. Deprived of any importance, it doesn't matter.

> **Bob:** *I'm not talking to any body, I'm not talking to any mind. I'm talking to that I Am that I am. Just this. Nothing else.*

If there is a receptivity, if there is a resonance, your attention will spontaneously shift upon hearing it to the source of all attention: to the sense of I am. If not this one, there are many others in Bob's bag of pointers! Try them all, try them again, they are alive and they carry the frequency to resonate with.

You may sometimes get lost in pointers, examples, explanations. You may get confused with vocabulary. But if listening to them puts you at rest, there is a resonance. Relax into it.

R – Rest, Relax

You may fall in, relax into it. You may simply rest in what is, as is. Recognition brings about the understanding that nothing needs to be done or gotten. Natural relaxation follows that recognition.

> **Bob:** *We are opposing what is. Resistance is conflict, and conflict is dis ease. When this conflict is going on,*

you are not at ease. Not being relaxed and at ease is dis-ease. Keep that dis-ease there long enough and it will manifest as disease in the body. So, simply relax, rest as That.

It may feel like this is an instruction to be followed by the mighty doer with free will to decide on following or disobeying instruction. It is not so. Only because of the structure of language is Bob inspiring resonance in this way.

To be more precise, we would have to point out all the contractions and tensions in the body and in the thinking. Showering them with enough neutral attention slowly relaxes them. It is so because the energy trapped in sustaining contraction is now used elsewhere – in neutral noticing.

Relaxing is not an action to be performed. It is an absence of its opposite, tension. Force applied to hold that false self-identity is to be recognized and left alone until it naturally ceases. All investment in maintaining this self-image is an energy, trapped and habituated. Resting, relaxing into plain being and relaxing out of this costume of concepts, brings peace.

When thinking relaxes, there is silence shining forth. When you rest your attention without following or chasing anything, there is stillness naturally there. When the body rests, tensions relax too. It is not an instruction but a pointer to the cessation of unnecessary unconscious actions.

> **Bob:** *Bankei told you, "Let it rest in uncontrived singularity", or "Rest in the unborn Buddha mind". I like to say, leave everything as it is, unaltered, unmodified, uncorrected. As it is. Relax. Release all resistance.*

R – Release – E X E R C I S E

We do not recommend any particular practices because they often come with expectations of attainment of an imagined goal in an imagined future time for the imagined 'me'. Identification as a meditator, devotee or practitioner wanting particular results in the nonexistent future is a cloud on the clarity and simplicity of being.

This is not to say that practicing won't or should not happen. The young eagle practices flying after leaving the nest. The dolphin practices bow riding whenever the opportunity arises. The little child practices walking. But they do not miss the present moment: they are it. There is no narrative setting goals and asserting doership of an entity or creating suffering when expectations are not met (because there were none).

Setting goals and expecting measurable results is not to be avoided, either. Who would be avoiding it? If these types of stories do arise in the narrative, leave them unaltered, unmodified and uncorrected. Just notice. Be aware. There is nothing wrong with any of the healthy, conscious and painless ways of utilizing reasoning capacity.

There are times when expectations (or goals) motivate but also when they cause frustration and resistance. How and who is there to release it if nobody has done it to start with? But there may be a tension in the body at times, and in thoughts and emotions. Life has done it. It has done it in response to itself and it can undo it if directed this way. Here is how life does it.

Please clench one of your fists for few seconds, as hard as you can. Apply force, as much as you can, count to five and stop. Notice sensations of natural release.

Now tense your body, all muscles on the face, eyes, lips, neck, shoulders, arms and legs, back, belly, buttocks, feet – and hold for five-ten seconds and stop. You can repeat it couple of times to notice more details.

A nice variation of it is this: when you wait for something, sit or lie down and run that tensing energy throughout your body, part by part. You could tense your foot for five seconds and stop. Stopping automatically releases the tension. Then tense the calf. Release. Hip. The other foot. Calf. Hip. All the leg, then both legs. Stop tensing and feel the difference. Do the same with the rest of the body, part by part. It is quite pleasant and pretty educational!

> **Bob:** *You don't know how to release or let go? Nonsense. You do know how. When you hold your breath for too long what do you do? You simply stop holding it and it releases, it lets go on its own.*

The same principle can be applied to any physical echo of raw energy of emotion in the body. Let's try low level irritability. In my body, it lifts and tightens both shoulders and shortens the breath, at times even stopping it altogether. Breath is somewhat contracted and goes in with some difficulty and a slight whistle.

I can tense my shoulders even more, make the breath whistle and go in even slower and tighter, and shivers of fury show up in my back. I ignore the label, take it off. Now I like to close my eyes and tune to each vibration of this symphony of pulsating, throbbing life. I amplify it (using intention) for another 10 seconds and stop. Release happens automatically. And what a learning experience!

Now every physical manifestation of emotion reflected in the body has become my friend for whom I wait to study even more. With increased sensitivity, amplification is no longer required. Now, no emotion is unwelcomed. Whatever Life serves, Thy Will is my will, because there is only one of us.

> **Bob:** *Try this: Just make it worse, what can happen? The worst case scenario is that you will faint, fall unconscious for a moment. Is that so bad?*

As you gain confidence, you don't mind — or almost invite the vibe of anxiety, panic attacks or phobias, just to learn more. If the emotion makes you wave your arms, you may wave them wider. Just watch out not to hurt yourself or anyone. It is an experiment. It needs boundaries of safety. It is to release trapped energy, not to even up imagined scores. If you are moved to do this exercise, remember what it is for. Especially when you play with emotion that is reflected in thoughts.

Emotions embodied physically are to be released first. Emotions sustained by the story will then be lighter, less sticky. Written contemplation is a good way to play, also.

If I hold the story that I'm unworthy of love, I first look for the area in the body where that story causes contraction. The body is like a mirror, which reflects any belief in the form of sensation. I scan it to find the reflection. In my case, the sense of unworthiness or low self-esteem was held in the heart, making it smaller, tighter and more painful. I would have a lump in the throat, my eyes would well up, and my forehead would wrinkle. My shoulders would lean forward and my breath would be short and shallow. Others may experience it differently.

Initially, I was addressing each sensation individually. First, it had to be noticed in all details, then strengthened for few seconds, and then let go. Later, exclusive neutral attention became enough to release any tension shortly after it appeared. Today, I don't see these thoughts anymore but other thoughts — like verbal threats — are a source of yummy variety!

> **Bob:** *I will hammer it to you until it sinks in: what is wrong with right now if you don't think about it? Nothing at all!*

Remembering that — and playing with the concepts and images **after** the physical residues are gone is pure fun! The exaggerated story becomes grotesque and makes you laugh. Instead of feeling more right and justified, you see the ridiculousness. You could make a comedy skit out of it. Release is automatic.

We have seekers reporting that some physical pains, including chronic pains, may be approached this way. We do not strengthen pain by putting salt into the wound but by monitoring throbs, pulsations and vibration and then amplifying them for few seconds in the mind if or when that is available. At times mere attempts to amplify pain bring back the recognition of non-doership, absence of control.

It is interesting to notice how attention wants to vacate present sensation and go back to the head, to the story. It is fascinating to notice the tendency to flee discomfort by seeking refuge in mental distractions. It is a wondrous capacity which protected us at some point in life when we couldn't deal with emotional pain or recognize sustaining story as story yet. It became a habit but the habit can now be broken through conscious recognition and release. We start from its reflection in the body.

R – Reflection

Just like the body is a mirror for the thoughts and emotions, and just like how the people we meet are screens for our projections – all the manifested world is a reflection of that wondrous omnipotence of Life.

> **Bob:** *Nothing has ever been created. It only appears to be so. Have a look at the reflections in that mirror. Has the mirror created the reflections? It may appear to be so, but the mirror does nothing, it just is. It is glass covered with a polished reflective surface. When you look at it, reflections are there. But when you come close and try to grab one, you will see that you can't, so they are not really there.*

Like everything in the manifested world, reflections appear to be there but they are not really there. Things neither exist nor don't exist. This applies to everything. Thoughts seem to be there but you can't grab them. Fear is only a story, not a fact. Its reflection is not fearful at all; it is a sensation. Things you see, taste, touch and hear are sensations also.

Material objects can seemingly be grabbed (which is just more complex form of sensing) but they are transient, changing as you do (including the hardest of rocks). Subatomic particles constituting solid objects are made of pure energy. There is no solidity to anything, just like there is none to reflections in the pond of water or dew drops.

> **Bob:** *So, in reality, nothing has ever happened. Patterns of energy appear, patterns disappear. It is still the same life, intelligence energy. They appear just the same way as the reflections appear in the mirror. What has happened to the mirror? Is it*

287

affected, touched or changed by any of the reflections? The mirror is self-shining and reflections appear in it. Is the mirror concerned whether or why there is a reflection there or not?

Space is like a 3D invisible mirror. Everything is reflected in it, but nothing contaminates it. Body is just a reflection in space. Thoughts and emotions are just reflections in the body. The whole world of forms is just a reflection in and of the cognizing emptiness.

Dreams appear in the space of awareness called the dreaming mind. This dreaming mind is a mirror for images and experiences reflected on it during the dreaming. Daydreams or past memories and options for the future appear in the waking mind. Present experiencing is also a reflection appearing in the mind. Mind is a multidimensional space, a field, a reflecting surface for things to show up. It isn't really a thing.

This afternoon I was sitting on the comfy brown recliner opposite of Bob for a couple of hours. At some point the thought appeared that I should inspire Bob to take our daily exercise walk before it started raining again. I heard myself describing out loud to him the gentle warm breeze on our faces, the sunshine on our backs and the smell of jasmine. I heard myself painting a seductive picture of us enjoying the autumn weather, but to no avail. He didn't feel like going. The daydream ended. I returned to my more immediate waking dream of being on the brown recliner, watching Bob do his crossword puzzle with our ginger cat on his lap. And I'm typing this chapter right now, this is the present dream. Gone by the time you read it!

These are dreams consciousness has. It dreams itself a body-mind of Kat and Bob, able to see, hear and feel. It projects and plans the walk, rejects the daydream and returns to the waking dream of simply being. But this whole scene is also just a reflection in this 3D mirror of space that you are. What are these dreams made of?

> *Bob: You are total awareness, always and ever. This body also — the front of the body which you can see — all these things are like the reflections in the mirror. The nature of the mirror is to reflect. It is just clear and empty but it is reflecting whatever comes near it. The things in the mirror don't contaminate or touch the mirror, either. Just like Awareness is not contaminated or touched by anything that is reflected (appearing on it). But this analogy has a certain limitation. The mirror needs something outside of itself to reflect in it. Awareness doesn't. It is all there is. You are That.*

You are the awareness (knowingness) and nothing is outside of you. Body (or ego, if you believe you have one) is not outside of you. Any self-image or center, any preferences and traits of personality (conditioning), are merely reflections; echoes. If you are awareness, you are also the awareness of everything that comes and goes. And that every-thing, when looked at closer, is a no-thing; a dancing pattern of energy; merely reflection.

> *Bob: A little child, prior to identification, is just living from the natural state. You can take a two year old, put him in front of a mirror and mark his face with paint or something. He will not know it is himself! He'll see the face, but he hasn't realized that "that is me" at that stage. There is awareness there. He is aware of the reflection in the mirror and what it looks*

like, but there is no self-awareness there at that stage.

As Life has it, this relationship is to be established first before it is dispelled. The dream has to be firm and convincing for the awakening to be valued appropriately. So, relationship forms itself and a reference point comes up.

R – Relationship. Reference Point

Bob: *The relationship is the problem. Notice: every problem is a problem of relationship. It is always related to the 'me'. Everything is relative. Relativity means me and the other. But we point here that there is only one. How can there be a relationship if there is nobody to relate to?*

Once the reference point of an entity or a little controller inside is seen through, the story loses its validity but life carries on as it always did. The sense organs, which are located in the body, are still transmitting signals. That may sustain the illusion of location and limitations in the same way that the sea continues to appear blue even though we know the water is transparent, colorless.

Bob: *It is all based on that seeming self-centre, 'me', and the 'not-me'. You see, as soon as there is a 'me' which is a reference point, then there must be the 'other'. If there is anger then there is only a 'me' that can be angry. 'Other', in that relationship, is anger or the seeming source of anger. If there is fear, then it can only be a 'me' that can be fearful. If there is*

290

seeming depression, then it can only be a 'me' that can be depressed. That 'me' is based on the past.

But what is that 'me' made of? Memories? Where is it? Is it something solid or fluid? Is it a feeling or image? Where do memories appear? Aren't they floating in the knowing-of-being? Could that knowing ever be limited by any floating ideas?

> **Bob:** *But when it's referred to a reference point, that reference point discriminates what the other thing is: "I don't like it. I know it because this thing happened to me before". Or, "It is good". "It is bad". "It is pleasant"; "it is painful"; "I hate it"; "I love it"; or whatever. As soon as those ideas come up, we try to alter, modify or correct what is. With that trying to alter, modify or correct what is, there is a resistance to what is. Resistance, conflict and disease.*

A conceptual reference point requires maintenance. It is evaluated, compared and attempts are made to fix or upgrade it. It has certain assigned attributes, qualities and self-esteem, which are varying depending on external circumstances.

In nature, every pair of eyes is viewing the environment from a certain perspective, so that the whole appearance is being sensed, perhaps even covered with appreciation. But a bee or a mouse does not narrate the story in which actions are related, credit is given to some entity in charge, and meanings are assigned. (This much we know about the neuronal structure of their brains, which lack the language networks capable of retaining symbols).

To dispel the illusion of relationship between subject and object, please simply register how the body is being lived. It is being lived no different to bodies of cats, trees, cells, clouds or comets. Notice how seeing is simply happening and how within it the story arises about me, the seer and seen. Simply register the relating habit, the self-referencing pattern.

R – Register – E X E R C I S E

> **Bob:** *The mind is simply translating what is being registered.*

Please give yourself a few minutes for this little experiment.

> **Bob:** *Now, briefly look around the place where you are right now, be it a room or yard or wherever you are, and register as much as you can, fast, without naming or labelling anything. Now if I asked you how many things you saw roughly, you'll say, the lot. But if I ask you to name them all, to label them, you will have trouble, you will skip many of them and will have to look again. Everything got registered but not everything got labelled.*

In the same way, animals register everything, even though they do not have a narrative self to whisper the names of things to themselves. They know what everything is. They won't walk into the wall, even though only humans call it a wall.

The world is made of registering. Perceiving sensations, sights, sounds, thoughts — registering everything. Registering is asserting its existence. If there is no registering, there is no registered appearance and no registering consciousness.

Now, register the content of your thinking for a moment. When thought or image arises, tell them, "Next, please" and wait for the next one to be registered. Do not dwell in the content of the thoughts; register them and move on. "Next, please". "Next, please". There may be a moment of silence and no images; register that, too, and if there is the commentary "Oh! No thoughts!" register that thought also and say, "Next please".

I was very grateful for this exercise; it was my lifeline when I was following my Indian guru Sirshree. It made my daily meditations easier and brought about some realization about the existence of gaps in seemingly continuous flow of chatter. I played with it further experimenting with registering sensations in the body without dwelling in them or labelling them.

This is particularly helpful when a very strong emotion (vibration) shakes the body. You may scan the whole bio-machine and register the movement of energy in every part of it. Once you register the strongest one, say "Next please" and move on to the subtler one.

In the case of so-called anxiety, the first thing to register may be contraction in the chest. Next, please. Next is registering of breathing, shallow and short. Next, please. Stomach, nauseous vibration. Next. Subtler tensions in various muscles, shoulders, next, eyes, next, neck, next, even subtler kind of a sound, whistling high pitch, next.

Learning to register without labelling — or, at least, without taking the label all too seriously — gives us more free attention. We re-discover the scene as fresh and new. It helps distancing from the narrative and therefore registering it in an impersonal manner, with genuine curiosity in place of judgement. It lessens the suffering and enhances natural resilience.

R – Resilience

The Mayo Clinic defines mental health in terms of resilience or the ability to adapt to difficult situations. When stress, adversity or trauma strikes, you still experience anger, grief and pain, but you're able to keep functioning--both physically and psychologically. It is an adaptive mode of thinking which without nondual understanding has to be developed gradually, alongside techniques for improving one's initial response to something uncomfortable or unwanted.

Studies have found that more resilient people are more motivated and build better working relationships and ways to protect themselves from stress. To a certain extent, it looks like it is a natural talent or learned skill. However, it can also be viewed as a natural capacity that has been obscured by a learned habit of trusting negative thinking. Once that habit is recognized and starts breaking up, natural resilience shines forth.

> *Bob:* Look out there in nature. There is resilience in-built in every creature. The instinctual love for life is there but animals don't have a story about 'poor me'. See the deer eating the grass. A moment ago it was chased by the lion and ran for its life. One of its colleagues got captured and killed. But for this one the danger is over, so it returns to its life, which is feeding. It doesn't go for therapy and doesn't tell the story over pints of beer for years about how it escaped death. Life is much simpler and much more present for it.

Animals are very resilient and very present in absence of distractions coming from inner talk. Resilient people are those who forgive and let go easily, which means that they don't hang onto the victim story about the past. They move on as life moves on. They go with the flow of life.

> **Bob:** *Take a bucket of water out of the river and put it on the bank. What happens there? The water is dead, is not moving anymore: it is stagnant. It may soon start stinking. ...And what do you do when you relate to this image of 'me' from the past? The image is static. No wonder you cannot keep up with life. You are always behind, trying to catch up.*

Living without self-centre is allowing the natural resilience (the natural love of being) to shine and express. In this natural flow of up and down, good and bad, winter and summer; nothing is excluded, all is interchanging as it must. There is great value in overcoming difficulties: a great appreciation of life that comes from gaining strength after great loss, crisis, injustice, disease or divorce. Positive life experiences like childbirth, flying, winning battles or lotteries will impact the flow as well.

> **Bob:** *A river is flowing merrily along, sometimes so very slowly that it almost stops. Sometimes it goes through rapids, waterfalls; and it goes through the forests at times, or cliffs, deserts or sandy banks. But it is alive, and water in the bucket is dead.*

Relating to that stagnant water in the bucket and falling behind the flow of life is the opposite of resilience (rigidity, weakness). Yet, this is not to say that individuals who did not develop this kind of stamina, who have been bent or broken by life, are any less beautiful. Freedom or bondage is/was not up to them. If suicide ended their life, it was Life expressing in this way, too.

Otherwise, quite often, reviewing the whole life from a death-bed perspective reveals the beauty which is not always obvious in the midst of calamities. That perspective is the standpoint of no-future, a standpoint of freedom. Life can end now and nothing will be lost. Now, that's a profound realization!

R – Renate's Realization – E X A M P L E

Renate is Australian born with a German background, a retired music teacher. She is heavily built, with a bunch of beautiful, silver-blond, spring-like long hair, always a bit wild. She is reaching 80 now, but her spiritual search ended after 3 years with Bob, about 12 years ago.

Her past as a seeker is really impressive! After leaving a Benedictine Abbey (where for five years she was a devoted Christian nun), she followed Rajneesh (Osho) to India and America for another 4 years. Later on, Renate converted to Judaism for a short and painful marriage. Then she tried lengthy Zen and Dzogchen retreats. She also became a Bhakta/lover of Krishna, and lived in various ashrams where she meditated, chanted and had all sorts of Kundalini experiences.

She blew a small fortune and spent about 20 years in various therapies before and after she first met Bob. Renate heard Bob speak for the first time when she was in her mid-50s but, after hanging around casually for few months, she disappeared for another 10 very bitter years.

For those 10 bitter years, though, the pointers were working in her, dissolving her like a doll made of salt dipped into the ocean. She didn't see that. She still believed she needed to be fixed. Renate thought she must be almost there, but not quite yet.

She had done much digging in the past (through methods like psychoanalysis, family constellations, radical forgiveness, gestalt, cognitive behavioural therapy, psychodynamic therapy and many more), which brought some relief but also strengthened the habit of looking for answers in the mind. She had blamed the seeking pattern for the failure of her short marriage, for never having children, never pursuing a real career, never making money and never actualizing her gifts and talents as a music performer.

In these long years of spiritual obsession, she went through very ugly, messy fights in court, missed the death of her sister, got rejected and estranged from her mother and went through two rounds of breast cancer. Her suffering was amplified and therefore easy to pin-point and see through.

Bob showed her that every time she hit a brick wall in her life, there was a humbling reminder of non-ownership hidden in it. Life had turned it around for her so many times, it won't stop now. She did not attract these calamities; she did not choose to start the search or to invest all the attention in it. It was Life that had it this way.

She heard it. She accepted guiltlessness and non-doership. She understood that choices and decisions were made but she wasn't the doer. Life was and always is the omnipotence. She 'got' it as she was walking out of Bob's house many, many times. Yet, often a day wouldn't pass (at times only hours) and Renate needed to call Bob again asking for reminder, lost and

297

devastated with a story of "why am I like this and how do I change".

For three years, Bob patiently translated Renate's every thought and every action a few times every week. When she was full of regret that she had yelled at her neighbour, Bob reminded her that it was mechanical pattern surfacing, not her as a doer. When she had a decision to make, Bob reminded her to create the space for this decision to arrive. When she didn't know what to choose and was vacillating between options, Bob would show her the vacillation pattern happening in awareness.

Over time, Renate didn't need Bob's translation. She could do it on her own. The illusion of control is still there today, but there is no belief in that illusion anymore. Without taking it seriously, the illusion only makes her marvel and appreciate the brilliance of such a convincing show. There is still reaction to pain and there is still anger and mild habitual impulses toward self-punishment for errors but today it is all laughable; unbelievable.

The way Renate looks back at her life today is free from bitterness. She doesn't need to be fixed or understood anymore. Her years of seeking (instead of "having a life") are now viewed as an amazing adventure rather than wasted potential. She remembers it with warmth in her heart now rather than with resentment.

She can recall long years of being penniless in India but still moving through the night with a small group of friends to get Sri Amma to her first public speech. She cherishes the feeling of when she was sitting high on a throne next to Gangaji as her sister. Countless times she was accepted in the homes of loving strangers, given food, air-plane tickets or invited to conferences and festivals.

This continues to happen, even after she has turned 80 years old and has slowed down her wild life on the road. She still marvels at the ways Life provides, plays, twists and turns and she knows beyond doubt that it is none of 'her' doing. She is being lived. She knows there is no her, even though there is an illusion of being an entity with free will and control. She loves how convincing and realistic it all is: just like in the dream at night. She is free. Instead of being resentful, she is radiant.

R – Radiance

Bob: *The Sun is radiant and with its radiance it creates heat and evaporates water, forming clouds that seemingly cover it. Radiance is a characteristic of life. When the burden of self is gone, it shines of its own.*

Bob and I have a faceted crystal hanging on thin rope in the dining room window. When the sunlight falls on it at just the right angle in the early afternoon, the walls and ceiling are covered with beautiful little rainbows. There are between 20 and 40 of them, and the colors dance around when moving leaves on the tree outside filter the sunlight. It is the radiance of the Sun that creates all these colors.

Bob: *You see these little rainbows everywhere, but go and try to grasp them, you can't. They are there and they are not there at the same time. They are just an appearance. More-over, go to the crystal and look at it. See if there are any colors there. You won't find any. It is clear. Look inside, check all the facets, you'll find no colors. They are nothing other than the Sun's rays.*

299

> *So, this pure awareness or Shakti is dancing around there as you and around here as me, Bob. Over there, as the tree, or cat or tram. Has it changed its true nature? After some time, the Sun's rays are on a different angle and not touching the crystal. What happens? The rays are not shining through that particular form and there are no colours. Have they been lost?*

Just like the radiance of the Sun breaks into colors when filtered through faceted crystal; it breaks into colorful impressions (scenes, sounds, sensations, smells, scents, thoughts) when filtered through your body-mind. Body is like a crystal. Crystal changes white transparent light into red, orange, yellow, green, blue, indigo and purple. The body changes transparent, tasteless, pre-sensory being into seeing, hearing, tasting, touching, smelling and thinking.

You are that self-shining radiance, not the crystal which makes it visible, not the body which makes it experience-able.

This radiance shines of itself. It doesn't 'do' it, it *is* it. Once readiness is there, it is clear.

R – Readiness. Ripeness

Nisargadatta used to refer to the metaphor of the fruit on the tree, Bob told me. No matter what it does, its ripeness doesn't depend on it. It is the sun, the rain, the soil, the health of the sap in the tree, the shade, the season, the gravity, the pollution — all of it. That is, all of it — including any ideas and wishes that the fruit would have if it could! But these wouldn't be of the fruit's or even the tree's doing, anyway.

> **Bob:** *The whole universe depends on that life essence,*
> *intelligence energy, which constitutes everything.*

In the same way, "When the student is ready, the master arrives", they say. Yet there is nothing to be done by the student for him or her to become ready. What does the child have to do to mature, ripen and become adult? Nothing.

Just like the fruit on the tree, the young seeker matures and becomes ripe, depending on that sunlight, soil and the environment. It is simple, straight forward and guiltless. Earnestness makes it sweeter, but even that is either there or not there, regardless of the will or wish of the phantom called 'me'.

The whole universe is collaborating and the outcome is in the universes' hands. If a silent retreat is required, it will become irresistible and it will happen. If it doesn't, it wasn't needed. Even the ideas of 'required' or 'needed' are simple after-stories. Life just plays out as it does. The conceptual story in the seeker's head is akin to the story a walnut or pear might have if they could.

Many fruits won't ripen at all and in that nothing is lost. Awareness is intact. It returns to itself inevitably when the body ceases, be reassured of that.

R – Remaining R's

R – Reassurance

A mentor, guide or friend is a reflection of you, of Life remembering the truth. They have appeared in your world and you in theirs. If you have that someone you trust, who remembers who you are even when you forget, you were granted a gift. Use it for reassurance. Anything can be a reminder! So, there is nothing left but to rejoice!

R – Rejoice

Once truth is seen, known and lived, there is nothing left but rejoicing. It is not a promise of bodily bliss or the absence of pairs of opposites (pains and pleasures). It is a position of no position where things are dancing in joy. Once you cease believing in the conceptualization, joy will "speak for itself" and there is no need to romanticize it anymore.

R – Romanticizing

Attractive ideas, as a sale's pitch for the quest for enlightenment, are often the starting point of the seeming journey. Romanticizing gurus and guides as supernatural, superior and almighty — making them a parent-like or god-like figure — seems popular amongst less mature seekers. Seeing through helps to unlearn these romantic, beautiful myths and to stay unadorned, naked with what is. Romanticizing Life or God (as just or man-like) is another idea along the seeming way. The same applies to the immortality dream, the story of re-birth.

R – Reincarnation. Rebirth

> *Bob:* To re-incarnate is to 'in-carnate' again, to return into the meat-body. But what is born in the first place? What is re-born? Is there a separate entity that travels? Is it memory? Is it a thought or bundle of thoughts? Where does the identification with the body go when the body goes?

If I is Life, I- Life incarnates in every form simultaneously. There is no re-incarnation, but incarnation. It is always fresh, always new. I-Life incarnates in every image, giving it colors and shapes. I-Life seemingly incarnates in every form, every single body, so it can see and feel itself.

It is not re-born because it didn't die but it is born fresh and new every moment now. It incarnates but it doesn't reincarnate. It doesn't re-breathe either, because every breath is fresh and new. And so is every improvised role.

R – Roles

I am Totality. I am emptiness and form. I am divinity and humanity. I am That. That represents everything. I am every role I play, every costume I wear. I am an ever-changing, never changing, chameleon, shape-shifter. I am a woman, a body, a mind, a thought, a feeling, a breath. I am a wife, a daughter, a servant, a master, a lover. I am white, I am married and I am fond of such and such entertainment and a graduate of such schools and courses. Yet, I am also the opposite. I am not a woman, not a body, not a thought, not a sound, sensation, role, costume.

I am the emptiness in which the dance appears and I am the dancer as well as the public. I am every single man and every mosquito and all their perceptions, also. I am the choreographer, the music, the screen, the projector and the projected. I'm the whole rainbow.

R – Rainbow. Razor's Edge

The rainbow is a beautiful optical illusion. There is no pot of gold at the end of it because it has no end. It has no existence; it only seems to be. A rainbow is just like the world and everything in it.

The "razor's edge" is a metaphor that is sometimes used in Sufis' contemplative poetry. It points to the fine line of 'relaxed being' between the pairs of opposites. Enlightenment lies at the very edge of the (internal) abyss. In the Buddhist, Islamic and Christian traditions, there is mention of a narrow path that is precarious and difficult to remain delicately balanced on.

The razor's edge is the relaxed state of being that is between or besides future and past; between or besides inside and outside; between or besides in-breath and out-breath, or incoming thought and outgoing thought. Only direct experience makes it reliable.

R – Reliable

Ultimate reliability lies in direct experience, which is not interpreted or contrived by any story. At all times, it is there to rely on it. The being-knowing, the awareness of presence, is absolutely reliable and on demand. Nothing else has ultimate reliability.

We all give certain reliability to our currency, politicians, time measurements, science, technology, food factories etc., and that is part of the dance, the dream. But we do get let down and that is a humbling reminder of the nature of the manifested world. Everything is impermanent here. Things once broken can't be fully restored; only no-thing can.

R – Restore

Restoring means re-establishing, returning to something or repairing. As a reminder, it may serve in each of these definitions.

As a baby, the natural state was inborn, established. Before the verbal conditioning has put an overlay of narrative onto the experienced world, things were registered but not related to. Returning to the natural state means disregarding this overlay of language. Re-establishing the truth is the exploration of silence.

Repairing is a big word but it can be stretched as a pointer to put the mind in its rightful place: as a servant, not a master. It doesn't take fixing but recognition. Respectful one.

R – Respect

Respect is a feeling of deep admiration for someone or something, and is elicited by their abilities, qualities, or achievements. It also means due regard for the feelings, wishes or rights of others.

To live the life in which everything is respected as the manifestation or extension of god, is to live a beautiful life. To respect the un-manifested (or emptiness) is also called rigpa.

R – Rigpa

Rigpa is yet another label pointing at the knowledge of the background, basic screen. It's opposite, unknowing (marigpa) is not knowing the nature of mind. Knowing (rigpa) is the knowing of the original wakefulness that is personal experience. In Dzogchen, a fundamental point of practice is to distinguish rigpa from the grasping mind. But how about the body?

B – Sailor B-OB

B – Body

There are many ways in which body was viewed in ancient eastern and western scriptures. It was a friend in some metaphors; in others, a temple or a barometer of the soul. It has also been presented as a donkey, a poop-factory, a meat-sack, a machine, a car, a horse or a cart behind a horse (horse being an emotion in that analogy). Nowadays, we also use the metaphor of a costume or a virtual reality suit.

To treat the body as a friend is to appreciate and look after it. The temple symbolizes sanctification and God's dwelling place. The soul barometer or reflection of spirit shows its sentience, communicates feedback, and has the potential to express the highest qualities.

The donkey points to the animal nature of the body, with its urges and desires. It is dull; it is to be trained and used as a servant. Many more derogatory comparisons have been made in different places and times to express frustration and contempt towards certain instinctual needs of this sophisticated organism.

In all cases the body is always presented as a thing, not who or what I am. It is my temple or my poop-factory, but not me, not myself. Each of these analogies may be a useful pointer if the seeker is lost in any strong belief. All being so self-contradicting, pointers are to unlock any fixed ideas.

Bob and I like to look at the body as the means through which (and as which) the experiencing and expression happens. Intelligence energy forms this body, so every cell of this body and every part is it (this energy). Intelligence energy uses the body as a speaker, as a perception tool, and vehicle for all sorts of creativity. Body is made of Life and used by Life. You are that Life. Body happens within you. It is a masterpiece!

> **Bob:** *When you think of separation, you usually mean your body. So, try to separate your body from the elements around you. Everything there can be broken down to five elements and further down to subatomic particles and pure energy. So we have: space, air, fire, water and earth (or matter). Try separating yourself from the air if you can. ...Or stop breathing. Try to separate yourself from the water! Your body is mostly water. ...Or just stop drinking and see how long you will last without replenishing that element, water. And body temperature — the fire — without this, you get hypothermia and die. Try and get off the earth, leave space.*
>
> *See, you cannot separate yourself from the elements.*

Body is not separate or independent from its environment, but it is perceived by the senses as standing out from its background. In fact, it is constantly exchanging the elements. Millions of cells are dying and being replaced all the time. Energy for that comes from food, breath and various other processes. This energy gets metamorphosed into cells. The body is in symbiosis, the state of delicate balance between various forces and the environment. Yet, all these forces are just different vibrations of the One Essence.

Body certainly seems to stand out, otherwise it couldn't be perceived! But both the body and whatever is seemingly not the body are all one essence, interdependent and inseparable, existing within the field of awareness. Both body and the world are happening within the being-knowing that you are.

Also, most thoughts are about the relationship between 'me' (assumed to be the body) and environment. All problems are bodily problems but are called 'my' problems. It feels like body is a limit to the sense of 'me'. It feels like I am within my skin and that what is outside of it is not me. Only within my skin do I experience pain. I (my body) can sense temperature or other forms of energy from a bit of distance away. To explain that, I may assume and define some subtle body or aura outside the skin, but that's it. At a few meters away, this feels certainly not to be me, because body (including the aura) is not there.

This natural arrangement is for the survival and optimal functioning of the body. All sensory organs, the nervous system, brain etc., serve an instinct to protect it, as it may be at times endangered by external forces. It is a form, therefore mortal, transient and changing after all! That is why body needs to feel limited and located. It is the ananda aspect, the loving to be in action.

However, is the presence of awareness or consciousness (I am) limited in any way other than by mental image? Does it have the shape of a body unless you imagine it to have one?

Body can also be viewed as the gift that Emptiness uses to see, hear, taste, touch, smell and think. It uses it to project stories, perceptions and the world. Without the body, there is no consciousness, only awareness, which is quite unconscious of its own existence but complete, free and perfect. So, Emptiness vibrates to forms.

The body is a great wonder. Its structure, functions, organs, symbiotic relations with other organisms, enzymes and bacteria all reflect the complexity of the whole universe. It is akin to a holographic structure that is permeated with a great intelligence that grows it and lives it to experience and express its magnificence.

The body is and isn't at the same time because it can't stand independently, separately! It is a mirror for thought; it is a vehicle of expression. It is a transformer of pure being into seeing, hearing etc. It is a transmitter/receiver of various frequencies translated into experiences. It is a friend, a temple, a poop-factory, a horse, a cart, an energetic feedback mechanism, a coat, a car, a house. It is all and neither. It is a mystery. A masterpiece.

So, is the body in consciousness or is the consciousness in the body? Is the consciousness dreaming the body right now without its past? Or does it dream it with the story of growing it slowly over time from a one-celled organism?

How is it in the dream when I sleep? Was the dream-body I use to fly or run when my physical body sleeps in bed also born in time? How does the body begin? How does 'I' begin?

B – Beginning. Birth

Bob: *Every fairy tale starts with "Once upon a time…" There is no such thing as time, so there can't be a beginning. Can you see how every fairy tale is just a bundle of conceptual images? No time, no mind.*

But the Bible tells us, "In the beginning was the Word, and the Word was with God, and the Word was God". What does it mean? It means that God is the word. Beginning is also the word. And without the word there is no beginning

Let's explore a few more fairy tales to dispel the myth of birth, the beginning, and of time in its entirety. Let's look how it is created by the act of belief, by projecting past, by the conceptual mind, the narrative. Let's look closely at these beautiful stories about the origin of God, universe and individuals, in this moment: now. Let's look and marvel, but also recognize that beyond the mind none of them has any reality. The past exists only when I think about it.

> **Bob:** *They say that this universe as we know it started off as a Big Bang or something and that it is still expanding. The original so-called beginning is fourteen billion years ago. Before that there was no time. But is there a time today unless we conceptualize it? They admit it is just a theory, not a confirmed fact.*
>
> *How did you begin? You tell me you began at birth, but can any one of you remember your birth? You can't. You didn't have any words to store that memory. And just before the birth, wasn't the body already formed in the womb? So, you can go as far as your father and mother, where the food they have eaten and the prana they breathe formed that microscopic particle in their bodies, called the sperm and the ovum — both cells suffused with great intelligence which told them what to do.*

We can say that the body began at conception, but this is only a convention, an agreement. As Bob shows, the ovum was already there before conception. It was there even at the mother's birth. Her own foetus in turn came about because of great grand ancestors, their food and prana, their peripatetic events, climate and everything else. One might say that the body began when life crawled out of the ocean, but you know life was there before that.

Bob: So, when did you begin and what was born? People tell me what happened to them in the past, so I ask, "How do you know?" "I was there", they say. What was there? Did you have the same body when you were child? Did you have the same self-concept or image of yourself? What hasn't changed?

On that unchanging awareness, the thought 'I am' was born, and that is what dies. It happens at about the age of two, when the child has enough words and labels to separate itself with. They test it with the mirror, by marking the child's face with colour and checking whether it recognizes the reflection as 'me'.

So the 'me' seems to be born and die. Recognize it now and be done with it. In St. Francis' prayer it says, "For it is only by dying that I can have eternal life". He wasn't talking about the physical death, but dying to that sense of self, that 'me'. St. Paul said, "I die daily". It is the dying to that idea of 'me'.

With the love which we share for the stories, we invent beginnings, levels, stages and phases in life. They all seem very real in the appearance, valid in the waking-dream. They are useful on this apparent "vacation from eternity", which so convincingly seems to have a duration...

Bob: When does this moment NOW begin? Now. And as it begins it is already ending, so it has no duration. The Buddhists call it 'unborn'. 'Unborn' means unoriginated. That means it has no origin. It has no beginning. It is beginning-less and endless. It is timeless. It is space-less. It is bodiless. It is mindless. It is no thing. Yet, it is the essence in which everything appears and disappears. That is what you really are.

311

You are beginning-less, endless, unborn. What a blessing!

B – Blessings

My dear friend Bruce, a man in his 80s who spent most of his life in wheelchair after polio, realized the truth in the conceptual framework of Christianity. With heartwarming authenticity, in most gloomy, rainy days he calls to rejoice, because this is the day the Lord has made. The Lord is always present and Bruce is always aware of the Lord's presence. He is blessed with presence-awareness. He takes no credit for remembering God but is immersed in gratefulness for that fact.

However dualistic the division between Lord and Bruce seems to be — split between omnipotent omnipresence and its admirer — Bruce is abiding in the natural state. The narrative is full of bliss, love and gratitude. He sings in the shower and says grace before meals. He gives thanks for abundance and asks for blessings for everyone he knows and loves. And he loves everyone he knows. He never asks for himself, for he is acutely aware that that grace is being showered upon him constantly. Bob and I feel blessed for Bruce's prayers for us.

Is love for Life any different than love for the Lord? It may be different in the form it expresses, but "By their fruits you will know them". Bruce has no fear of dying, for his life belongs to the Lord already and there is no-one to resist when the Lord comes to claim it. Bruce doesn't need to teach or convert me, for he can see how my heart sings with him the hymn of glory for the miracles of Life.

I told Bruce once that my human adventure is seen now as a story of good fortune and luck. He reframed it gently, "I'd say it is Grace, not luck. You are not lucky but blessed, it is God's plan". How gorgeous! Who would ever dare to challenge beautiful faith like his and what for? This type of an overlay of narrative brings up the most precious qualities of love, gratitude and joy. There is warmth and sparkling loveliness to this way of consciousness' dancing life.

Jesus is very much with us when I visit Bruce. He is as real as the walls in the house. We both feel him and love his presence. There is an open 'YES' felt in my heart to this interpretation of space. When I leave Bruce's house, I leave Jesus there. Jesus and Bruce disappear and my motorbike shows up to take me back to Bob.

In no way is my view or Buddha's understanding more precious than Bruce's. God abides in him as him, undeniably. In the love affair between emptiness and form, father-sky (spirit) and mother earth (body), what a blessing this manifested world is!

> **Bob:** *Count your blessings, they say. Notice the goodness, the beauty, the love. Look around, you may just start seeing it everywhere. Get yourself out of the way and you will see greatness and miracles everywhere.*

World views, interpretations, choices of values and meanings are transient and updateable, provided the universe conspires towards it. The Holocaust survivor who life moved to feel lucky and grateful will have different experiences to one who pursues vengeance and remains bitter. Absence of forgiveness may locally seem like a worse experience, but in the long run it may affect more people, raise awareness, change history and delay the next holocaust. Life's intelligence is immeasurable.

So, no judgement is ever true; the process of making choices is recognized as improvisation by life. Reframing your outlook on reality is beyond our interest. To see, to recognize (and therefore disbelieve) certain tendencies is enough to alleviate its consequences as psychological suffering.

> **Bob:** *There is a famous quote by Dale Carnegie, "Two men looked out from prison bars; one saw the mud, and the other — stars".*

If Life moves you to experiment with re-programming the body-mind, remember to give credit to Life. You are that Life embodied!

B – Being Embodied - E X E R C I S E

Please sit in a relaxed posture for a few minutes. Focus an attention on your feet. Feel them, feel the throbbing life energy inside and feel the touch when they meet the surface. Ask yourself, am I these feet? Am I in these feet? Are they me, myself? Is the sense of 'I' located in them? Had I lost them, would I be diminished in any way? When they get numbed or forgotten, am I less because of that?

You remember, you call them 'my feet', so they are not you. They are yours. The sense of 'I am' is not located there. Notice how the experience of feet touching the ground is just one sensation, not two.

Please examine your whole legs in the same way. Feel them; feel your ankles, your knees, the muscles in your calves and your toes. Feel the life in them. Ask yourself, "Am I in these legs? Am I these legs? Am I experiencing the world from this location? If I had no legs, would the sense 'I am' diminish? When I don't feel them or don't focus on sensations in them, am I less of myself?"

Please experiment with your arms in the same way. Look at your hand and feel it. "Am I in this hand? Is the sense of I located there? I call it 'my hand', so it is something that I have, not something that I am. When I get my arms numbed or too relaxed after intense workout, is there less or more of the sense of me?" No? Know it for certain.

Check the same with your back and your chest, stomach and inner organs. Are you in your left lung? Are you your left lung? If your lung was to be transplanted, would the sense of presence change? Check in your head, ears, nose and lips. If you were to have plastic surgery, would you stop being you?

Confidence might go up or down depending on the result, but the sense of presence, aliveness — would that change with a change of face? Does the sense of presence change when you put on a wig, makeup or suntan? Does the sense of presence depend on your height or skin colour?

> **Bob:** *Children tend to ask adults whether they would still be themselves if they had different parents. They intuitively know the answer, they are pretty close to it still. They know the sense of presence doesn't depend on the looks or age of the vehicle of expression, the body. They would have a different look, but they would still be themselves, the 'I am'.*

When you were little, your body, your thoughts and your self-concept were different, but you knew you were you. You know innately you are the same you, even though the costume is different. You may also have noticed that the sense of presence is not ageing with the body.

I had many dreams in which I had a different body. At times I had a glimpse of it in a mirror. I had the body of an animal or a male body but it was always 'I' having it, wearing it.

If that sensationless sense of presence is independent of the shape and form of the vehicle, could you sense the presence in other bodies? Would that be any different 'tasteless sense' of presence (being)? Could you sense the presence of the tree? Would that be any different than the being of a cat, a sky or a rock?

Please find out for yourself. Wipe yourself out of the way and be present with what you see and play. Embody other bodies. It is all you. You are the totality. Nisargadatta suggested starting from touching index finger and thumb and interchanging between what you call feeler and felt. Make your thumb the feeler experiencing your index finger for a moment. Than change and make you index finger experience you thumb.

This experiment is not essential, it is just a bit of fun that relaxes rigid thinking and bodily identification. It is fun to sense the being of the ocean, flower, rock, ant, your dad... If you taste any differences, imagination has crept in. That's okay too, nothing is wrong. You didn't become anything you imagined or sensed, being is changeless.

B – Being vs. Becoming

Bob: If you are seeking truth, God or whatever you like to call it, I suggest that you start with the only reality you are absolutely certain of: that is, the fact of your own BEING. I'm talking about the feeling, not a thought 'I am'.

There is a sense of presence; knowing that you are. There is a presence of awareness here now. That is the only reality we are absolutely certain of. Nobody can truthfully say 'I am not'. Even to say it, they would have to BE there first. That knowing is constantly and ever with us, and that is why we say that what you are seeking, you already ARE.

Bob likes to play with the word 'Presence', pointing out its origin could be PRE-SENSE. It means "Being preceding senses", prior to any sensation. For any content to appear, the capacity of being has to come first. In it, thought or sensation (scene, sound, scent etc.) is known.

Can you be certain of anything at all except for the simple fact of being? What else is certain? Let's look at an idea: "I'm a human being".

Is that an experience? If you close your eyes and feel how it is to be you, is there anything 'human' about it? What does it even mean? Isn't it just somebody else's belief that you acquired or learned? Who told you that? Did you ever question this concept? What is true without this conditioned thought, memory, image of being the body?

Bob: You put all these labels on yourself and the worse one is "After all I'm ONLY human". You call God

"Supreme being", you call yourself a "Human being".
Take away these labels 'supreme' and 'human' and
try to separate anything in that being right now. Are
you separate from God (or whatever you like to call
it) without that label?

Unless you take a thought, can you say anything at all of what
or who you are? When you exclude and question every other
possibility, you will know that being is the only thing that can
be known directly and without learning or believing somebody
else's thought. And it is the only fact that can be trusted. The
Absolute Truth is the fact of your own being. In the timeless
eternity of now, this is what we call Reality. The conceptual
future where the body will be no more is only imagined now.

Bob: Being is not becoming or was-ing, or will-being.
To become something or someone you need future,
you need time. But what is time? Can you show me
time right now? Time is mind only. Without the mind
there is no time. Without the thought there is no past
or future. It is the immediate moment now. In this
moment what you are is all.

There is no need to become realized or enlightened.
Everything is already here. Being is already here. Realization is
a recognition of it. This goes with the recognition of no need
for this moment to be any different. To see the completeness
of this moment now, and to drop any agenda of trying to fix it,
alter, modify or correct it, is enlightenment.

Bob: There is only being, there is no becoming. There
is no future, only in thoughts. Mind can't grasp it, so
it creates all sorts of stories, afterlife, heaven and hell
or reincarnation. For the mind it is always becoming,
instead of being. It is becoming something else in

some projected future time. There is no future time to
become in. The actuality is right now.

'Becoming' is a valid term for communication in the appearance. Body-mind becomes proficient in driving with the experience in time. The pregnant woman becomes a mother; the teenager becomes an adult, and then elderly and then a corpse. It is only the self-realization which is beyond time, beyond mind, beyond becoming, beyond building up and gathering experience. There is no 'I' there to become some better or brighter 'I'. It is a realization of no self: realization which is not happening through the 'I' but in complete absence of it.

Bob: *If you don't START from being THAT already, you may try 'becoming' THAT. The idea of 'becoming' sets up the future, the need for effort, the path. It also reinforces the doer, the goal, the desire.*

Being is an ultimate truth. Being this or that is a belief, illusion. A moment ago you might have been hungry (believing you are the body) or sad (assuming the being of person or ego). Becoming happens in the space of being. Being seemingly becomes something or someone. Being, Emptiness, becomes form. But does it stop being?

An actor becomes the hero or the villain. Screen becomes the story. Becoming is a dance in the manifested dream. Becoming is an expression of being. Becoming is like a cloud appearing on the sky, formed of the sky. Becoming is an illusion. Being is reality. Nisargadatta was told to stay with the being and in three years the clarity unfolded. Abiding in Being is bliss.

B – Bliss

There is a possibility of simply being undistracted, being like a sky, being this space of seeing, hearing, tasting, touching, smelling... Being open, empty, still, silent space. Sat-Chit-Ananda. In that Being there is an obviousness that we are — and a subtle bliss/joy. There is a contentment in conscious being — wordless recognition that there is nothing wrong.

Without the thought telling us that something should or could be better, Life is. Love is. On that pure screen of awareness, everything appears. In the space of seeing, forms appear. In the space of hearing, there are sounds. All content comes into play in changeless, blissful stillness.

Yet, this is not the way we expect Bliss to be, right?! We are waiting for pleasure beyond measure! I did... It was my bait. It was to be eternal or at least long lasting. Contrary to common sense and simple every day experience, ecstasy was to be detectable for the senses — even if its level were constant. This would somehow also not cause the brain to shut down due to severe serotonin shock. Additionally, I believed that the background of its opposite wasn't necessary to define it.

I love how wrong I was! What a sweet dream to wake up from to even sweeter, subtler truth! All is as it is. Blissful in its tastelessness. The way body-machine is constructed, projected pleasure wouldn't be detectable anyway if it was constant and the brain survived it. It would fade to the background and become invisible, like space. Strong smells and loud noises also turn into undetectable background when we are exposed to them for long enough. This is the same for the stillness, which is the true subtle bliss. It has only been misconstrued by the imagination to be something overwhelmingly pleasurable, like an everlasting orgasm.

True Bliss which is beyond thought, feeling and sensation is never far away. Just withdraw the attention from all distractions and wait in your heart. It will shine forth.

Bliss or Love (which is your essential nature) may seem to forget itself; it hides from itself and longs for itself. Recognize and discard distractions and it is there — here — in every breath.

B – Breath

Bob: When you breathe in, you inspire, when you breathe out, you expire. Let the thought ride on the breath. Every new breath can be inspiration. Old thought may be exhaled. Let it go with the outgoing breath.

This suggestion often works literally. Many people have developed trust in Bob's pointers so on hearing the instruction to breathe out that painful thought, they simply follow it. "But, Bob, they did this to me!" Breathe it out. With new breath a fresh and new thought will come. It may be similar, but it is new. Breathe it out. Exhale. It expires.

In Hinduism they call it 'prana', meaning life force or vital principle. In the Bible's Book of Genesis, God made man of clay and breathed life into him. In the Judaic and Christian traditions breath means spirit. In various traditions of meditation it is akin a bridge between matter (body) and

321

consciousness. It seems to be voluntary and controllable to a certain extent, and automatic when no intervention is made.

Breathing exercises can alkalize the body and create various experiences, including temporary bliss. They can also unlock and heal certain traumas. Breath is used as an object of focus in mindfulness training. It changes while singing or chanting. It is instantaneously affected by any change in psychophysical state. It is easily detectable and therefore helpful in breaking the pattern of thinking.

Simply switching attention from distressing thoughts to the breath establishes one in the immediacy of perceiving rather than in the mental activities of interpretation and internal discourse. Breath can also revitalize, energize and supercharge the body. There were cultures in which breath was used to energize visions in order to actualize them.

> **Bob:** *Energy comes into the body through the breath and goes out through the breath. This energy goes all through the body to the ends of your toes and fingers. It also radiates out to all those around you. It shines out of your eyes.*

A similar simple 'trick' I heard Bob recommending to people was to use this reminder, which is like a mantra: "In the mind, no mind; in the thought no thought". Who repeats this mantra? Life, of course. There is no one else. It may seem like there is a little human in charge who has control and who chooses to repeat that mantra or to remember to exhale, but there isn't actually anyone there.

It is just that same brilliant illusion which makes the sea and sky look blue even though there is really no blueness there whatsoever.

B – Blue

Please remember these powerful metaphors every time you see the colour blue. It is relatively rare in nature, but it is abundant above your head when you are outside in day-time. Look upwards every once in a while. Vastness and spaciousness brings about the metaphor of the basic screen but the colour blue has special significance. It reminds us about the illusion.

> **Bob:** *Sky appears to be blue when you look at it. You do know that it is not blue. Sky is only space. When you get up in an airplane at thirty thousand feet with space all around you, it is still clear and empty: the blue is always further out. Blueness doesn't come in through the windows, does it? We understand that it is not really blue, but we will still see it as the same blueness. ...But you know full well the truth about it.*

In the English language, the word 'blue' can be used to mean 'sad'. If I say, I'm blue, or I'm feeling blue, I'm pointing at depression. However, it is the 'me' that is the cause of this apparent sadness or blueness, and this cause is fictitious.

> **Bob:** *There is a perception of the blue sea. It appears blue. You can't help but see it this way. But if I told you, go down and get me a bucket of blue water out of the sea, what would you answer me? You'd say, don't be stupid, you know all too well the water is not blue. It is clear: you have seen it many times. You have investigated it. ...But it doesn't stop appearing this way.*

> *That 'me' is an image also. That is like the blue sea and the blue sky. You have got to see through that idea, too.*
>
> *It is what Christ meant when he said: "Know the truth and the truth shall set you free". No matter how it appears, you know the truth about it. There seems to be a 'me', but it is an appearance only — just like a rainbow; just like a mirage; just like the blue sky.*

The sense of 'me' is just like the blueness of water and air. They are transparent and only appear blue. The 'me' is also transparent; it only appears to have this strange flavour of contraction, dissatisfaction and incompleteness.

Presence is clear as well, it is pure existence, knowing of being. It is not 'me being' but being. 'Me' is seemingly colouring the Presence. 'Me' is like the seeming blueness of the sky, which is not real: it is not blue, it is not even there. But look! It still appears so! What a beautiful, brilliant illusion!

B – Brilliance and Beauty

Bob likes to call it Intelligence Energy: the energy that makes everything alive, vibrant and tangible. This energy flows and changes with great creativity and wondrous intelligence. This Intelligence expresses itself through patterns and as patterns of incredible variety and complexity!

There is the beauty of the night sky; the brilliance of planets revolving around suns; the wonder of tides, currents, tsunamis, winds, clouds, plants and insects; and the genius in how bacteria and worms decompose life into minerals that fertilize the soil to promote more life! There is the incredible continuous symphony of bodily systems and the miraculous functions of the sense organs and their relationship with thought. Indescribable intelligence suffuses every particle of creation. This intelligence knows what a particular form needs for its survival. It equips tigers with stripes and birds with wings. It brings about the colours on a peacock's tail and gives dogs an incredible sense of smell.

It shapes itself as the reasoning capacity in humans. It gives them the ability to remember stories and compose new ones. It enables them to form societies; farm lands; create new species of animals to work for them and feed them; create means of communication (verbal and non-verbal); build complex structures (physical and intellectual); and to invent gods, devils and even separate selves through the power of imagination. Their lives are complex, multidimensional and abundant in relationships with other humans, animals, plants and things; as well as ideas, institutions, opinions, preferences.

The brilliance of this diverse and complex arrangement is undeniable and hard to be overlooked. Beauty is in the eye of the beholder. This world is a reflection of 'I Am', and in it there is a beauty and greatness for anyone to see. When I look into the sky, I'm looking into a mirror. Sky is my reflection. Ocean is my reflection. So, too, though, is all the wildness of erupting wars and pandemics. It is the flow finding its balance, even if that means ice-ages or the implosions of whole solar systems; or the emotional floods and fires experienced by 'my inner child'.

> **Bob:** *If the planet was to explode right now and everything would turn into dust, there would be nothing lost, not one particle would be missing, because energy cannot be destroyed; it remains: embodied or bodiless.*

B – Bodiless Being – E X E R C I S E

Investigate: Without thought (or mental image), and only in your direct sensory experience, do you have a body at all? Let's start from the face. Please close your eyes for a while and move aside any image you may have of your face. Notice what is present, what is the content of awareness when the eyes are closed and thinking/imaging is paused or put aside, unattended.

There may be some buzzing life vibrating, or some other sensation there. Rather than 'there', though, it really is 'here', right here — the same 'place' where the knowing of it is. Sensation may intensify with the movement of muscles, which may bring back the image of the face. This picture would only come from memory, from the reflection we remember seeing in the mirror or captured in pictures. But if we park it aside and take the label 'face' off it again, what do we find?

Now, please try to sit with no thought, image or label of the face but with the eyes open. Please make sure there is no reflection of your body available anywhere. Don't look at anything specific, just investigate what's immediate. What is the experience of the face without having a mental image or reflection to reference?

What is the experience of the source of seeing if you don't project any eyes that are doing it?

Where is the seeing coming from?

What is it that is seeing?

How does it feel behind the eyes?

How much of your faceless body can you see?

There is no need to conceptualize or describe; experiencing is all. We won't find face in the direct experience anywhere. In fact, we find no head. I used to entertain myself with drawing what I see of my body — sitting crossed-legged while driving the ship for long hours from mighty controllable super-chair. This is long before I heard about nonduality. Those drawn to drawing often discover it too.

> **Bob:** *Douglas Harding is the one who came up with and described the idea of "the headless way". I found it very simple, very clear and very direct, so I helped to organize his visit in Melbourne when he was still around. We really got along, he was a beautiful, humble man with great sense of humour. He was 98 when he died in 2007!*

My eyes are open right now and I see the edges of my glasses. When I look down, I see fragments of my torso and where my arms and legs are sticking out of it. Looking is coming from where I used to project the image of my face. It is the wide open window of my gaze; a window of seeing with blurred edges. I cannot see my face. All I know is the pulsation of life. I can see the tip of the nose at times, but without the label, it is just some shape and colour. I can feel a sensation which comes with the image of my lips touching each other. There is also tension which comes with the word 'jaw'. This appears in the open space where one is projecting the head or the face.

In the same way, other sensations come with images interpreting, explaining and narrating the meaning of them. There is sensation here (always HERE), which labelling translates to weight on the chair and the texture of the seat, but without the mental overlay it is just one sensation being known, not two. There is no chair and no bottom on it: there is just one inseparable buzzing in the field of awareness. There is just the content of being-knowing; just sensation — here.

When I look ahead, in my direct sensory experience, I have no body in the same way as I have no face or head. I am that being-knowing, and every sensation here is a passing phenomenon appearing in what I am, being-knowing. Experiencing goes on, ever changing in the immovable background of 'I Am'.

If you still feel like you are having a body or being a body, let's experiment further. Pause and see what your first-hand experience is. Without the thought or mental image from memory — are you male or female? Is your body male or female without the concept? Please notice the difference between direct sensing and thinking.

Is your skin fair or dark without the image or thought of comparison? Can you say anything about it? In your direct experience, do you have skin unless you apply a thought?

Without the story, are you single or married right at this instant? Are you a daughter or son, a wife, a father or an employee? Are you even human without the concept, idea or image?

Pause for a moment and see what you know about this body without past learning. Stop thought and see if you even have the body or if you are the body without taking a thought. See what is true without the narrative, the mechanical commentary. Don't go with the story, with what thoughts are telling you, figure out what is the reality without believing. Strip off the belief and see.

B – Belief

Does Ocean know itself to be an ocean displaying waves? Does the dog know itself to be a dog? No. They just are. Thought is required to know things but not the fact of being. The fact of being doesn't depend on thought. It is known directly.

How do I know to be a person? Somebody must have told me that and I innocently believed it... Would I still know myself as a person without that belief? With no thought or label, what would I be? What am I without my story? I was being in a baby's body once, with no ideas or identification. I had no beliefs. I had no cares or concerns and life was looking after all my body's needs.

> **Bob:** *The root cause of all your problems is A BELIEF that you are a separate entity, an individual, a person. This is just a belief. Check up your dictionary definition of belief. Belief is an unquestioned acceptance of something In the ubsence of reason — acceptance of an alleged fact without positive knowledge or proof.*

It has not been questioned! Something has been alleged. When you look at some of those alleged beliefs and question them, they will fall apart under investigation; they won't stand up. The false cannot stand up to investigation.

What do you believe to be true? You know that you exist, you know that you are. This is not a belief, but experiential certainty. Without any thought (belief) you still are. Without thinking, Being is. The bodily senses are working. There is seeing, hearing, tasting, touching and smelling. There is no thought about 'me' being the doer of sensing, so things just are. Things are and are known non-conceptually.

But what do you believe about yourself and about the world? Do you still believe you (as the body-mind) and the world are separate things? Do you know it to be a functional belief, or you are taking it to be reality?

Specifically, what do you believe to be true about you and the world? Do you believe in science or other religions? Do you believe in the past? Do you believe you are deficient, limited or incomplete? Do you need fixing or should you be different, better, more deserving? How did you come to believe that? Do you believe you are any of the roles you play or costumes and masks you wear?

Do you believe in other separate people? Do you believe there is a 'you' who has these concepts? Do you feel you choose them? Do you believe you know what thoughts or feelings other people have? Do you believe you know what their concepts about you are? Do you think you know how it is to be clear, realized or enlightened? Do you believe there is something to get? Do you believe in future? Do you think you know you are not That just yet?

What are your beliefs, rules and conditions that you may think need to be met for you to know you are That? How did you get them?

How about belief in the existence of a chair or any other inanimate object? Do you believe you know what anything is? Do you believe you know what they are for?

What do you know that is original and completely 'yours', as opposed to learned from other people (or understood using such knowledge)? Who told you so? What do you believe about things? What stories, associations, meanings? Just notice, without dwelling. What are you covering the mystery with?

Do you believe that you and this thing are separated by space? Do you believe you are the witness, the subject, the seer and that this is the witnessed/object/seen? Who told you so? Who/how would you be without these beliefs?

> **Bob:** *People used to believe that the Earth was flat, but they have investigated and found it is not so. All sorts of beliefs they had about evil forces which now we call bacteria or viruses. But not many investigate that idea of being body or mind. Why? Belief in this apparent 'I' is the cause of all your problems.*

Everything behind the words 'I Am' is a belief — an unquestioned allegation taken to be fact. Once they are known for what they are, beliefs are benign and there is no reason to avoid using them in communication. The whole world is collectively believed into existence and sustained by these beliefs. Body is a belief, disease is a belief and the cure for the disease is a belief. They are not chosen but pre-conditioned. Some can be undone and others won't.

Medical, dietary and scientific discoveries are experiments affected by the presence of observer's expectations, so they are technically beliefs actualized — not discoveries of things which existed before the observers named them. The placebo effect is an example of supportive belief. Nocebo is akin to the virus of the mind. As an example, Life expressing as Bob and I shares a belief in Vitamin C as an immune support and anti-constipation agent — and it serves us well, even though we know it is part of the dream, illusion.

We didn't invent or choose that particular belief. We discovered it there, acquired by some kind of resonance. We have questioned and recognized it as a belief. There is no intention to do anything about it. There is no-one to do anything about it and no such need. It is very handy and we are grateful for the effect it produces in (believed into existence) bodies.

The dream is known to be the dream and embodied characters are playing along with the illusion, flowing with life, choicelessly. Bob is Life playing Bob and enjoying itself. It knows it is a play but it doesn't spoil it because that's the game. There is just Life. We could guess that if the body wasn't believed into existence, the world couldn't be projected into being. They are interdependent. We could speculate: without them, experiencing and expression would not be here.

Some beliefs, like these in Santa Claus and the Tooth Fairy are no longer available to us. Belief in the little man in the head is no longer available to the Life in us. Belief in an ego narrating, choosing thoughts and "driving this bus" had dropped away. There is only Life and I Am That. Life in others may still experience some 'buts'...

B – But. Because

> **Bob:** *People may be open to some pointer — really receive it and get some shift in perception — and then they begin with their doubts: "But what about..." or "Oh yes I've seen it and understand it, BUT..."*

An often recurring concern is the future. People say, "I see it now, BUT when I leave this room..." Or, "It is easy now, BUT what about when I'm at home or at work, where I'm bullied? How can I remember then?" Or, "It is easy here, BUT there are hungry children in Africa..."

Questions and doubts like these seem reasonable and valid. So, it may sound dismissive when we say that nonduality pointing is "not about then and them". It is about present recognition, here. 'Then' you may or may not remember (it largely depends on habits of attention). It will be evident when 'then' is now.

Right now is the time to be tuned in to the clarity and certainty of being. Now is the time to be grounded rather than conceptualizing hypothetical situations in an imaginary future. When present recognition is habituated, it is more likely that 'then' will get resolved from that habituated recognition.

> **Bob:** *We don't realize what we do in that. We immediately leave the immediate, the pure resonance, and move into some conceptual idea or image of what we think it should be or what we would like it to be. This resonance is what pointing is all about. The spiel is not for the logic to learn. Don't trade this immediate recognition for thoughts of 'ifs and buts'!*

333

Trying to understand nonduality with WHY-questions and BECAUSE-answers is missing the point. 'Whys' and 'what-ifs' and 'becauses' are valid in the appearing world and useful — helpful in many fields of life. Conceptualisation is to be honoured and appreciated as part of the miracle — but it won't help to recognize this open space of being beyond the mind. In fact, it will cloud it and veil it from recognition.

The WHY-question invites the mind into the picture. Mind is a creative tool and it improvises an answer if none is readily available in memory. BECAUSE gives excuses and justifications, also from this creative improviser mind (think-ING).

> **Bob:** *Did you ever smoke cigarettes? Yes? So what did you do with the butt? You threw it away, didn't you? When the cigarette is consumed, the butt is thrown away. Consume, digest the pointer and throw away the BUT. Stay in the immediacy. Give it a chance, it is not boring.*

B – Boredom

Boredom (as I understood and imagined it) used to be one of my greatest fears. For a ship's officer on the ocean, it meant careful preparation for every trip. Devices, chargers, batteries, options to read, listen, write, paint... I used to think about the future, plan future activities and fear potential future boredom. I used to plan it and fear it more than I planned for or feared for the challenges of my actual super-demanding job! Upon realizing that fear in my early 30s, I had to face it. Meditation training was a must.

In conventional usage of the word, boredom is a state experienced when an individual is left without anything in particular to do; is not interested in the immediate surroundings; or feels that a day or period is dull or tedious. The opposite of being bored is being entertained. Boredom has been associated with increased drug and alcohol abuse, overeating, depression, anxiety and an increased risk of making mistakes. Boredom is often conceptualized as "the aversive experience of wanting, but being unable to engage in any satisfying activity". It is clearly a resistance to what is. It is a subtle desire for this moment to be different, more pleasant, more entertaining.

When I sat my first Vipassana, I found no boredom to face. Practise was demanding and kept me very busy. Further, meditating in many sanghas, ashrams and monasteries dispelled this fear completely. Boredom was nowhere to be found. For me, it existed only as a concept, only in the imagination. The so-called inner world was as rich and juicy to explore as the outer one. My love affair with pure being-ness started. Even though the meditation practise has dropped away with the meditator, that love shines forth ever strong.

Bob: They say, "Face your fear of death and the death of fear is certain". Face your fear of boredom. Go into your fear and amplify it. The worst that can happen is that you faint. Allow yourself to faint and it may not even be the case. These imaginary psychological fears can be easily dispelled and be rid of. Once dispelled, what is left? Call it the unborn, or Buddha Nature, if you like.

B – Buddha Nature

Buddha-nature is just another label for the same. It is also a philosophical concept used by wise scholars. It may help to illustrate the difference between direct knowing and intellectual dividing, distinguishing and grasping.

"Buddha nature" is a term used to refer to the indescribable realm or ultimate substrate, also called the womb or embryo (tathāgatagarbha and buddhadhātu): the luminous nature of pure, undefiled or "unborn" mind. It is considered the natural and true state of the mind; an emptiness that is a non-implicative negation (Madhyamika).

Sometimes Buddha nature is described as a true or original self, and sometimes it is said that everyone 'has' Buddha nature. Every sentient being — even insects — either have or are Buddha nature, depending on the sect and its language of pointing. The seed of Buddha means consciousness; the cognitive power; the seed of enlightenment.

According to the Lotus Sutra, all living beings possess Buddha nature. Buddha nature is understood to be completely present but obscured by our delusions. However, an essence or element that beings possess makes it something like a self-essence, and this puts the principle at odds with another important Mahayana teaching: shunyata, or emptiness. Shunyata says that all things are empty of any self-essence. In the Mahāparinirvāṇa Sūtra Shakyamuni Buddha said, "Living beings are all Buddha nature. The Tathagata is continuously abiding and not subject to change".

Certain schools proclaim that Buddha nature is a potential to be developed via rigorous practise and discipline. Buddha nature is a topic often placed within the philosophy of the "third turning of the wheel of dharma". In the first turning, all is a process, with emphasis on renunciation and the refutation of the illusory self (associated with personal identity). In the second turning, all is empty; it is a union of emptiness and compassion but not a nothingness. Mind is inseparable from the qualities of transcendence, therefore, in the third turning of the wheel of dharma, all is luminous and radiant. Clarity restores immediate experiencing, free from the adventitious techniques of analysis that were utilized in the traditions of the first and second turnings.

The Tibetan Buddhist traditions employed useful pointers such as "empty of self" and "empty of other". According to the Dzogchen-teachings, the Buddha-nature has three qualities: 'essence' (oneness or emptiness), 'power' (universal compassionate energy), and the fact that it is unobstructed.

Zen Buddhism is a mixture of Indian Mahayana Buddhism and Taoism. It began in China, spread to Korea and Japan, and became very popular in the West from the mid-20th century. The essence of Zen is attempting to understand the meaning of life directly, without being misled by logical thought or language. Not much is said about flavour-less ungraspable realm beyond the mind.

Another B-label for ineffable reality is the Hindu term Brahman.

B – Besides on B

B – Brahman

Brahman is the oldest known Hindu label for the One: the whole and only reality underlying all phenomena; a stateless state that defies the limited conceptions of existence and nonexistence. Everything else, including the universe, material objects and individuals, is false. Brahman signifies the infinite, omnipresent, omnipotent, incorporeal, impersonal, formless, transcendent reality that is the divine ground of all Being.

Brahman is also described as Neti-Neti, meaning "not this, not this", because it cannot be correctly portrayed as this or that. It is the origin of this and that, the origin of forces, substances, all of existence, the undefined, the basis of all, unborn, the essential truth, unchanging, eternal, the absolute. Brahman is also beyond the senses: attempting to perceive it is akin to a blind man trying to correctly describe colour. It is the basis of the material world, which in turn is its illusionary transformation. Brahman is not the effect of the world. The Upanishads (commentaries on the Vedas) call it the eternal, conscious, irreducible, un-locatable spiritual core of the manifested universe that is marked by finiteness and change.

B – Background. Basic screen

This pointer is another metaphor attempting to bring attention to that which 'is' always here: the substratum or base presence required for anything to exist. Without 'it', nothing is. Yet, in itself, it cannot be viewed as existent or existing. It can be hinted at through language but it isn't perceptible by the senses. It cannot be experienced but it also cannot be negated or denied. It may seem to exist conceptually since there is a word used, but it cannot really be imagined, because imagination only works in limitation and relativity.

What is imagined, is not it. It doesn't have shape, form or colour to exist objectively or as a thing. It is not IT. To turn toward the alive wakefulness of presence, or the most basic sense of 'I am', is to turn toward it. But it is not located in the body. It is not sourced by corporeal brain.

B – Brain

Medical science tells us that the brain is an organ of soft nervous tissue which is contained in the skull of vertebrates, and which functions as the coordinating centre of intellectual and nervous activity. This practical-for-daily-use definition has its own applications and implications. Brain surgery or brain damage can extensively affect personality!

But what is the direct experience? Can you experience your brain? You were told you have it and by saying 'yes' you accepted it into being. Now it has an existence. So does every other brain in every other body. You accepted its role and function in explaining the universe. You credited it with conception of science, invention of future and past. Now you blame it for your nightmares.

Once believed so strongly, it is not an option of explanation anymore but a fact. Brain becomes real. The more attention is given to that version of the story, the more detail is being created, diseases named and cures searched for. There is nothing wrong with this picture! This version of agreed reality is quite amazing and certainly very successful in being incredibly convincing! Brain science is enchanting indeed!

Direct non-conceptual experience however doesn't contain having a brain. There is freedom in being able to alternate between the relative and ultimate perspectives. This happens spontaneously, without any doership or decision-making process. This is balance.

B – Balance

Balance is a state of equilibrium or equipoise; the equal distribution of weight, amount or value. It signifies mental steadiness or emotional stability; the habits of calm behaviour and proper judgment. It is also a state of bodily equilibrium. Balance is a right proportion between known and unknown, metaphorical black and white, warm and cold.

If we look at nature, in the long run it balances itself out. There may be ice ages and periods of global warming; implosions and explosions but, as a rule, energy seeks equilibrium. In the air-element, atmospheric pressure seeks to even up (causing winds); in the water element, rivers flow to level up; in the earth element (matter), force seeks the path of least resistance; and in the fire element, temperature always equalizes with the surroundings. It is a motion, a seeming process in the motionless space element.

Every contraction in human body is an energetic imbalance as well. Non-judgmental, curious, child-like attention directed towards the whirlpool in solar plexus, heartbreak or knot in the gut will even up the imbalance causing healing. The same applies to any call for attention, including bodily sensations sustained by negative narrative.

Natural balancing is instinctive, self-regulating and beyond control.

B – Before (Prior). Beyond.

This pointer is used for want of a better word and does not suggest time nor space. Bob doesn't use the word 'prior' to mean a certain time before. Bob is talking about registering prior to labelling; plain being before the thought 'I am'; space prior to content; awareness before consciousness. It is pointing to the 'underlying' factor.

When a book is printed, its pages with their content come out of the press simultaneously. We say that the blank page is prior, even though the book wasn't a book then. We say that blank awareness is more basic than the consciousness of things.

It is the very capacity to know — the necessary prerequisite. A page without print is possible, but print without a page is not. Consciousness appears in awareness like print in the book. There is no form without emptiness, there is no consciousness without awareness, and there is no labelling before registration.

'Beyond', within the context of nonduality, doesn't refer to a location in space, but to the necessary prerequisite, much like in the case of 'prior'. "Beyond the mind", "beyond words" and "beyond language" point to a non-location location that cannot be conceptualized or imagined. It is a metaphor.

B – Butterfly Metaphor

The butterfly metaphor is a beautiful illustration of self-transformation. Bob uses it to show that things often aren't what they seem to be and that all change can be a powerful force for growth and transcendence. The key is not fearing or fighting against it, but releasing the old to give way to the new. It may require effort, like the effort that is made by the butterfly to break free of its cocoon (which strengthens its wings in the process) so it can fly. Without self-centre or ownership, each effort is effortless.

Bob: Look at the caterpillar, the ugly colourless grub which, due to that innate intelligence, knows to build

341

the cocoon around itself and in it, it becomes a liquid, soupy substance. Transformation takes place and out emerges a beautiful butterfly or moth with all these colours on its wings. It died as a grub. It died to itself as that ugly form. It broke through.

B – Breakthrough

Breakthrough is defined as a sudden, dramatic and important discovery — a development or event that helps to improve a situation or provide an answer to a problem. This word is often used by seekers and therapists to indicate an insight they've had. It is also used to connote the realization of something profoundly deep.

If there was a single event that dispelled the whole illusion of self-identity, it is often called a breakthrough. Otherwise, small insights, soon forgotten, also get the same label. Language is where they belong.

B – Belong

In human psychology, belonging is defined as a need. It means the sense of fitting in or feeling like you are an important member of a group — especially with friends, family members or other sympathetic folks. Fitting in is helpful toward seeing value in life and in coping with painful emotions. The social ties that accompany a sense of belonging are a protective factor helping to manage stress, which we can even see in other tribal animals. When we feel we have support and are not alone, we often cope more effectively with difficult times in our lives.

With self-realization, when there is no one to belong and no longing to belong, that need is addressed in action rather than in a self-victimizing narrative. Some seekers report initially feeling isolated and lonely, having difficulty sharing their insights with people of other interests.

The more mature seeker (as well as the 'finder') will rather observe than preach (listening rather, and hearing the same life in others). Furthermore, there may be no urge whatsoever to communicate the nondual nature of reality to others. Abiding is often enough.

Recognizing this inherent sense of completeness does not need to result in obvious and irreversible change to the personality. However, when people begin to exhibit new or rare levels of joy and other desirable qualities, it naturally invites the curiosity and interest of others.

> **Bob:** *Initially, people may pull you out of clarity back into illusion but, once it stabilizes, they will see your light and come to you asking for what you've got. They will come to you rather than you going to them. They will see your benevolence.*

B – Benevolence

Once you realize there is nothing separate and apart from you, natural benevolence is a by-product. This is not to say that the body must then completely give up its survival mechanisms and that you will then reflexively turn the other cheek to anyone who hits you in the face. Such self-disinterested pacifism does sometimes occur but it is not a universal rule. Rather, benevolence towards sentient and insentient beings comes from recognition of the beauty and lovability of the dance. Rather than being lost in a self-obsessive narrative, things are merely registered by the senses. The silence/stillness/space — in which all phenomena manifest — is known and loved. It is known as the Beloved.

343

B – Beloved

Once the nature of everything is seen clearly as a reflection of No-Thing — which you, yourself, in truth are — everything is recognised as the Beloved. As Rumi said, "If the Beloved is everywhere, the lover is a veil, but when living itself becomes the Friend, lovers disappear". The lover of God, the worshipper of the Beloved, melts and merges into all-pervading space. Separation was only apparent.

In that oneness, nothing is lost. Neither is the story, the biography.

B – BONUS: Biography of BOB - E X A M P L E

This book would not be complete without at least a brief synopsis of Bob's extraordinary life story. Bob was born in the winter of 1928, and grew up during the Great Depression: the era of food scarcity and tension that would soon lead to another, even more devastating world war.

His father, a Gallipoli survivor, was a farmer in a small country town not far from Melbourne. His mother was a caring housewife and a loving and fair-minded matriarch to her four children. Bob had two older sisters, one younger brother and a few cousins. Uncle Arthur would often take the boys rabbit hunting and tree climbing to collect bird's eggs. As a kid, Bob had too much energy to sit in the classroom, so he struggled to receive eight years of (minimal) formal education.

Bob was still too young to join the army when WWII started. He was a teenaged boy stuck helping on the farm while his blood boiled with patriotic frustration. While picking fruit he met a lot of crazy people — alcoholics, dead beats, draft dodgers, traumatized war deserters and criminals on the run. They taught him to smoke, drink and fight (he needed to self-defend whenever he opened his mouth). In 1945, when he was 17 years old, he was finally able to join the navy and was sent to Japan with the occupational forces.

In 1948, after a couple of years on the destroyer Arunta, Bob was disciplinarily dismissed from the navy for drinking. It was for 16 years altogether — he was a no-hoper — a social outcast. To get money for a buzz he took many short-term jobs. He travelled with other drunks around the country working as a gun-shearer, seaman in the merchant fleet and a contractor at various construction sites and factories.

Eventually, however, his addiction left him unemployed and unemployable.

When Bob was in his early 30s, the Alcoholics' Anonymous program (still young and new in Australia) helped him stop drinking for a time. Still anxious and arrogant, Bob decided that he was cured and left AA after nearly a year of sobriety. It didn't take long before he was back on the streets — drunk.

Fortunately, though, a path out soon presented itself. Upon returning to his life-saving 12 step program in 1960, Bob was handed the book *Sobriety and Beyond* by an alcoholic priest. It was the author, Father Doe who pointed that some of us get a second chance in life. He also posed a challenging question: "How well will we use it?"

It was like a lightning strike in Bob's stomach, a turning point. In that moment, Bob realized that the only way to use his second chance in life was to find out who or what had given him this second chance. This faint idea initiated a relentless spiritual search. He was 32 years old when a couple of his fellows, whose own stories closely mirrored Bob's, took their lives. One had jumped out of a window and the other had shot himself.

As a committed seeker, Bob explored many spiritual paths and disciplines for another 16 years. He looked into various sects of Christianity first (Catholicism, Protestantism, the Salvation Army, Scientology, the Quakers and Christian Science). He then became interested in mystical Indian practices such as those taught by Paramahansa Yogananda, Maharishi Mahesh Yogi and Swami Muktananda.

The real game-changer, the end of the search occurred in April of 1976, when Bob met Śri Nisargadatta Maharaj in Bombay. Life has arranged for repeated synchronicities and "too many coincidences" to override Bob's deep loyalty to his 'kundalini guru'.

It happened at last when familiar Librarian in Bombay (as many had before) suggested he look through "I Am That". Bob opened it and the first lines he read resonated with him profoundly. Nisargadatta's address was written in the book and Bob went there immediately...

Life works in an amazing manner! Bob's decision to drop everything, leave Australia and lock himself in an ashram in India had come after the devastating heartbreak of having his beloved first wife, Barbara, leave him for another, wealthier man. Although a painful tragedy at the time, it proved to be a good fortune, as she returned to him a year later. Barbara also experienced transformational grace from this humble, ordinary, approachable, little great man, Nisargadatta Maharaj.

Back to April of 1976. Bob sat down on a wooden floor in a hot, tiny room filled with dense smoke from cigarettes and incense. A couple of young kids were crawling over the shoulder of a brown skinned man with no shirt on. Seven to eight other people sat around with devotional looks on their faces. Bob desperately needed answers to his burning questions, so he took place in front. Relying on translators, Bob and Nisargadatta would have many fiery but loving dialogues!

"You think you are this body, you think you are this mind, but are you? How could you be what you are aware of? You are not the body! You are not the mind!"

Bob: A-ha! Yes! I see now!

I've heard it before — many, many times — but now it strikes home! Somehow, now I know it to be true!

Of course! I'm not this body! I'm not this mind! Now there is clarity; certainty! Now I will never get trapped in the mind again!

"Who won't get trapped? Mind will continue to vibrate and when it carries on, you just look again, and again, until the habitual pattern falls away", translated Mullerpatan. Yet, as soon as Bob left the tiny room, he was back in the narrative.

It wasn't the same, though. He couldn't truly believe it anymore. He couldn't fully believe these thoughts. He looked again and there was nothing there, no one there. There was only freedom; peace; awareness of being.

Over the next 12 months, Bob took many fortnightly trips by bus and then train to spend a few days each time with the passionate Indian who quickly became his guide, mentor and dear friend. Profound insights were flowing through Bob, and he shared them out loud, but Nisargadatta continuously brought him back to non-conceptual space instead. He was pulling out everything from underneath Bob's feet. No word or description was good enough comparing to silence.

Maharaj used to 'blame' Bob for bringing many other grateful Westerners during these 12 months. On their last day, during a little farewell snack party that the guru arranged for Bob, they embraced with tears in their eyes. The connection and love between them grew solid and unshakable.

Back in Melbourne, in 1977, Bob wanted to shout the truth from the roof-tops, but very few could hear the message. These few formed a group and that group is still alive to this day. Just as cells in the body are replaced by new ones, so are members of the group. They would get some or complete clarity, leave, and then fresh new seekers would appear to replace them.

In the meantime, Life goes on in all its diverse dualism of interrelated opposites expressing. Bob spent a few more years with the seaman's union, which earned him the nickname 'Sailor' to comply with anonymity requirement in AA. Then he spent a few years on the agritourist farm, had couple of prospering health food stores after, and few other businesses with some losses and some gains.

Bob also persevered through various incidents, sicknesses, fires and floods. He always felt that Life was looking after him. Twice Bob and Barbara lost everything they had, and twice Life found another way to provide for them and return them to safety.

Clarity of understanding brought about a curiosity to find out how things resolve themselves, and to this day things continue to do so. Things turn around. Conflicts resolve. Long, debilitating sicknesses or weaknesses end. Feelings and thoughts change. It is indeed amazing!

Seeing patterns in life brings natural serenity and humility to human viewpoint and brings a sense of awe in the Space-like perspective. Seeing patterns in things from the immovable background of awareness of presence is a waking dream — an incredible dream which is all no-thing but which one still can't help but love.

Bob: The way in which life looks after this pattern called 'me' or 'Bob' is utterly amazing. Now, as the body is expected to fall apart, it brought Kat into my life, and she got me fit again and there is still joy and love regardless of the pains and aches of old age. It

349

will end one day and it doesn't bother me in the least.
What I am was never born and it can never die.

Bob is available for anyone who would like to connect over the phone or video call.

Epilogue: Kat's abbreviation of the acronym 'Sailor Bob'

S – Smooth sailing

Everything used to be about me. Because other people might think something bad about me or push me away, I didn't ask questions. Other people could talk about me behind my back or confront me, reject me, belittle me, so I felt invisible and acted as if I were. But I was still the most important person for myself, no matter how small and inadequate I felt inside. Quite early in life I discovered that others often feel the same way or worse, so I became a caring, giving person who was comforting and fun to be around. It was because I wanted something in return. I wanted to belong, I wanted love, appreciation, validation. Friendships would keep my fears quiet, I thought. Thrilling adventures, spiritual search and obsessive planning of more pleasurable options would keep me away from the unbearable void of self-doubt.

Now all there is — is just smooth sailing (passing occasional storms) — the seeming journey through time-space. Things come up, thoughts come up, the weather changes and feelings change, but there is no relating going on. Nothing is about me. The beautiful story unfolding for this body-mind is known in more details than other stories or other body-minds, but it doesn't make it more special or more important. What's beyond the story, where the story unfolds from, here I abide; from here I appreciate an appearance.

A – Appreciating an Appearance

It seems like this is what the dream is all about here. Once it is clear that *what appears to be* is transient, mortal and momentary (even if only on planetary scale), I cannot help but to appreciate it fully.

How well done it all is! How real it looks and feels! How amazing, complex and deep! How brilliant! What a way for this incredible Intelligence to see itself as other in so many forms, shapes and patterns... Life: magnificent movement of subatomic particles at the micro-scale, and the movement of galaxies at the macro scale. What a dance! The appearance is appreciated from its opposite, the No-Thing, the Cognizing Emptiness, the I Am.

I used to hate and fear certain things: noisy machinery, football, self-shaming, rejection, powerlessness, the poverty of others, sickness (suffering in general). Now nothing is wrong any more. Some things are less appreciated through this particular body-mind, but collectively everything gets appreciated in the appearance.

Bob is the pinnacle of appreciation here, the best mirror, the deepest mystery, the most marvellous miracle. But warm cherishing envelops the whole nature, space, colours, music, cats, chocolate and all stories and feelings.

351

Who I am, is not just this one body-mind: all bodies appear in me. I have many eyes and they are not only human. They are deep in the oceans and high in the sky. I am the Appreciation itself, innocent in temporary costumes.

I – Innocence in Individuality

I remember taking credit and feeling guilty for something I used to label as imperfect. Many of my dear friends still struggle with that. It may be their relationship with themselves, their bodies, spouses, jobs, health, finances, friends... anything. It was all of this for me only six years ago. Today I remember who we all are and remind others of their eternal innocence.

How could anyone voluntarily blame themselves for thoughts they did not choose to think? How could they shame themselves for circumstances that created habit patterns that act out spontaneously now? Thinking patterns were formed to serve at some point but got mechanical through unconscious repetition, of which there was no doer and no choice. It is all pure innocence. Intent behind every thought and behaviour is always prolific, positive.

I love how different and how complex every individual is! I appreciate the ability of life in every form to see and recognize its innocence once it is shown. This is because of innate wisdom. Deep down in our hearts, we know we are good. Life always wanted good, Life always 'chose' what seemed best in every given moment with the knowledge and viewpoint available back then.

I love the uniqueness and depth of every individuality, every story. I love the Intelligence shining behind it with its creativity, always new, never repeating itself (even in snowflakes or fingerprints). And even more so is no 'awakening story' ever the same. Once one 'is taken', it won't show up again, it need not be longed for.

L – Listening to Longing

Everything is love. Longing for love is knowing Love, it is a 'hide-and-seek' play. Shame is love (longing) for perfection of oneself. Guilt is love for goodness of actions and behaviours. Anger may be longing for safety, justice or power. Everything is Love in many different costumes. Longing shows up in the colourful dresses of Maya (illusion).

I hear longing for perfection, peace, beauty, wisdom, freedom, security, completeness, love... It all comes from innate knowing that there is perfection, peace, freedom, beauty, completeness, love... I listen to people's deepest longings to show them how it is already with them. I listen for longing to see the aspects they want to express and embody. I tell them the same things Bob says: "You are Already so! Recognize it now!"

In here the longing has quietly subsided but because everything is me, I can taste longing in its reflection in others. The sweetness of longing is immense; almost overwhelming. I deeply appreciate it.

I am what I was longing for so desperately and so intensely! You are what you are longing for. You possess the qualities you are longing for too. As Totality, everything is that already: it is very clear. Longing for connection, for eternity, permanence, efficacy, safety, significance... Longing for celebration of life, for fun, pleasures... It is all 'mine'; it belongs to one openness of Life.

O – One Openness

In that openness, everything is welcomed with attentive curiosity. Everything is allowed, accepted, appreciated. Nobody does it, it just is. It is heard. Received. Loved.

It hasn't always been like this. I knew so many things for sure and wasn't open to question them! Better than anyone, I knew what to eat, what the best diet, supplements and exercises were, what the right moral approach or correct interpretation of facts were. So, I felt solid and closed-minded about it. I knew what was right for some others as well. I knew what they were supposed to think, feel and do, so was I mercilessly converting and convincing them to agree with me. They were more open minded and willing to hear, and I saw this as a sign of weakness. How different things are now!

I love not knowing, not needing to know and staying open! I love hearing what others think is true and do nothing about it (unless requested). Open curiosity is such a yummy attitude! Recognized strong opinions and meanings have relaxed now.

R – Relaxed Recognition

There is nothing static about relaxed recognition, even though it is a glimpse of static background when distractions are gone. Recognition is always fresh, new, surprising and wordless. There is no permanent "recognized state" but only stateless being with recognition, moment to moment.

It shows up as a recognition of Love; appreciation of complexity and intelligence. It shines as a recognition of the dream playing out — of everything being nothing and yet still somehow showing up. It appears as a recognition that no one is seeing it and yet everything is seen. It dresses up as a recognition that forms are emptiness; and it is space dancing in all these magnificent shapes and colours. In this relaxed being, in this ordinary awareness, it flashes fresh and new in many different aspects. Sometimes it flashes daily, sometimes hourly. No one has preference either way. Beauty is undeniable.

B – Beauty of the Beloved

I'm referring to beauty beyond the duality of pretty-ugly. It is about the beauty of recognition. The colourful, magnetic belly-dance of Maya: mystical, sacred and hypnotizing. The shocking beauty of nature feeding itself by killing 90% of its offspring to enable survival up the chain. The extinction of species. The tragic beauty of falling civilisations. Ice-ages. Exploded stars. The heartbreaking beauty of lost hopes; abandoned children; exterminated bee-hives; horribly polluted oceans and sky...

Seeing it as Beauty inspires immense respect for the magnificence of the Expression. Beauty is beyond judgement, so death and suffering isn't evil here, it is the Beloved. As it is, it is perfect. It self-organizes.

Wherever the attention rests it meets the Beloved. It is in violence on the human scale as much as it is in the violence of white blood cells fighting the poor innocent bacterium who just wants to live also. It is in support for the environment saving movement and in the pain of its destruction. Every heart-break, every motive, every fact and every story: nobody is ever a doer anywhere. There is only Life, only Nature, and it is AS-IT-IS. The beloved No-Thing expressing as Beloved patterns and forms.

Because all is viewed through bodily eyes, there is filtering going on. Microbes are conceivable and imaginable but not visible to the eye. Some colours are. There is a habit of active looking out for Beauty going on. Bob sees beautiful buildings, cars and trees; I see beautiful flowers, faces and dresses. We share it and appreciate it together. I notice hundreds of points of beauty every single day. They are both, ordinary and outstanding.

O – Outstanding vs. Ordinary

To be fresh and new, Life flows, floats and vibrates. It shifts from outstanding to ordinary countless times every day. There is no judgement or preference to either.

B – Benevolence of Being

Benevolence is our natural state. The animal who is not traumatized, hungry or agitated due to seasonal conditions — who has safety and position assured — also shows signs of benevolence. Humans who do not live in their heads, who do not stress about what is not, are happier. Happy people tend to be naturally benevolent. Questioning the source of suffering brings back the joy of being. Sharing that joy increases collective benevolence.

The Spiel in questions for contemplation

1. Are you **trying** to **learn** or to **get** something here? Needing something new, exciting and entertaining? Are you looking for something you don't have yet? Or to **become** someone?

2. If the Reality is Sat-Chit-Ananda (as Hinduism calls it) — meaning existence (being), consciousness (knowing), bliss (loving to be or stillness), then aren't you already that **loving awareness of being** alive?

3. Can you **deny** your being? Can you try to **not be**? Wouldn't you have to be first to deny it?

4. Are you **unaware**? (Unconscious?)

5. Would you rather be dead now? If somebody puts a gun to your head, wouldn't you want to escape?

6. Aren't you THAT already? Aren't you? Are you?

7. If it is true what they say in ancient scriptures, that the Great Mantra (Mahavakya) means I Am That, wouldn't it be essential to look what the word 'THAT' represents? What is THAT in our language? What does it means? What does it point to?

8. What is **not** THAT?

9. What is a word (any word) after all? Is it anything other than **sound**, subtle vibration, a line of letters or symbols?

10. What is the **word** 'I' or 'me'? Is it who or what I am?

11. Were you born with any words?

12. How were the words acquired?

357

13. If Buddhism points to it as "non-conceptual, ever fresh presence awareness and nothing else (just this)", are you **not aware** of this presence right now? Are you not IT **already**?

14. **What else** do you expect if you hear they say, "Just this, nothing else?" Does it resonate?

15. Christianity points to three aspects called Omnipresence, Omnipotence and Omniscience: what do they mean?

16. Isn't 'Omnipotence' the TOTAL power? Is there any room for Higher Power, will-power, power of thought or power of any separate entity doing anything?

17. Is there any **other** power running the universe, moving planets, galaxies, cells and atoms and maintaining your body and thoughts?

18. Are you **doing** (do you have power to do) digestion or growing finger-nails and hair?

19. Are you doing the seeing or thinking? **How** do you do it?

20. Isn't 'Omnipresence' the TOTAL presence? Can 'you' be separated or excluded?

21. Isn't 'Omniscience' the TOTAL intelligence or TOTAL knowing?

22. Is any belief **ever** the actual? (For example: flat Earth, Santa Claus). Is that true when investigated?

23. What is a belief?

24. When we seek to become whole and complete (when we want liberation), who is that **for**? Who is the 'we' wanting it? Is there a personal self?

25. Is the 'Person' ever a reality? Where did that word 'person' come from? Doesn't it mean THE MASK in Latin (per-sona)? Isn't it a Mask of a concepts?

26. Isn't the conceptual image **based** in believed past? Isn't the past dead? Is there any freshness or newness in old memories?

27. Relating to the false image: what are you going to liberate yourself from?

28. What is to be realized?

29. Liberation is to be **from what**, and **for who**?

30. Do you still believe you **can** find the answer in the mind?

31. Do you think you can **get** peace of mind?

32. What is the nature of mind? What is mind apart from thought? Can it stop vibrating between opposites and still exist? Can it work in **any other way** than movement, vibration?

33. **What** is there when vibration ceases for a moment or is not attended to?

34. If there was an answer in thought, how long would that be valid for? Would that complete, fulfil or satisfy you truly and for good? Wouldn't you have to **hold on** to that thought all the time?

35. Why hasn't anybody found the answer in the mind yet?

36. Is the word the actual thing? Can the word 'water' make you wet or the word 'fire' burn you?

37. Is it any different with the rest of the words in the manifestation? Are they the real things or just symbolic representations? Do they have **any power**?

38. Is this **word** 'I' or 'me' even alive, as I am alive and conscious?

39. Isn't the manifestation a dream-like illusion projected and sustained by **the energy of belief** (attention)?

40. Is there **anything** permanent or static in the manifestation? Anything solid? Anything that doesn't change?

41. Do you have the same body you were born with?

42. Where is that **original cell** (formed from joined sperm and ovum dividing into a foetus) right now?

43. Did the body start at birth or conception; or much earlier? Could you say it started when your parents where eating food and breathing prana which enabled these cells to form? Or was it even earlier? Can you trace back **the beginning** of life spark?

44. What is the body anyway? What is it **made of**?

45. Are any of the elements in the body (air, matter/earth, fire/temperature, water, space) **separate** from the totality?

46. Can you separate yourself from water? (The body is mostly water! What would it be if you removed it (dried the meat) or stopped replenishing it?) Can you separate the body from air? (Can you vacuum it or stop replenishing by breathing?) Can you isolate solids, heat or space?

47. Can you live **without** any of the elements? Can you leave earth or space?

48. Can you function if you **stop exchanging** the elements with surrounding environment?

49. Isn't the body just a vibrating pattern of energy if you look closer, use tools like microscope?

50. When you break it down to elements, or further to subatomic particles, or to waves or to pure energy, isn't it as they say: **the no-thing**?

51. Isn't it the same with **every** form in this manifestation made of phenomena?

52. What is a phenomenon? How does the dictionary explain it? Isn't it that which only appears to be? Doesn't 'only appear' mean that it is **not** what 'is'?

53. So, are you this body?

54. Don't you call it 'my body' just like 'my coat' or 'my car'?

55. Could the body be **a kind of** coat or car?

56. Doesn't language suggest it when you say you are **an owner** of the body or a coat or a car?

57. Who is that owner?

58. Are you this mind?

59. Don't you say 'my mind' in just the same way?

60. What is the mind? Can you **show me** your mind?

61. Is there anything **else** other than thought or image, one at the time?

62. What is thought? Isn't it a subtle sound, mental picture or vibration of **energy**?

63. How did the idea of separation and identification came about **after** the baby was born?

64. What can you remember **without** words, before reasoning and storing memory was possible? Can you remember your birth?

65. How did you learn you are a person? Who **told** you so?

66. What else did they say you were?

67. What did you **add** to it and how?

68. **What** are you relating to as 'me' right now?

69. Isn't it all relating to past events? How else would you know what you like or dislike?

70. Isn't this reference point a dualism?

71. Can there be a duality in nonduality?

72. If ego is a problem, can you get rid of it? Who would be **trying** to remove it if not ego itself? Does it have any power? Is it real?

73. Is there such a **thing** as an ego?

74. In relating to past images of what is good or bad and wanting to keep the good and push away the bad, aren't we in **conflict** with what is right now? Isn't it RESISTANCE?

75. Doesn't conflict make you anxious, depressed and uneasy?

76. Isn't un-easiness a dis-ease?

77. Isn't all the **psychological** suffering a conflict or dis-ease?

78. What if you don't relate anything to a reference point (me)? Where does it go? Who does it affect?

79. How about Nature? Does it **relate** anything to anything?

80. Doesn't it also vibrate in **opposites**, day/night, summer/winter – but **without** any conflict?

81. Does silence fight the sound?

82. Are you anything other than Nature?

83. How do you do investigation? Look: Are you seeing right now?

84. Did you decide to **start** the seeing in the morning? Or was it there, already available — the same as the rest of the functioning?

85. Isn't it **the same** seeing with you right **now**? The content is different but has the seeing capacity changed?

86. Isn't it the same with hearing, tasting, touching, smelling?

87. Does your eye tell you 'I see'? Does it **say**, "Look at this, look at that?"

88. Isn't the thought 'I see' merely a translation of the mind creating a subject-object **split** in plain, singular seeing?

89. Can that thought 'I see' **actually** see? (Close your eyes and check!)

90. If the eye is only an **instrument** and thought is only a **translation**, WHAT IS SEEING?

91. Does the thought 'I hear' — actually hear?

92. Is the thought 'I'm aware' itself your awareness?

93. Is the thought 'I choose' itself the choice maker?

94. Can you **choose** thoughts?

95. Would you ever have unhappy thoughts if you could choose them?

96. How many thoughts can a CORPSE have? How much can it see or hear, even though all the **organs** are there?

97. How much information can you get out of the computer if the power is **not** ON? Can you see the analogy? Are you the **vehicle** or the animating power — the life **essence**?

98. How long have you been searching? Could it be that you are seeking in the **wrong place**? Could mind be the **wrong tool**?

99. Do you think you can find the answer in the future?

100. Where is the **future** if you don't think about it (don't imagine it)?

101. Are you trying to become something **other**? What or Who?

102. Is becoming the **same** as being?

103. If it is to be **found in time**, could you ever trust it? Wouldn't it be lost in the same way? Is anything time-bound even worthy of perusing?

104. If it is to have a starting point, wouldn't it be just another passing phenomena, a mere **temporary** experience?

105. Having a beginning, wouldn't it need to have **an end** as well?

106. Isn't TIME mind? Is there a past or any other time than now if you **don't** think about it?

107. Who are you if you don't think about it?

108. Who are you without your past?

109. Do you understand that there is ONLY ONE thing that needs to be understood in the mind? Do you see that this one thing is that the answer **cannot** be found there?

110. What is wrong with right now if you **don't think** about it?

111. Can you find curiosity to **pause** the thought and see if you still **exist** without thinking? What does it really mean? Aren't you **already** That?

Acknowledgements

The whole Universe has contributed to the appearance of this book, not a single factor: thing or event could be excluded without affecting the final outcome. The whole seeming past, long hours put into its content and structure, are included in its present existence now.

Having said that, there are some influences that stand out and shine brighter: Bob is the most obvious! Apart from him, I would like to wholeheartedly thank my wonderful editors/proof-readers Jeb Webb, John D. Weekly and Tristan Foy. Their priceless service was contributed freely — Bob and I can never be grateful enough for being looked after by Life so generously.

Gentle invitation and encouragement coming from some of you, guys, potential readers, were super motivating and stimulating. Thank you! Life in me is lovingly acknowledging Life in you. Beyond mind there is no separation.

Printed in Great Britain
by Amazon